DATE DUE

DEMCO, INC. 38-2931

DRAMA TEAM HANDBOOK

ALISON SIEWERT
AND OTHERS

InterVarsity Press
Downers Grove, Illinois

InterVarsity Press
P.O. Box 1400, Downers Grove, IL 60515-1426
World Wide Web: www.ivpress.com
E-mail: mail@ivpress.com

InterVarsity Press® is the book-publishing division of InterVarsity Christian Fellowship/USA®, a student movement active on campus at hundreds of universities, colleges and schools of nursing in the United States of America, and a member movement of the International Fellowship of Evangelical Students. For information about local and regional activities, write Public Relations Dept., InterVarsity Christian Fellowship/USA, 6400 Schroeder Rd., P.O. Box 7895, Madison, WI 53707-7895, or visit the IVCF website at <www.ivcf.org>.

Scripture quotations, unless otherwise noted, are from the New Revised Standard Version of the Bible, copyright 1989 by the Division of Christian Education of the National Council of the Churches of Christ in the USA. Used by permission. All rights reserved.

Permission is granted to perform the sketches in noncommercial settings as long as one copy of the book is provided to each actor. If a ticket fee is charged, then please contact InterVarsity Press for permission.

Cover design: Cindy Kiple

Cover and interior images: Jim Naughten/Getty Images

Cover and interior photos: Dan Pinka and Andrew Craft

ISBN 0-8308-2364-6

Printed in the United States of America ∞

Library of Congress Cataloging-in-Publication Data

Drama team handbook / Alison Siewert and others.
    p. cm.
Includes bibliographical references and index.
   ISBN 0-8308-2364-6 (pbk.: alk. paper)
  1. Drama in public worship. 2. Drama in Christian education. I.
Siewert, Alison
BV289.D73 2003
246'.72—dc21

                                                 2003010876

P	23	22	21	20	19	18	17	16	15	14	13	12	11	10	9	8	7	6	5	4	3	2	1
Y	20	19	18	17	16	15	14	13	12	11	10	09	08	07	06	05	04	03					

With love

For Derek and Micah,
who keep the drama moving

For Dan,
who coaches the actors

CONTENTS

PART 3: ACTING

PART 4: DIRECTING

APPENDIX A:
BIBLE STUDIES FOR DRAMA TEAMS

PART 1

DRAMA AND ITS USES

1 THEATRICAL GOD

Alison Siewert

All of creation is a theater for God's glory.

JOHN CALVIN

The Bible's story is utterly, profoundly, fundamentally dramatic. Think about it.

ACT ONE

The houselights dim. On the stage, all that's visible—and it's barely visible—is a vague, dark, scary-looking mass of . . . well, you're not sure. It doesn't have much shape. It's not a place you'd want to be. In fact, if you got up close to it, you'd find it's somehow *actively* dark. You can't see to navigate. This picture lingers—and you wonder if this play is going to be any good at all. There are no words. Nothing's happening, nothing breaks up the ominous murk. Perhaps you misunderstood— maybe it's a horror story. Or a bizarre, abstract . . . what? You can't even really describe it. But you don't like it. At all.

Just as you're about to get up and go home, you stop. Where there was silence, you hear breathing. Rhythmic, patient breath. Sloshing. A voice.

"Light."

Who—? A pinspot of light—dim at first— grows slowly, almost imperceptibly, brighter. You don't realize how strong the beam is becoming until all of a sudden you can see what was sloshing around up there. You were right: it's a deep, dark, surging mass of . . . wastewater. Ugh.

The breathing, speaking, lighting force acts. "Dome."

A spectacular effect: Suddenly a large blue dome rises out of the murky water, taking half the water with it and sealing it, somehow, in the flyspace.

"Earth."

Platforms, places to stand, rise out of the water, creating islands, where you imagine the action will take place.

Now things move more quickly. Grass actually begins to grow—*how did they do that?*— on the islands.

"Stars! For signs and seasons."

Sparks appear in the blue dome—so many stars, with a sun and a moon.

You have to look twice—and yet again—to believe there are actually fish now visible in the water. In the watery, lifeless place there are now hundreds of species, colorful, swimming. And birds swoop from the rafters onto trees, which, you realize, have grown while you sat there. And these aren't just pigeons, but birds you've only ever seen in *National Geographic*.

"Be blessed, be abundant, make more! Fill up the space."

The voice, again, "Creatures."

From every corner of the theater, animals make their way to the stage. Tapirs. A couple of toads. Capybaras. A zebra. Several capuchin monkeys. An enormous ox. A pack of Siberian huskies. A long green iguana. What do you say? It's like . . . a zoo—except the animals aren't in cages, and even the bright orange tiger looks calm, collected and not at all interested in eating you.

The animals actually take their places, as though they've been rehearsing for weeks. The lights shift. The voice:

"We will make humans. Male and female, in my image. Like me."

And it happens. A woman and a man rise from one of the dry places, looking around at the animals, the dome with its stars, the water, each other.

"Be blessed, be abundant, make more! Fill up the space. Eat from these plants. Be my partners. Keep this place, its animals, its beauty."

And that's the end of the first act. God is a creator, an artist. And that is dramatic.

ACT TWO

The stage lights come up. We see the world just made. It's beautiful, alive, perfectly balanced, abundant. God made people and made them the keepers of this place. It's all theirs, save for one single, solitary tree. They are set up for life, God's partners. They know God personally, intimately. He walks through the garden in the cool of the day, just as night-blooming jasmine gives off its scent and crickets start their song. He has come to meet them, to spend time with friends.

But on the other side of the stage there are the people—God's partners, the ones he's waiting for. On the other side of the stage, something else is happening. By that one tree, a conversation is taking place between the people and a snake. The snake says—no, he sibilates—that maybe God hasn't really set these people up so well. Maybe this isn't such a good deal. Perhaps this "God," as he insists on being called, is actually out to use these two, to keep them down so he can pump himself up. Maybe this is all an elaborate way for God to fill his résumé. "God is keeping you from the fruit on this tree, and it's the best stuff in the whole garden. He's keeping it from you. Think about it. He's using you."

The conversation ends when the people buy it. They slurp the suasion whole and take the unthinkable step: they commit outright treason. They cross the line. They decide they don't need a "God," thank you; they can do it on their own just fine. They dis God. And they make the down payment on what will cost them all of their life—their garden, their God, each other. They eat the fruit.

They are no longer who they were. The garden is no longer their warm, spacious, green, sweet home. Now it's a place of terror because—*what was that noise?*—they might encounter God. And they will know it is all undone. Undone. They panic. Maybe they're not—*get a leaf!*—maybe they're not quite able to manage on their own. The whole of creation is threatened. Will it revert to the dark, dank abyss? Will the lights go out, the dome collapse, the sun bears and rhinos and geckos and snowy owls be crushed under the weight of the stars slamming down? The crickets stop, the jasmine closes; will it all—just—end?

No. The voice, now walking—like us—comes searching. He finds them, his pathetic creatures, shivering now in their leaf-clothes, defeated, small, dorky. And he speaks again.

"What is this you've done?"

Thus begins the conversation of the rest of the story of God and his people. We are left wanting. How will God respond? Will he end the whole thing right there? How could you possibly get back to the way it was? Who could repair this damage? It seems beyond rescue.

But it's not. And the play returns after an intermission.

ACT . . . THREE?

God is a great hero, a rescuer, a repairer, a physician. And, as we all know, when you have people in a terrible predicament, you need a hero. It makes for great theater.

The story of God is theatrical. Every part of it could be its own play. Perhaps you've seen one of God's stories played or have been in one. Or perhaps you've noticed how the stuff that happens to biblical characters is so much like the stuff that happens in your own life. The story of God is theatrical, universal, good for all time. We know what those Bible stories are talking about. We've been there, shivering in the fig leaf outfit, feeling stupid, aware we've blown it, searching for a way out . . . looking for the Hero to make his entrance.

WHY DRAMA?

God is theatrical. And we need drama. Drama is the compression of human experience into a story we can view on a stage. It's a way of communicating what is and has been important, of describing our condition, of making symbols and stories in which people can find meaning, release and hope. Drama is a means of evoking our deepest longings and greatest need.

Dramatizing our experience is an important way we understand the world. We do it subconsciously every day. Have you ever told a story? Then in some sense you've done drama, or at least you've dramatized. You've chosen particulars—details, feelings of an event—and told the story in their terms. It wasn't just a long book about clown ministry; it was an unbelievably loooong book on clown ministry. And in the last three-and-a-half seconds of the game, you didn't just make a basket: You looked left, pivoted right, reached past the guard, caught Kevin's pass . . . and got the ball off for three a split second before the buzzer sounded. Drama describes our lives.

DRAMA REVEALS

Drama helps us see ourselves. It suggests that life is bigger than we are. It makes space for all that's ambiguous, thrilling, painful, uncertain. Theater helps us know life. It draws our attention not only to our own personal reality, but also to the bigger world outside us, to our context. It gives us the chance to see our lives differently. It says things to us that we desperately need to hear, and says them intuitively, by pointing rather than explaining.

DRAMA ASTONISHES

Drama helps us see God. The woman at the well comes to know God because she admits who she really is—and in the very next turn, she hears Jesus speak who he really is (John 4). God makes no sense to a needless person. We have to know who we are if we hope to want and know God. Seeing the fullness of God prods us out of our cynicism and sloth and into amazement. We have to know who we are, and we have to be awake to hear and see who God really is.

DRAMA ENLARGES

The small story is really about the big story. The local is universal. This is why art makes sense even across time and culture. Our lives seem small in the grocery checkout and dull over morning coffee. In the giant picture, we are all alike in our shrunken stature and our vague regret. We all need rescue. But in finding ourselves small and leaf-covered, we also discover we have elicited the attention of the Hero and have become his mission. And as he approaches, we see ourselves reflected in the giant, shining eye of God.

DRAMA SPEAKS PROPHETICALLY

Drama interprets the present in God's terms and helps us know the future in his terms. Theater can ask hard questions by pointing to them on the stage, and we can say things in the context of theatrical dialogue that we would struggle to speak in any other context. Because an audience hears indirectly, observing characters talking to one another from the stage, we can offer people something that speaks to them without any finger pointing. We don't control this. The speaking is God's. But if we participate in it, both talking and hearing, we receive the Word too.

ABOUT THIS BOOK

This book is about how we can use theater to tell the story of God and people. We want to help you explore how to incorporate drama in your context—in worship, outreach, campus, church and arts events. Our focus will be on settings that use drama as part of a larger experience, rather than on full-length theatrical productions. We call this approach a mosaic, or aggregate communication pattern. We see drama as a piece of the whole, rather than the whole communicative process.

This book draws on our experience in community. Even before the Bible was written, it was memorized and spoken in communal settings, with one or a handful of persons reciting the sacred story as others watched and listened. In the Bible we receive the diachronic legacy of those who memorized and recited the great story of God. Theater gives us an opportunity to participate in the dramatic approach to God's Word that is our Christian legacy. Drama continues to make sense in the Christian context, because Christianity and theater are communal. You can't really perform alone. (Well, you can . . . but if your housemates walk in, you may need an explanation.)

Theater, like a good Bible study, is an opportunity to hear, see, experience and feel the story together with other people. This makes it inherently different from video, recorded music and other electronic media, which are usually created ahead of time and played as recorded performances. The kind of drama we're talking about draws on, and might incorporate, multiple media but centers on the live performer in the room with the rest of the community. In live drama there is something being created in our midst.

The story of God and people is not found only directly in the Bible. If you watch the news or read a paper, you know that people are still doing the same basic stuff they've been doing since they had coffee and donuts with the snake. And God is still, amazingly, working to bring people and creation back around himself so we can have the good he intends for us. Constant, basic themes of human struggle weave their way through all sorts of life paths everywhere and all the time. So we're not only going to explore traditional Bible dramas—we will do that some—but we also want you to stretch with us, to think about how God's story is getting worked out, day to day, in your life and the lives of people around you. Consider how the story looks in different places, told by different people. What does God have to say about what happened today? He does have something to say. And our task as dramatists is not only to say what's been said but to wake it up, make it fresh, let it grow.

We want to experience the story in ways that will impact, startle, renew, energize, anger, help, pester, move, surprise. We want the people who've been coming to worship every week for eight hundred weeks to find a new way to see God. We want people who've never been to worship, and who think they would never come to worship, to come to the theater to experience the story.

We wrote this book not because we have all the answers—or, really, even a lot of answers. Of course, there are theological concerns that we mostly leave to other writers and to Bible study (see appendixes A and E). And there are technical rights and wrongs, but we won't focus much on technical theater here. What we're really, deeply concerned for is people who want to take a risk and try to express their stories and God's in new ways.

We're looking for people who want to communicate to a world that's heard it all, who are willing to get uncomfortable, to go around the old buildings and muck through back paths and pathless fields. We're searching for people who are willing to work at making art. This book is not intended to help you construct pieces that always tie up in neat solutions; we will avoid any attempt to give you a big, neat solution to theater problems. Because there isn't one. There is only hope, good conversation, the Scripture, reflection and prayer—and, in the end, following our theatrical God in the risk of getting out there and doing the play.

If you're up for it, keep reading.

2 WAKING UP

Alison Siewert

My father says almost the whole world's asleep. Everybody you know, everybody you see, everybody you talk to. He says only a few people are awake. And they live in a state of constant, total amazement.

PATRICIA GRAYNAMORE TO JOE BANKS,
"JOE VERSUS THE VOLCANO"
JOHN PATRICK SHANLEY

The problem is paying attention. Look out over any average congregation on a Sunday morning as the Scripture is read. Anyone taking notes? Hear a cheer go up? How 'bout some generalized facial excitement? Not so much. Unless you're in an unusual church, Scripture reading is probably not the highlight of worship. People in Christian communities have heard lots of Scripture. Many of us had to do memory verses as we grew up. Maybe you even have some old Bible Bowl ribbons lying around. We know the Bible, right?

A missionary friend told me the story of Christians in a nation where faith is persecuted and Bibles are illegal. People have chosen Jesus there nonetheless, and soon after their conversions, many teenagers go out in pairs to evangelize other villages. They usually have only one Bible to leave in each village—villages where *many* people have begun to follow Jesus. So they carefully cut apart their one Bible into individual books and rotate the books each week so that every household can read every book over the course of time. Since most villagers have no other books, the missionary said, the Bible is read constantly and fervently.

Familiarity breeds contempt, it's said, and our culture is familiar with the Bible. Think of all the places you can find Bibles, or at least Scripture, around you. Motel rooms, bookstores, libraries, hospitals—all have full Bibles on hand. You can purchase Bible verses printed on bunny posters. A local Christian store carries cookies and mints inscribed with verses. One fast-food chain prints "John 3:16" on the bottom-inside rims of its cups. My kids received plastic clapping hands—the kind you win at carnivals—with Scripture printed on them. Even people completely outside church circles see Scripture plopped and plastered around them.

The problem is paying attention. Scripture socks and Bible basketballs are a far cry from Nehemiah's gathered community standing to hear God's Word and responding in worship. "There is no hearing of God's word apart from a people who are struggling to listen truthfully for God's word."[1] To hear God's Word requires attention. Jesus says it himself: "The measure you give will be the measure you get" (Mark 4:24).

The Bible carries our spiritual genetic code—it explains, often by the description of history, what it means to be God's people in the world. It proclaims that the meaning of the past is defined by the meaning of the future, which belongs to God. We are people who are going somewhere, who are in the process of being saved not only *from* something (our collective and personal pasts) but also *to* something (the kingdom future).

But we already know what the Bible says. It's old. And not only is the Bible old, information in general is getting old. We have so much of it. You can find out about anyone or anything: you can order wallpaper from Finland, Google your best friend, find out about the donkey sanctuary in India. Because we know so much about so much, it's difficult to sort out what we want to know, what we need and hope for and love. "It is hard to find those [authentic] moments in our culture because we think we know so much about each other."[2]

We know so much. But what we know is bound by gold edges, separated by numbers, made distant by tired reading and formal robes. What would it mean to make the Bible's stories real and tangible? What if we experienced them rather than sleeping through them? The writers of Scripture surely never intended their work to be considered dry, undramatic or boring. These stories were their lives: they painstakingly copied, carried, protected and disseminated the precious, powerful book—in pieces and in whole. Church history reminds us that people have died for the sake of making Scripture accessible. There must be something in there worth paying attention to.

When it comes to handling the stories of Scripture, American Christians aren't exactly the most enthusiastic changers. In places with less Bible and more strongly postmodern cultural drift, gospel communication has to lean out on some risky edges. Perhaps it's our Puritan roots (although the Puritans usually get a worse rap than they deserve). Maybe it's that we have so much communication going on that we don't feel the need to work so hard to develop new models. Either way, we suffer

from "an almost total anesthesia of the soul . . . [where] Christian bookshops, with their bookmarks, posters, furry animals with Scripture texts, and pantheistic record covers, are a dreadful reminder of what happens when [the gospel's call to see beauty and possess hope is] trivialized and isolated from the world we inhabit."[3]

When faith is a given, taken for granted, we don't feel compelled to invent new vehicles for it. American familiarity with Scripture creates a nice, familiar, conservative climate. It's not attractive to do something new. People might not like it. It might not work. But God "presses the church's speech to its imaginative limits. . . . The church loses its vitality when its speech is cleaned up, pruned down, domesticated to ensure that our relationship with God is predictable and nice. Today's church suffers from suffocating niceness and domesticated metaphor."[4]

It is tempting to trim down the dangerous parts of Scripture and stick with our favorite verses, our posters, what will fit in a two-verse song. But to trim the Word down is to truncate our personal and communal growth, our evangelism and our art. We risk becoming numb to the real stuff—the unpredictable, the dangerous elements of the kingdom.

Our culture-bound relationship with the Bible may be numbed into predictability, but it is not gone. We can act in faith. We can hope to wake up what is asleep, scramble what is overdefined, hang suspense where there is rote predictability, and leave silent mystery where the information yaks on ceaselessly. This is the call for Christian artists, and especially for those of us in theater art.

Drama is good at refreshing the overfamiliar. Art makes breakfast for what's asleep. How? Art nudges the sleeper awake, enticing with the scent of brewing coffee. Have you ever gone to a play or musical event and, upon leaving it again, felt it odd to be back out in the world, outside the theater? Theater creates its own realities. In drama we find "a breathtaking

HOW WE GOT HERE
Alison Siewert

What Christians ought to do with art is widely debated. It's not a new conversation. In fact, drama has been a hotly disputed topic for much of the church's history. It started with Greeks and Romans, who did a great job of communicating their religious values through this art. And—here's where we get in a lot of trouble—Roman drama not only exalted the pagan pantheon but also deliberately debased Christianity in grotesque and violent ways. So the first church didn't celebrate much theater. But eventually, because drama is so deeply rooted in human communication (storytelling, pictograms and ritual), the church did begin to develop its own dramatic values and forms.

Drama has been part of the Western church for a very long time. We could draw an only slightly broken line from the earliest church uses of drama in the early Middle Ages to the present. Of course, the nature and shape of drama has changed over the course of this history. Drama was first used in the Middle Ages by priests to express the Mass. Mystery plays followed, both in churches and on street corners. But the Reformation distrusted many art forms, including drama, which reformers couldn't excuse from its abusive and morally nasty history, and by 1642 the British Parliament closed all the theaters in that country.

During the Baroque era, many Christians wanted to use opera to perform religious stories. But theatricality was thought to detract from worship, so folks had to come up with a less flashy art form: oratorio. In oratorio, the characters don't express themselves through staging or costume—it's all in the singing. Drama went underground but remained alive. Even Puritans, who usually get the bum rap of being dour, sour and utterly without capacity for fun, had among them some supporters of theater. In 1665 the first play produced in the colonies, Ye Bare and Ye Cubb, was accused of being blasphemous, but after being performed in court (for the judge, who hadn't seen it), it was ruled not blasphemous, on account of its being entertaining.[5]

But the majority of churchgoers denounced theater and therefore renounced their place in its development and growth. In 1778 (during the Revolutionary War), Congress prohibited all forms of theater, a decision approved by most of the church. Theater happened anyway. After the Civil War, hundreds of entertainment troupes fanned out to the new territories, carrying minstrelsy, vaudeville, reworked versions of mystery plays, and social plays to the people.[6]

So . . . even though drama has been around, it hasn't always been welcomed. (And when it has been welcomed, it hasn't always been done well.) But every so often it seems drama surfaces in the church's mind and ministry and precipitates new growth.

moment shared by all. . . . It is the fruit of a relationship, personal rather than abstract, immediate rather than secondhand. The author speaks, rather than 'has spoken.' The play breathes, rather than mechanically records its message."[7] Drama changes our view of the world.

So . . . what if we take what is tired and dulled out and shake it a little, wake it up? It is possible—no, it's necessary—for us to do this. How can we do any art at all if the work of our greatest artists, the Scripture writers, goes untended? We, of all God's people, must pay attention.

3 DRAMA AND WORSHIP

Daniel Jones & Alison Siewert

It is my opinion that art lost its basic creative drive the moment it was separated from worship. It severed an umbilical cord and now lives its own sterile life, generating and degenerating itself.

INGMAR BERGMAN

Worship is coming to God and seeing him rightly. In the worship service we gather as a community to connect our lives with God's life and our stories with God's story. When we enter into worship, we enter into an encounter with God that changes us. Worshiping God puts God in his rightful place and us in ours. Worshiping offers us contact with God: we perceive what he's like and what he promises; we bow down and rise up in exaltation of a King who loves us and the world he made. While it can include singing songs and listening to sermons, it can also be a time in which we see and hear pictures of God and his kingdom. Worship celebrates the Lord of the universe and helps us see how we are woven into his story.

ONE STORY

When our church started a mission to young adults, we didn't set out with a well-developed structure for worship and theater. We simply wanted to see people in our generation receive the gospel. We had a group of artists: musical, visual and dramatic, and we wanted to find interesting, creative and artistic ways to tell God's story, translate it and make it accessible to postmodern people. We wanted to do this in part, although not entirely, in the context of worship. We wanted to create a space where people looking for God could meet him and have their story woven into his in a way they could understand and would respond to.

THIS IS NOT A NEW STORY

We see God's people attempting to engage in this kind of worship throughout Scripture. We see it in the sacrificial system. An animal was brought to pay for sin with its life. The Hebrews understood God's view of sin and their need to repent and receive forgiveness. They acted out God's redemption through the sacrifice of an animal. It was a communal activity, taking place in the temple in the midst of God's people. Its purpose was to remember and attribute worth to God.

When Ezra and Nehemiah called people from exile back to Jerusalem to rebuild the wall, it was an effort shaped entirely by their desire to belong to God, to worship him as his people. As the whole assembly gathered, Ezra read the law of God from early in the morning until midday. People didn't just get a three-point sermon. They got the whole law read in a way that engaged them for most of a day. Listening to the words of the law, to God's story, was an act of worship (Nehemiah 8:1-18).

When Jesus visited the temple, it was a visual experience. He overturned tables, knocked coins everywhere and sent birds flapping as he judged the use of the Gentile court for shopping. The temple was supposed to be "a house of prayer for all peoples [nations]" (Isaiah 56:7). Jesus' actions called people back to God and to true worship—which is not just about Israel but about all nations, all kinds of people coming to know God through worship. This is the worship Jesus sought to establish: what would allow people in Israel to worship and encourage those outside Israel to join in. The strip mall in the court was clearly in the way.

How do these pictures relate to drama in worship? They are all pictures of God's people telling stories, reading the Word, raising questions and leading people into the narrative of salvation history. This is how they came to understand and meet God in worship. This is how God led them back to his presence. This is how they came to acknowledge God's faithfulness and redemption. And finally, this is how they continued to live trusting God and to pass the gospel down to us.

HOW WE TELL THE STORY

It is important for us to recognize the reality of worship in the history of God's people. God is consistently at work. And we may need to rethink some of the ways we approach our worship gatherings and how we communicate the gospel. William A. Dyrness says,

It is true that the Protestant imagination has been nourished uniquely by the spoken and written Word, and therefore, we tend to think that everyone must be spiritually and morally nourished in the way that we (and our forebears) have been. Surely these verbal means are of critical importance. But our children and their friends have been raised in a different world; they are often uninterested in our traditional word-centered media. Instead, they are looking for a new imaginative vision of life and reality, one they can see and feel, as well as understand. . . . We must listen carefully to this generation and reread Scripture in light of their dreams and fears. Then perhaps we will present the gospel and plan our worship in ways that respond to their quest and reintegrate word and image. It is possible that we might actually win the battle of words but lose the battle of images. And losing that battle could well cost us this generation.[1]

Like those who have gone before us, we can get caught in a rut, telling the stories the way we've always done it. We can forget those who don't know God. What speaks to them? What does a hymn mean to someone who's never been to church before? How about a sermon on the doctrine of substitutionary penal atonement? We certainly don't want to discard hymns and atonement theology—these are crucial in the life of God's people. But could we make these accessible through drama, storytelling, dance and other communicative arts? Probably.

A NEW WAY

From the start of our worship service, we made drama a regular part of how we experienced God. We knew going in that our generation is a visual crowd, raised on TV and movies. This is a generation that experiences, interprets and understands through images, music and humor. And we knew that we had people who could bring these things together in the context of worship.

We met in an 1860s icehouse (where they used to make and store huge blocks of ice) on the banks of a river. The building had been converted into a black-box theater: a pretty hip, nonstandard setting. The theater space, our sanctuary, had uneven wood floors and lots of very old brick. It was flexible so we could recreate the atmosphere each week. It was an ideal place to explore drama in worship. Even our décor was theatrical. We used lights, pictures from magazines, sculpture and even a clothesline hung with socks at various times. The offering plate was a lunch box by the door. But no big flower arrangements.

We saw drama as more than a decorative part of worship. It was a way people came to hear God's story. We knew our generation needs multisensory communication—that's what we're used to. The multimedia-driven services and events we had experienced lacked a certain kind of authenticity we found ourselves yearning for. It struck us that video and other prerecorded art isn't live, and that perhaps *live* art was a missing piece we could try to include in our work together. So we committed from the start to making drama an equal part—along with preaching and music, fellowship and prayer—of the service. In fact, all these elements in balance began to flow in an out of each other. The worship became an integrated whole in which the gospel was translated through a mosaic of communication.

A worship service might look like this: An opening prayer flowing into celebration through music—new and fresh and unchurchy. Celebration turning to reflection and confession. We might respond with some more musical worship. A question of the week would be asked to give people a chance to chill with each other, and we would set up a dramatic sketch. The talk might flow out of the sketch, or the sketch might emerge from the talk, which might then move us to a song. We'd turn to reflection and confession, a sort of application time from the talk. Sometimes this involved drama too. We might respond with more musical worship. Afterward we encouraged people—both verbally and with the offering of good food—to hang out and talk, to let what happened in worship spill into conversation.

It didn't always look the same. Sometimes drama started the evening; other times it set up the talk; and other times it happened at multiple points throughout the evening. What did we discover? Drama is a way of pointing people to Jesus. It creates good questions. We don't have to answer all the questions in the sketch. The talk might explore the questions, and we give people time to respond in prayer, conversation, reflection and musical worship. There are ways people can respond outside a service, too: offering their time and resources to ministries of justice and help, learning to extend care to people in pain, taking new risks to apply the gospel to life, or dealing with deep emotional and spiritual issues by receiving healing prayer and counseling. The experience in the building and the experience outside it weave together the bigger story of life with God.

A REACHABLE, VISUAL GOSPEL FOR A DISTANT, VISUAL GENERATION

The sacrificial system must have been intensely powerful for those who witnessed the taking of a living creature for their sins. Jump hundreds of years down the road from the first account of animal sacrifice (say, to around the time of Malachi), and the act should have been no less powerful, but it seemed to become more of an empty obligation than an act of deep trust. The point of the law was to atone for sin and to help people to trust God. (Thus the offering of first-born animals and first fruits. Giving God your first one made you dependent for whatever came later.) Malachi chided Israel for offering not the unblemished lambs called for in the Law, but the sick ones who could be given up without great cost. And without much trust in God. Sacrifice had shifted from being a way to trust God to a way to look good.

It's easy for worship to become about us. It's attractive to make worship a place we feel comfortable, see our friends, hear something affirming. However, the purpose of worship is not simply to be blessed, but to honor God by blessing others. God's house is a house of prayer for all the nations. That means we have to think about who these people are, and what and how they need to hear the gospel. We could miss a generation if we fail to tell our story woven into God's story. Worship cannot, should not, get stuck in words. We must loosen our grip on our confidence in words and begin to think through creating live images aligned with words to invite people into the good news.

We need to translate the gospel to the least in this generation in ways that are relevant, understandable and not cheezy (our word to describe . . . cheez), in a manner that invites the nations into worship. In every age of human history, God has expressed himself in ways people can understand. He is a God who wants to be known. Theater and other arts are a clear way to make him known. May our worship reflect the great desire of God to have all peoples welcome in his house.

4 DRAMA AND MUSICAL WORSHIP IN CONVERSATION

Daniel Jones

It's easy . . . to think that the artist has in mind a clear image of what he or she wants and then, having acquired an assortment of skills, deftly imposes that image on the material. Most of the time, the truth is far other. The work of art emerges as a dialogue between the artist and material.

NICHOLAS WOLTERSTORFF

Drama in its truest form is about bringing people together around a story in which characters ask questions, deal with their fears and engage conflict that prompts the audience to respond. A good drama creates tension and elicits a response.

We approach drama in much the same way we approach musical worship. In worship, we gather people together around God's story. Worship leaders, through music, lead people into the reality and truth of God and the questions and challenges that arise as we encounter the gospel. If it's done well, tension is created: tension that leads us to yearn for Jesus and that makes us uncomfortable, like seeing our sin. Tension creates opportunity for people to respond to Jesus.

STILLNESS AND MOVEMENT

Theater and worship are both static and kinetic. Drama's stories can move you (the kinetic) toward something: a question, a theme, a way of thinking about your life. Without being direct about it, the audience is prompted to mull over something of life. And often we are mulling away when something surprises us—a thought, a realization, a question we didn't know we were asking—SLAM! We stop in our tracks (the static).

DRAMA AS PART OF A LARGER EVENT
Alison Siewert

There are many ways to organize and conceptualize events where drama is being used. Here's a quick overview.

Bypass

One way to use drama is to bypass an audience's defenses. In this paradigm, art connects with emotional life and forms a channel for hearing the gospel. Drama can open people to the potential of life with God. Usually the message is delivered by the pastor or speaker. Drama sets things up, opens doorways, raises awareness, creates identification for that Word. In this setting, theater is theater and preaching is preaching. The drama doesn't speak the whole message: Elements are connected in a generally linear fashion, so that each piece of communication builds on the next.

Dialogue

Another way to use drama in partnership with preaching is in a dialogue between media. The preacher might give an introduction and then stop as a sketch begins. As the sketch ends, the preacher picks back up until, at another agreed-upon point, another sketch arises. This produces a piece of communication that flows back and forth between modes. It isn't just a stylistic thing: It's a way of seeing art, and for that matter, preaching. This angle creates a more evenhanded perspective on communication, where art and rational discourse act as partners. Art can still be left to do its job, and preaching to its task, but the way they work together is more thoroughly integrated. If you're thinking, Wow, that's a lot of coordination, well, yes. This approach demands a preacher who is willing to be fully part of a team that builds the communication together.

This is something like being in a funhouse. It's like this: you're walking along slowly, cautiously. Perhaps you know something lies ahead, but you are not sure what. You come to a corner and you must turn to keep going. What lies around the corner both intrigues and scares you, but you're in too far. You have to turn the corner. You do and then you encounter it! You are horrified or surprised or angry, or it's the most hysterical thing you've seen, but whatever it is, it has stopped you in your tracks.

This is how we approach a play. This is how directors, actors and writers approach it and how they hope the audience will approach it too. You want the audience to keep rounding the corner—*what's ahead?* You hope they ask questions about their own lives. You want them to stop in their tracks.

Like drama, worship can be both static and kinetic. The role of worship is to attribute worth to God. Musical worship leads us by calling us toward Jesus. And as we move to-

Evocation

Sometimes the hope of drama is simply to evoke, or call out, a sense of experience, the scent of what's to come, a shared moment upon which other pieces of communication build. In this model, a sketch suggesting the Scripture or theme could show up at any point in the larger communication process. The drama is not necessarily directly referenced by the speaker and other communicators; it simply creates the idea, context or process that will later be elaborated through preaching, worship, other arts, reflection and other elements.

Provocation

Sometimes a talk is not the best way to start the conversation. If people aren't even thinking about a topic, for example, a sketch can raise it and create a felt need to deal with it. Drama can be fairly direct because it is fundamentally indirect. A difficult story told from the stage gets a better hearing, in many instances, than a story told directly—particularly if the intent is to provoke new thinking and action in a group. To use drama this way requires clear and thorough agreement on the part of all who will communicate during an event. If you're asking people to work with difficult material, the last thing you want to do is jar them with chirpy announcements, songs that don't fit or a spoken message that doesn't deal with the topic.

Straight-Out Storytelling

Theater can function as the main storyteller or as one artistic part of a storytelling event. It's useful and refreshing to depart from our standard service format or outreach plan sometimes—or maybe even all the time. We can trust drama to tell a story thoroughly and well. Many groups are experimenting with arts events that do not employ a spoken message, but rather allow drama and other forms to speak on their own. These can be mosaic, where various small pieces form the whole communication, or linear, where a single story is told in order, with contiguous characters and plot, over the course of an event. People can follow up with their friends in conversation or find opportunity for process and reflection afterward.

ward our Lord in worship, we should be stopped in our tracks to behold all God is.

If we are approaching worship as holy, it shouldn't be that far removed from the fun-house experience (although generally minus the strobe lights and freaky clowns). Don't we often turn the corner in worship and find ourselves completely giddy with joy or surprised or in awe or horrified or even angry? In that stopped moment we respond. Worship prompts us to move toward Jesus and to be changed by our encounter with him.

HOW WOULD THAT LOOK?

Here are some examples of how my community integrated theater and worship:

In one sketch, *Laundromat: 2am*, we move through the story of John 4, using a laundromat as a setting. The language, postures, clothing and surroundings are all present-day. We finish the sketch open-ended, leaving tension as the woman drops her laundry basket (her water pot) and exits. In the final moments, as the woman tries to take in what just happened, we see her recognize her emptiness. With fear, hope and curiosity, she tries to respond to Jesus. Music rises out of the silence as the woman leaves. Our guitarist plays a long introduction to let the theater hang in the air and to leave room for people to move from observing to responding. The worship team begins to sing and people may feel free to sing with us, stop and pray, or reflect.

The first time we did this sketch, people in our community were able to identify with the woman and grab hold of what Jesus was offering them in that moment. The sketch, combined with musical worship, fleshed out the picture of the woman's encounter with Jesus. It also gave room and space for individuals to respond immediately. They were able to respond to what God was saying to them in the sketch and what he continued to say as we moved into worship.

In another sketch, we used the picture of David dancing before the Lord to open our worship time. Dave is dancing around in his, um, skivvies, unashamed and unabashed. This was our call to worship. We were inviting our community to let loose in worship, to stop and see a picture of someone responding to God by celebrating. I played David, wearing my Tongan lava lava, a men's skirt (we figured boxers were a little over the top for our setting), and dancing the mashed potato (a '50s dance) through the entire sketch. I was also leading worship and invited folks to move from the sketch into a time of celebratory worship.

On other occasions we've had sketches and monologues rise out of worship sets. The worship team (including myself) finishes the set, and another member of the team invites folks to sit. Then we begin the sketch or monologue. Because we established early on that the worship team would lead worship *and* do sketches, people went with us and easily made the shift—creatively and communally. We found it wasn't distracting but rather integrated the whole of what we were trying to do and say in that space. It allowed people to move with us from one picture of response to another.

NEW OPTIONS

Approaching worship with drama in mind gives you a number of creative possibilities for telling God's story. We've found it to be a helpful and contextually relevant way to think about worship and art. In many fellowship contexts, worship and theater function as two separate entities: this can be fine. However, one or the other can feel a bit detached from the whole of what you are trying to communicate. We have enjoyed the ability to integrate a whole service, as we work with all the elements rather than just being in charge of one. (Our preacher is usually on the team with us, both for planning and for execution.)

We continue to explore ways of weaving theater and musical worship together. We don't have it tacked down, but it has been fun to see what God does in and through our journey. It continues to excite me about the possibilities for telling the story of God and helping people enter into response.

5 TRANSITIONS

Alison Siewert

When worship preparation is seen as an art, as an experience to be wisely and lovingly curated; when its shape, style and content develop from the context of the lives of the community coming to worship; when thought is given to incorporating the total environment and all the senses in the worship experience, then worship that encourages a loving of God with heart, soul, mind, and strength will be hard to avoid.

MIKE RIDDELL, MARK PIERSON,
CATHY KIRKPATRICK

Transitions organize and communicate. They are important. If you are planning drama for use in worship or in any event larger than the drama itself, you need to think through how you will transition into and out of the performance.

We performed a collage in the midst of a worship time at a conference. The sketch was Jonah's prayer from the belly of the fish, spoken by one person, and that prayer simultaneously danced by a second person. The worship time was already a bit crowded with activity. The conferees had just heard a challenging talk and were taking time for reflection. We had decided the sketch would rise out of the silence of reflection, the same way Jonah's prayer rose out of his utter isolation inside a fish under the sea. This meant that the guitarist would begin playing a simple, quiet introduction, and the actor would begin to speak the prayer. This would alert people that something was happening and they should look up from their prayers or notes.

The point was to draw the reflective process of an entire group together, to develop community in response to the challenges of the talk. We wanted people to be led by the sketch, to be encouraged into prayer and worship by

Jonah's experience. They were ready, and so were we. But at the moment that should have been silent, a voice started talking. We looked up. The conference emcee announced we'd continue reflection time, to a song the worship team would now play; then he proceeded to read the words to the song.

Whatever chance we had of drawing people gently into worship was now shaky. And then it was toppled completely: "Okay, um, now some drama people are gonna do a skit for us." Oh well.

We have the opportunity to build lovely moments—points at which people can connect with God, open their hearts and minds, and receive from Jesus. It's not that every sketch has to be a Moment. But some can and should. Give some attention to these points:

◆ Decide on a transition and plan for it. Know why and how you want to move from one thing into the drama and from the drama into the next thing.

◆ Communicate the technical transition to everyone involved, including announcers and especially sound technicians. You can't lead a transition if your mic is off.

◆ Prepare the teams to be in place and ready

to go at the right time. This doesn't need to be panicky, but it does need to be clear.

◆ Talk with the emcee about the content of the transition. Does she need to say anything to introduce the sketch? Will she begin with a Scripture reading? And what needs to happen between the sketch and the next step in the service? Make sure this person knows the tone and point of the sketch so she can speak appropriately to the moment.

◆ Or ask the emcee not to speak a transition. Consider not announcing the sketch. People will figure out that it is a sketch, right? And sometimes letting the picture rise out of silence or singing, background music or conversation, is more powerful because it's not announced. It can surprise and refresh people to have the transition made dramatically, which is what will happen if it's not announced.

◆ Practice the transition so it goes smoothly.

◆ If you are in on planning a service, consider not only distributing the script but also having the cast, or even the staff, read through it aloud. We performed a sketch that ended leaving some people so sensitive they left the room crying. What followed it should have been silent or quietly accompanied reflection. What did follow it was a loud, hard-hitting video. The video was awesome, but the emotional power of the sketch made it hard for people to take in, and left the audience craving time to think and talk about the sketch.

◆ Place sketches well. You've worked hard on them because you believe God speaks through your art. The team has spent its energy preparing because it wants to bless. Creating appropriate space, time and transitions paves the way for that blessing.

6 CREATIVE INFORMATION

Alison Siewert

You enter the extraordinary by way of the ordinary. Something you have seen a thousand times you suddenly see as if for the first time

FREDERICK BUECHNER

It can get old having someone stand in front of a service or meeting week after week, droning on about what to pack for the retreat, which letters of the alphabet bring what to the potluck, where to turn in your Sunday school registration forms, when the broomball tournament starts. There are ways to make necessary announcements more interesting.

There are good reasons to use drama in this functionary way. It presents an opportunity, especially if you're working with a new or inexperienced team, to get people up and practicing. Doing a sketch about the spring car wash and sock sale is much less threatening than playing Jesus during Easter week. If you see these openings as opportunities to try things out, to learn, you'll be blessing your fellowship and developing your theatrical skills and ministry all at the same time. Very cool.

Another, yet more major, reason to communicate some things theatrically is that you can often say more and say it better by showing rather than telling. And if your congregation is announcing events that include developing people's spiritual growth or introducing people to Jesus, then of course you want to communicate with the most energy and care you can muster. A sketch that introduces a conference theme could also paint a picture of what it's like to choose, for the first time, to go away for a weekend with a group of people you don't know very well. Which in turn will communicate to your audience that we all have these fears and it's okay to work them through.

CHOOSING WHAT TO SKETCH

It's very easy to announce too much. Whenever you're planning announcements, keep the context in mind. If people have just sat listening for thirty minutes to a talk or sermon, don't have someone stand up and yak through a bunch of details. Consider spacing announcements, especially at the beginning and end of meetings. If you're planning worship, make sure nothing disrupts participatory worship time. It can be downright uninspiring: You finish singing "All Creatures of Our God and King" and someone sits you down to tell you about the Senior Bowling League Awards Burrito Banquet coming up (get your tickets from Erv in the front row tonight). And how often, after a list of announcements, have you been asked to stand back up and get into worship again? Ugh.

Think about the flow of the event and where announcements can land unobtrusively but memorably. Obviously people are

more likely to retain the information if you announce it toward the end. But there might be times when sketching an announcement early in a program allows for appropriate reflection and response—especially when it's done dramatically.

MAKING A SKETCH

Once you've identified what you're announcing and where it fits, you need to decide how to say it. What information must be included? And most importantly, what can we possibly leave out? Too many details will swamp both a sketch and its listeners. Sketches are good at communicating meaning, making things inviting and relaxing people's fears. Figure out what you're hoping to do and what information is needed in order to do it.

Next, think about how to communicate it. Most announcement sketches should be comedy. Why? Because if you lay out a serious, deep or challenging theatrical picture and then "just happen to have" a conference coming up that can "solve" the problem presented, your group will likely feel manipulated, or at least cheez'd. If you're going to announce something, you can detract from the fact that you're announcing something by making it funny, by taking yourself less seriously even though you're making an announcement.

For example, our ministry offers a conference at the start of the academic year. It's designed to invite new college students into fellowship, help returning students reconnect and introduce people to Jesus' life. The camp where it's held is called Refreshing Mountain Camp. Now, if you're in a room full of 18- to 22-year-olds and have to tell them they're invited to something called Refreshing Mountain Camp, you should tell them with a light heart. Because college-culturally speaking, it's a slightly awkward name.

It's also a true name for the place. It is actually refreshing—a great facility with staff who love to serve their guests. It was funny, but we didn't want people to feel jaded to the name. We came up with a lighthearted refrain—the announcer saying, "Refreshing Mountain Camp," followed by the characters (and eventually the audience) responding, "Ah! Refreshing!" It's not profound material, but it got into everyone's heads and they showed up at the conference. Refreshing.

Another time our church wanted to announce a series of talks on the Ten Commandments. When you say "Ten Commandments" to Americans, many think of Charlton Heston in a long robe, or rules about thees and thous. Very few people in our society have really studied that part of Exodus. They think they know it already . . . but they don't.

So to announce this series, we picked up on what people think they know. And to get everyone loosened up and ready to really listen, we made it funny. It's hard to translate how funny it was, because humor is contextual and part of what works in these sorts of pieces is who is playing what part. You can do a lot by bending people out of their normal roles. Commandment Bob (in a striped mylar coat with large blue glasses) was a mild-mannered Sunday school teacher until, struck by the realization that people didn't know the Ten Commandments ("Pull yourself up by your own bootstraps" isn't a commandment?), he set out to help people know what they're really about. His assistants, Bible Power Princess Claire and Rila, Love Warrior, helped him get his message out. It was campy, but it was funny. And people got it.

UNSKETCHED BUT CREATIVE ANNOUNCING

Not long ago we showed up for a performance at a small college. And guess who else showed up? A guy in a cow suit. With an udder. A six-foot-eight-inch-tall sophomore, well known at the school for his basketball prowess, sense of humor and dramatic talent, was assigned by the Christian fellowship to introduce our performance. We were in the middle of the student union, in perhaps the most visible venue on the campus. About a hundred students had gathered, talking and rustling as the time neared. And then John appeared onstage in his cow suit, carrying a guitar. He took complete—and completely funny—authority: "Cell phones? I don't wanna hear 'em. Dogs? Send 'em away. Need snacks? They're on the tables at the back. And now, a song." John proceeded to perform a short, funny song about Jesus ("He was the star of his high school basketball team . . . led Jerusalem for three seasons . . .").

Now, I've never been introduced by a guy in a cow suit before, but I have to say it was one of the best announcements I've ever seen. John was funny, but not, despite the suit, completely flippant. He got all the information across quickly and painlessly because people were laughing so hard but also wanted to hear what he said next. The cow costume created expectation. It made people want to listen.

Not many people should make announcements in cow costumes. It takes a certain comic élan to pull that off. But it is a good model of thinking beyond the obvious, outside what's traditional, and with buoyant hearts, about how to get people knowing what they need to know, almost without them knowing they know it. With a little creative application, you can come up with announcements that fit into the context of your worship—and help your group to remember where to get those Senior Bowling League tickets (from Erv in the front row). For a sample announcement sketch, see the script for *Sketchimony* on page 183.

7 DRAMA AND EVANGELISM

Jenny Vaughn Hall

The purpose of art is to lay bare the questions which have been hidden by the answers.

JAMES BALDWIN

We've all seen them. Good-hearted, well-intentioned attempts at "being creative" about presenting Jesus.

You know what I mean: dramas that try to capture what it means to be lost and then found. A woman on the verge of a breakdown who comes to know Jesus because her Bible falls to the floor and happens to flip open to John 3:16. She then falls on her knees and weeps while "Wind Beneath My Wings" is sung karaoke style by Bertha the soprano.

Okay—maybe this is an exaggeration, but let's face it. Sometimes it sure seems like friends shouldn't let friends mix art and evangelism.

When art gets mixed into evangelism, the art often becomes clichéd and the evangelism cheezy and forced. Now, who am I to say that Bertha's rendition of the old Bette Midler tune couldn't touch someone who doesn't know God?

But even when we hope and work to make art that will engage people with the gospel, we can miss the mark. We've all seen that badly crafted or misplaced art can turn people off to the good news. Can we hope for something better? Yes!

The relationship between art and evangelism holds incredible power to draw lost people into the arms of the Father. Artists and evangelists need each other. And lost people need the relationship between artists and evangelists to

work. There is a great model of their marriage in Acts 17:16-34. Paul is in Athens and is disturbed by all of the idols he sees around the city. He ends up in the Areopagus, the place where philosophical debates take place in town. As he looks for creative ways to affirm the Athenians' search for God, he alludes to an altar with the inscription "To an unknown god" (Acts 17:23), as well as a line of poetry that they are familiar with: "'For in him we live and move and have our being.' As even some of your own poets have said, 'We are his offspring'" (Acts 17:28).

Paul does two very clever things here by using the art already present in Athenian culture. First, he points out that there's something missing in their spirituality. The artists who designed this altar didn't know who the unknown god was, but they did know they didn't have all of the cosmos figured out. This altar was a reminder of that to the public. Paul then says, "I do know who this unknown god is; in fact, he is the God above all other gods, who created the world and everything in it." He goes right to the missing piece they themselves have acknowledged.

He uses their own poet's truth as a springboard. The poet captures in abstraction the reality that a god is everywhere and we are "in" him—gaining our life, movement and very being from his power. Paul affirms the part they understand and fills in what they don't—starting in their terms.

The artists of the city have raised the right questions about God and captured the abstract reality of God. Paul enters the scene, begins to answer those questions and adds dimension to their picture. Without the artists it would be very hard for Paul to convince the Athenians of their need for the one true God. Similarly, without the evangelist, the artists would leave the Athenians groping for the unknown god but never finding him.

The hardest thing for any evangelist to do is to help people see and believe that they have a need for God. This is the uphill part of evangelism. It is difficult to get people to admit that they want something more in their life. Most people are "far too easily pleased," as C. S. Lewis says—satisfied with way too little.[1]

A friend of mine wasn't a Christian but would come to a Bible study that I led with some other friends. He got high every day because he was bored. His relationship with his dad was painful and broken. He even drew a picture of himself digging a hole in the ground, with God crying up above him. He clearly wasn't satisfied with his life. And yet for an entire year, whenever we talked about his soul, he would just say, "It's all good. Whatever. I'm cool." If people have no sense of need, it is difficult to get them to pay attention to Jesus.

On the flip side, one of the hardest things for *art* to do is call people into a wholehearted commitment to Jesus. The role of art is to disturb, provoke and raise questions. What would it look like for a drama to lead people into some kind of call to commitment, where the characters suddenly turn to audience and challenge them to commit their lives to Jesus? The audience would likely feel betrayed and manipulated. Drama creates a kind of safety that allows people to open themselves up to the process on the stage. If, suddenly, the very characters who operate on the stage, from a safe distance, break open the

fourth wall and challenge people directly, the audience will balk.

But herein lies a match made in heaven. An artist's strength is her capacity to unveil the longings in people's souls. Drama can get beyond non-Christians' defense mechanisms and help them admit they don't have all the answers and they don't have it all together.

I once did a dance to a Sarah McLachlan song at an evangelistic outreach. The dance was part of a talk with art woven through it that was geared toward non-Christians. The dance captured my own weariness with life and heartache and how much I longed to be loved by God but was at the same time scared to be vulnerable before him. All of this was done through choreography and patches of light on the stage, which I entered and left. A woman dressed in punk clothes came to me afterward and said, "You just danced how I feel about my life. I left the room crying because I want exactly what I saw you wanting." She became a Christian later on.

Could the talk itself have allowed the woman to open herself up that vulnerably? Perhaps, but I believe that the art got under her skin and in her soul, and mirrored to her the ache she felt inside but had been unwilling or unable to admit.

An evangelist's strength is inviting people to say yes to Jesus and entrust their lives to him. Evangelists need artists who are willing to let their art disturb, provoke and raise questions about spirituality and life. Artists who have a heart for lost people need evangelists to reap the fruit from the seeds that they plant through their art. How incredible to see the fruit of your labor in the lives of people who come home to the Father!

Artists and evangelists need each other not because their friendship is efficient for the reaching of people but because they are both and all part of the body of Christ. Another way to see this relationship is simply to say that our gifts complement the gifts of others. If artists are doing their work, expressing themselves, engaging the gospel in their lives and therefore reflecting it in their art, they will draw people to the truth of what life, in its pain and joy and searching and longing, is really like. And they will also, quite naturally, open pathways attractive to nonbelievers who are searching for what's real. And finding that God is the most real of all.

Evangelists, likewise, will find that as they seek ways to love the lost, art can speak in an experiential way that appeals not just to the rational but also to the intuitive and emotional realms of the soul. Art will not necessarily explain, but it can evoke. If evangelists are open to—even eager for—the partnership of art and artists, they will discover themselves inviting people into conversation who have already begun to respond to truth at a deep level.

This will call for a willingness to approach evangelism in a way that's more generous and process-oriented than many of us have been taught in the past. But if, as William Dyrness says, the rising generation is shaped by and drawn toward the aesthetic, our work together, artist and evangelist, will be a more apt communication of God's love.[2]

8 DRAMA ACROSS CULTURES

Alison Siewert

If we want to understand what makes other people tick, if we want to get inside the mind of someone of another gender, race, age, or religion, we can do it best by fiction. We can experience circumstances we have never encountered. . . . We can see both sides of the story.

HILARY BRAND AND ADRIENNE CHAPLIN

Most of us, dropped into a Japanese Noh theater performance, would have no idea what to think, even with subtitles. We might follow certain lines and general senses, but we'd struggle to grasp the meaning of the play on a deep level. We could be mystified by an Iranian film narrated by a girl who comes alive from a *gabbeh*, a storytelling rug. Or we might hear the performance of a hip-hop poetry troupe from Philadelphia and not be sure what they are really saying. "This is a country of many tongues, even if we stick to English. Placing myself in other people's words, as in placing myself in other people's shoes, has given me the opportunity to get below the surface—to get 'real.'"[1]

Culture isn't just from other countries. It's everywhere and all the time around us. You don't have to go very far to find someone who is very different from you. And every culture has its own performance traditions—ritual, theater, storytelling, dance, puppetry. Theater is about communication, and every culture communicates. In many cultures, theater plays a more significant role than it does in our own. It carries responsibility for transmitting major cultural values and articulating what's important to a people.

START WITH VAUDEVILLE, END AT THE CINEPLEX

The emergence of multicultural cities gave rise to vaudeville—from the French words for "voices of the city."[2] Groups of performers would perform comedy, sketches, dance and music from their home cultures (in the beginning, mostly Italian) in their new country's urban centers. Even though people couldn't necessarily understand the languages, they could enjoy one another's art and lives through performance. Between the end of the Civil War and 1930, vaudeville nurtured creative people and expressions of immigrant cultures in crowded, communal settings where you couldn't help but get to know one another.

Once films and recorded music developed—and especially once television and home stereo systems gained popularity—people could narrow their viewing and listening to just what they liked best or were most comfortable with. Today we have more choices but more segregated entertainment. Films, television and even theater are marketed as mass-market (dominant—white, male culture) or as ethnic (African American, Asian or Latino). Films are evaluated and marketed based on what production companies think will bring in cash and crowds.

THE RISK-TAKING GOSPEL

Marketers make their predictions based on numbers because they don't want to risk losing money on small audiences. We, on the other hand, are called to risk—all the time and in all parts of our lives. We can take risks by hearing, seeing, learning, sponsoring and advocating other cultures' art. Find out where dance, theater, music and visual art from other groups and places will be shown. And go there. Even in the middle of Pennsylvania—hardly the multicultural melting pot of my hometown, Los Angeles—we can find Korean music at outdoor festivals and a resident African dance and drum company. Find out who's writing and producing theater, and see if there are ways you can develop partnerships and extend yourself in service to those people.

Crossing cultures is good for audiences and great for artists. A sketch I've included in this book, *lifeDesign*, was performed by a black woman as Miriam and a white man as Moses. While the historical Moses and Miriam shared their racial heritage, their lives were socially, economically and, by virtue of Moses' adoptive status, ethnically different. A friend whose student actors performed the sketch said, "It was really good for the students who did it. The experience and emotional/thought processes Moses and Miriam go through over the course of their words were pretty similar to those they'd experienced in their own path of racial reconciliation. As I was helping them prepare, we had some deep moments of connection with the text helping them understand their experience and vice versa . . . which amounted to their performance being richer for them, and as a performance."

Whose voices are speaking in your city, and what are they talking about? What concerns them? What are their hopes and fears? If we never listen, we never know. Talk to people; get to know artists from other communities. Ask questions. Help out. Look carefully at how cultures express themselves. The form of the art may teach you as much about a culture as the content of the art.

THE STORIES OF PEOPLES

Bangarra Dance Theatre uses ancient aboriginal and Torres Strait Islander movements, symbols and dance traditions to interpret the contemporary experience of Australia's aboriginal people groups to audiences. In one piece the company explores how aboriginal people were weakened by the introduction of flour and sugar to their diets by European settlers. By the end the dancers have covered themselves in flour—a picture of what happened to their people.

> Initially the rations were accepted and welcomed because it was seen as a giving gesture, it was sharing—a big part of indigenous culture is sharing amongst each other so when these other people came in offering these things, it was welcomed . . . but the settlers didn't truly want to share. The settlers wanted to give the rations but not share the land. . . . They took priceless artefacts in return for flour, water, and sugar.

As the overtaking of aboriginal lands progressed, people were blocked from ancestral lands, hunting and rituals. "They were in this limbo zone, like a dead person walking between two worlds."[3]

These are deep, painful issues that generate unjust systems as well as personal grief. They need to be addressed in many ways and on multiple levels. Art, for its part, allows people with aboriginal ancestry to see their heritage, to have the story passed on to their children. The choreographer of *Rations*, Frances Rings, said, "It makes me understand my mother . . . why we are what we are today . . . you have to walk through it, you can't jump over it."[4] Through her art, young Australians will have opportunity to understand their history.

This art also allows nonaboriginal people into the pain in a setting that also interprets that pain. It's a more compelling introduction to watch someone enact the process of aboriginal loss than it is to listen to a lecture about it.

Art convicts; it can motivate people to seek more, to question how we might address the pain and redress the injustice. Art sings a prophetic role among the voices of our cities.

Theater can also help us retain and pass on what has been most significant to a people group. August Wilson recalled "James Baldwin, in particular his call for a 'profound articulation of the black tradition,' which he defined as 'that field of manners and rituals of intercourse that can sustain a man once he's left his father's house.' I thought, *Let me answer the call*."[5] August Wilson set out to celebrate and articulate the endowment of his heritage—onstage, as people live it. It's unlikely we'd find a book on how to keep home training, but to see the tradition of manners presented in the form of a story we can take in—in a live setting with actors—makes it accessible to people within and outside the culture. A story onstage communicates more than a discussion of traditions. Drama communicates the meaning of a cultural experience in terms of that culture's traditions, offering a richness and texture mere description could never approach.

THE LEARNING CURVE

The vibrancy and uniqueness of a people shines when artists are given space to speak from their vantage point to a wider audience. And for many rooted in dominant culture, theater and other arts may be the only way they get to see. In some cases, dominant culture folks simply refuse to extend themselves and learn about other people. In other cases, through lack of knowledge and experience and the overwhelming presence of dominant expressions (and thus, relative hiddenness of other ethnic expressions), they simply don't know how or where to look. Theater can change that by nurturing a variety of cultural expressions from the stage.

I had the experience of having parts of a play I wrote used in a Muslim society that I've never been to. I wasn't even there, but my

EXPRESSING ETHNIC IDENTITY
IN DRAMA

Jess Delegencia

After performing dramatic sketches at a large conference, I was surprised to find that most of the specific feedback I got was about my ethnicity:

> *"Great job Jess! You don't know how much it meant to me to see an Asian face up there!"*

> *"It's about time a Filipino was up there!"*

> *"Jess, I'm an (Asian) actor myself, and you inspired me!"*

> *"You go, Asian brother!"*

> *"Thank you for being there and representing Asians!"*

Many of the Asians who approached me and who responded with such enthusiasm know that it is rare to see a face that looks like mine doing what I was doing at that kind of event. Bruce Lee and Jackie Chan aside, how many Asian men would you consider household names? My face represented an affirmation of Asian culture and Asian people.

As an actor whose face is not mainstream, I know that there are projections, hopes and ideas attached to my face that go beyond my performance. The invisibility of Asian American role models has a profound impact on many young Asian Americans, and I have realized that my public performances serve an extra purpose: to be there as a visible model to my Asian American sisters and brothers.

Theater and drama also have the power to be a progressive platform for culture. Consider the Hollywood movies that have successfully introduced America to its ethnic subcultures: The Joy Luck Club *(1993) about Chinese Americans,* Mi Familia *(1995) about Mexican Americans,* Smoke Signals *(1998) about Native Americans and* My Big Fat Greek Wedding *(2002) about Greek Americans. These were all commercially successful films that showcased the uniqueness of cultures. In 2001 the first full-feature film about Filipino Americans, called* The Debut, *was released. It was an opportunity for my friends to know me more and to understand and appreciate Filipino America.*

Our cultures form us and offer us our first views of the world. It's normal and important for people to connect with how God meets and works through their particular experience. Seeing a face like your own is a point of connection to God and ultimately to the global, multiethnic community of saints.

drama on Genesis 1—3 was. A friend had taken a group of students for a cultural exchange project, and they had opportunity not only to learn language but also to share some of their faith experience. They did this mostly through relationships, but they also used art. Here's how it went.

> We introduced the montage by giving a little blurb about common stories and defining Yahweh Elohim as the name for God/Allah in the original texts. We told them to just use their imaginations as they listened to the first section. So with lights down, two students read the creation sequence. The audience pretty naturally closed their eyes and just let it soak in. They loved it, particularly the poetic feel, since poetry is big in their culture.
>
> We didn't remember how you originally blocked it, but when we did the sketch about the Partner (the creation of Adam and Eve) we played around with it and figured out something that worked, exploring the newness of a gendered relationship without having it feel culturally offensive to them. Once they were created for each other, we had Adam accidentally drop Eve, laughing the whole time, and changed the mangos to watermelon (since they don't know mango).
>
> This was their favorite sketch, largely because of the action of the drama. It was also the one that seemed to affect them the most. Art is a great way to get under people's skin and deal with their prejudices. It was fun to offer some very counter-cultural and very Christian thoughts and images to them without being at all offensive, and then to have opportunities over the next couple days for further discussion (there'd already been a lot) about human value and gender as we Christians see it.

Genesis, written down by Hebrews living in the midst of other nations, communicates the story of God's people in the most basic terms. And because they are basic, they are profound. Genesis makes sense. It applies to everyone. Every human can find his or her story in its verses. Being able to put that story into a form accessible to students who would likely never open a Bible is a thrilling prospect.

Here is an opportunity to risk. Culture is part of the journey. Art can help us get there. Step into your own city and see what voices are speaking—and what voices are still to be heard. This is the call of art and also the call of the gospel. We not only disserve people if we do not listen to them—we also lose out. We stand to learn everything if we attend to one another; and lose our way if we ignore the people God has placed all around us.

9 BUILDING A PERFORMANCE TEAM FROM THE GROUND UP

Alison Siewert

We must reconsider what is meant by "talent." It is highly possible that what is called talented behavior is simply a greater individual capacity for experiencing.

VIOLA SPOLIN

I can't think of any Oscar winners at my church. There's one guy who did community theater once, but . . . nope, no Oscars. We'd all love to have big teams of well-trained, confident actors and technicians to work with. But many of *us* aren't even all that well trained or confident. So that can be a problem. It's not impossible, however, to develop people, along with material they can perform well. The key is to think developmentally—start with what people can do, and go from there.

There are some things you can do with lots of inexperienced people. One church did dramatic outreach with large public performances using animals and a live orchestra set in an outdoor venue. It was enthusiastic, heartfelt and full of effort, but in the end it wasn't theatrically compelling enough to be effective. Few were reached. And in the end the pageant fizzled out. And the church was left with a group of people who had exerted such immense energy building the physical event (tents, live animals, chairs, technical equipment) that they lost sight—or perhaps never found sight—of the building blocks of a team.

Could a pageant help build a team? Yes, if you use it developmentally. That is, if you approach every part of an event as a learning op-

portunity and a training ground. Even a sketch or a big hi-tech event that goes "badly" can be very useful in the process of developing people. God wastes nothing. Every experience can contribute to growth. If we're thinking about developing people, we will spot moments when we can point out a new way to think or work, an opportunity to adjust or improve.

WHERE DO WE START?

First of all, know that your team is out there—in your fellowship. The task is to find them.

Talent and its illusions. Talent is a nebulous category filled with people who seem to have a knack for whatever it is we're assigning talent for (baseball, basketry, theater). Certainly there are folks out there who carry a combination of gifts that make them particularly well suited to drama ministry. We should look for gifted communicators. But acting is more of a discipline than a phenomenon. Sometimes mercurial people end up having less to offer, because they've not disciplined gifts that they experience as natural. Without discipline to shape them over time, gifts can weaken. Three people on our team used to be reasonably good gymnasts; now none of us can even start a back bend.

Talent in the popular cultural imagination often has more to do with attractiveness than with an ability to apply skills and intuition to a particular art. But in our context, attractiveness is less of an issue, and skill is more important. Our hope is to communicate the stories of God and life in an effective, useful, arresting way. Our actors need, more than talent, to be disciplined, humble, responsible and willing to serve. If they are gifted communicators, if they're learners, lovers of God, and enjoyers of art and other people, they're probably who we're looking for.

Set the bar high. Apply yourself to finding the best people you can—from the start. One director I know produced a church's first play using ringers—hired actors from outside—to play key roles and make it really excellent. I don't love that approach, but I have to admit it worked. When the ringers left at the end of the project, the congregation knew what they were aiming for because of the professionals' example. They aimed high, and over time they got there. The church ended up with a first-rate drama group. Gifted people attract gifted people. If you build something that looks good, people who know what good looks like will get interested.

Start small. You probably won't attract everyone immediately. That's okay. If you think of this as a building process, you'll be able to hang on through the length of a team's development. Your fellowship's expectations will grow with your team: it doesn't have to happen all at once. The point is not to have the most professional thing going. The object is to create drama that evokes truth and sheds light. Excellence is only a means to the end of beautiful, God-filled art. Take time to develop a capacity for beauty by developing the size and skills of your team.

Look for key people to build with. Locate a couple of really gifted, mature people who can work with you to get things started. It's much better for you not to be the sole standard-bearer. Holding that thing up will make you tired! You'll have more fun and develop more community if you have some partners. See if your fellowship includes any solid believers who are also identifiably skilled theatrical artists. These are people who have done professional or semi-professional productions, have training or are otherwise gifted. Get to know these people. Get to know their skills.

Start by doing. Don't talk quite yet about your hope to build a drama team. Rather, start by doing. Have one or two of the partners you've sought out begin working on monologues or simple sketches. This will give you a sense of what their gifts really are. You have to see people work—preferably more than once—to assess their ability and skill levels. Invite them to perform something as a part of worship or another event. Begin to build a vision for drama in your fellowship. People won't know what you mean by "drama team" until they see the beginnings of one. Work with your partners to make your first performances the best they can be. This picture will live on in the mind of the church and set a precedent for others who want to participate.

Cast vision. If you find these first few people are a good match, talk with them about your interest in developing a team. Since they've been doing some of what the team would be doing, the vision will seem intuitive to them. As you invite others to join the team, they, too, will get the idea through the doing of it—intuitively—rather than through explanation. Your vision will be built on solid drama already in progress rather than on abstract notions. You see Jesus do this all the time: he shows, and *then* he interprets. Jesus invites the disciples to be with him (Mark 3:14-19), and they see him do a lot of things they don't fully understand until later. Sometimes they have to jump into ministry, doing things they've seen Jesus do, when they don't feel they understand. But this isn't a ploy to exasperate them: it's how Jesus teaches. Create vision by doing vision.

WORKSHOPS:
NON-AUDITION AUDITIONS

I'm not a huge fan of auditions, because they can be intimidating and discouraging to people, and they tend to exclude people who've never done them before. Auditions are certainly valid (see Judges 7:4-5), but they feel out of place in fellowship settings, where our normal ways of discerning people's calls and gifts lean more toward praying together and affirming what we see in one another.

Auditions in some form are, on the other hand, really the only way you're going to know who can do what. It's just not the norm for folks to be strolling the streets reciting monologues, so we rarely get to see nonperformers doing scripted drama. One of the ways you can work this out is to hold workshops where you apply audition categories without the pressure of auditions. I've seen this done successfully with both musical worship and drama, so I pass it on to you with hope.

Here's how it works. Invite the drama team, if you already have one, and anyone else from the congregation who's interested, to spend part of a day looking at new scripts together. There is no promise of team membership implied—just an opportunity for folks to get in on the process and see what they learn. This works best if it happens on a somewhat regular basis, such as once a quarter or twice a year.

As people arrive, you can allow for a few minutes for coffee and milling, during which you (and perhaps a trusty assistant or two) check in with new people and find out a little about them. If you are working with a large crowd or a big church, you might ask people to fill out a brief information card giving you their contact info plus answering a question like, What do you like best about drama? Or, What has been your experience with drama? Either way, getting a sense of who's in the group will later help you to assign work and keep track as you assess potential.

Your first goal is to help everyone relax and have fun. Welcome people in. Gather to introduce the time and each other, and to pray. Do some warm-up exercises (See "Ten Best Warm-Ups We Ever Warmed Up With"). Start out easy, of course, and work up to something challenging. Some will be ready to sink their teeth in. Give them something that's harder to do so you can see who tries, how far they get and how they respond to success or failure.

Once everybody's warm, pass out scripts you have chosen for their straightforwardness and accessibility. Having observed well, you'll have some sense of who to group up for some rehearsal—and later, performance reading—of several sketches. Ask experienced team members to lead the groups.

Send people to side rooms for thirty to forty minutes, and while they work, cruise around to watch. (Trusty assistants may fan out too.) See what people are doing with their scripts. What's their comfort level? Are they trying new things? How's their tone and inflection? volume? enunciation? What do you observe about how they work with others in a group? Take notes. You might get new insight on people you already know!

Bring people back together to perform for each other. Ideally you can have each group run through their sketch twice. After their first run, give them some feedback and have them try it again. You'll be able to see how well folks translate your feedback into their adjustments and actions. Let the crowd cheer people on. Keep taking notes.

Finish off the workshop with some more practice. Choose a couple of exercises that will loosen people back up, relax them and help them to have a good time. End with some food and time to hang out. Keeping the atmosphere friendly and adventurous makes the process attractive. Even if some aren't ready to join the team, they might grow into it over a year or two, so you want them (most of them) to come back.

In many cases, you'll know right away who you're interested in bringing on the team. It is very useful to sit down with the trusty assistants, if you have them, and debrief the workshop. They may have observed what you did not. Discuss people's gifts and teachability. How did each person do at trying new things? Taking risks? Playing as a team member versus being a star? Did you observe any struggles with self-consciousness? And did you notice any extraordinary, surprising or new gifts?

You will need to do more to find out about individual spiritual lives too. After you narrow your focus to the few people you're interested in pursuing, you can use an interview process to further explore how team membership might fit their lives and help them grow.

As your fellowship sees performances, others will become interested in working with you. When people indicate interest, you may want to set up an audition process. You can begin by talking with them and observing them to gauge their readiness for membership on a team. There are also lots of people out there who have gifts in the dramatic realm but have never had the opportunity to try them out. They may have been intimidated. Perhaps they had a bad audition experience and never tried again. Or they may simply never have thought to try. But they're out there, they're game, and some of them will make great team members.

WHAT ARE THE QUALITIES OF A GREAT TEAM MEMBER?

Here's what I look for in potential team members.

Gifts that have been developed. Experience and background are great but don't necessarily translate into the kinds of experience and background that will help you develop a working team in your context. For example, someone who has done mostly Gilbert and Sullivan operettas might have trouble, or even disdain for, adapting to the contemporary edges you're exploring. And there is a lot of bad drama around, so it's also possible that someone has had lots of experience in a low-quality context. On the other hand, it's also possible, and even likely, that some people's backgrounds will be a blessing.

Freedom from self-consciousness. I look for people who are unself-conscious. This doesn't mean they're not aware of themselves, but rather that they're not caught up in how they're coming across. People who are constantly afraid of how they look in front of others will have difficulty acting. If they're prone to attention getting (the flip side of fearful self-consciousness), they'll likewise have trouble acting. Unself-consciousness often translates into a freedom to do the unusual before others.

Truly unself-conscious people have the freedom to try different things, to get goofy, to take risks in front of others.

Expression. I also look for people who are expressive—that is, they show a range of expression when they are telling a story or talking with other people. (Some people, by contrast, are just naturally more stoic.) To be helpful, the expressive quality also needs to be genuine. I want to know if this person's words, face and internal reality match. Does he or she seem authentic?

Presence. "Presence is that quality that makes you feel as though you're standing right next to the actor, no matter where you're sitting in the theater."[1] There are some people who, when they walk into a room, change the social dynamic for the better. This often indicates an intuitive ability to gauge other people, to tune into human emotions. People with presence are often outwardly focused. Their presence doesn't demand, "Hey! Look at me!" (That's insecurity, not presence.) They bring grace and depth into a room because they're able, without being threatened or competitive, to enjoy the presence of others.

Talking gifts. Volume and articulation of speech are also important for drama team members. You can always learn to speak more loudly and enunciate more clearly. But often, people who are already loud and clear are also more confident.

Transferable skills. Some drama gifts show up as transferable skills. For example, an introverted interior designer might be able to use his connections with people's wants, his sense of space and shape and art in general, to engage in drama. An executive might use her skills at painting vision for other people, rallying workers and listening carefully to others. These don't look like dramatic skills, but in the right person they can be transferred and used in new ways. Keep your eyes open for non-acting gifts too. You will need some people who really like working with props, technical equipment and media, sets, and other parts of the process beyond the writing, acting and directing.

Artistic inclination. I keep my eyes open for people who are engaged by art. People who are into art are more likely to enjoy engaging with others in doing art. Drama is harder work than most people think, so anyone who likes the process of making art, or at least appreciates it, will likely manage the tedious moments with greater enthusiasm.

Life with God. Up-front participation in worship is a form of leadership. The drama team will be in front of your fellowship frequently. Even the behind-the-scenes folks are helping to put something in front of the group. Whether they expect and like it or not, people will see them as contacts and leaders in that setting. Witness the way our culture treats entertainers: they're role models and trendsetters. It's not that our groups are insensitive to the differences between the Brat Pack and the Drama Team. However, we are culturally predisposed to equate up-front presence with authority. Our team members need to be able to handle that, both in their personal lives and in their relationships.

A team member's ability to deal with ongoing sin problems, such as lust, idolatry of wealth or looks or career, gossip, coveting others' positions or roles—make the list as long as you like—is crucial. Not dealing can wreck the dynamic not only of one life, but of the whole team. If any one person cannot trust any other one person on a team, they will not be free to work together on a common goal—least of all drama, where everyone is asked to become vulnerable and to trust their teammates.

As you observe candidates, a good question to ask is, does the person apply the same energy to pursuing God as to pursuing drama? I look for people who are able, by putting it in context, to avoid idolizing the drama ministry. That is, they see and understand the world and God's work as much larger than their own sphere, and take active interest in hearing of and praying for God's work in the world. If people only ever talk about and work with drama, they won't have much to bring to the ministry. It is real life, and our willingness to give ourselves to God on a daily, unglamorous basis, that give meaning and charge to our art.

Teachability. Team members must be willing to learn, to try and, failing, to try again. Drama requires great levels of risk taking and can make people feel exposed. When we're in that kind of space, when we need to keep going over the scene, does the person stay in it? Of course everyone gets tired. But the key is attitude. Does the person maintain a posture of humility? Is he or she willing to learn?

One of the best actors I know is also one of the most teachable people I know. Given her monumental gifts and experience, she could easily insist on her way. But she is always the first person to ask, "Is there anything you think I should work on more? Do you have any input for me?" You want this kind of person on a team. These people model for others and build trust in the whole team's process.

Flexibility. Teachable people are also usually flexible. Drama can be bumpy—you don't always know exactly how long a sketch will take to rehearse; you may on occasion have people switch parts or adjust lines. Stuff goes wrong. Team members need to be able and willing to manage the rough spots without resorting to anger, freaking out or shutting down.

Commitment to the team. Finally, team members must be reasonably willing to submit their personal agenda to the team's needs. Even the best actors in the group have to show up on time, with their work done and their spirits ready for rehearsal. The strongest people need to be at rehearsal more, not less, than the weakest. They may not need the extra rehearsal time, but they do need to help the team along with their disciplined, caring, humble presence.

WRITING SCRIPTS

10 WHERE TO FIND SCRIPTS

Alison Siewert

> There is virtually no time when I am not writing. Reading is writing. Cooking is writing. Listening is writing. But what is writing, exactly? Nothing more than getting things straight. That is the job of the writer—to get things straight—things that people say, things that people think, things that people feel. I might as well be working as the straighten-out girl in a room full of hand-knitters.
>
> MARSHA NORMAN

Where can I find good scripts? Everyone wants to know.

[Pause]

Write them.

Of course there are some good scripts out there. Actually, there are some great ones. And you can certainly obtain and perform a good number of them. However, you will likely run into trouble with prewritten material, at least some of the time. Quite often I have encountered scripts written for a completely different context than my own and which therefore don't work for reasons of style, content, tone or resources. This can mean they

◆ seem cheezy, cartoonish, campy or otherwise inappropriate

◆ are cool, but don't fit our aim

◆ are poorly written

◆ require actors we don't have (either in number or quality)

◆ seem preachy or instructional

◆ require formal tone, bathrobe costumes or other features we want to avoid

◆ need technical support, props, sets or other material beyond our scope

Here's some encouragement for locating good scripts: Write them. You can learn to write scripts. If you have an ear for how people really talk (dialogue), how life really goes (story) and how to work in your context (timbre), you can learn. We can't, of course, work it all out on the pages of this book. But we will try to help you get going.

GETTING STARTED

A good script is the right luggage well packed. What are you writing for? Take stock of the context you're working with. Unless you are working on a play that is to be independently mounted in a theater (in which case you need a different book), you need to assess the placement, timing, format and feel of the situation in which your script will be performed.

Riding Lights Players points out that in street settings you must get the audience to stop and pay attention to you right away. Performances need to start with something loud and lively enough to attract notice and interesting enough to warrant the audience's delay from whatever they were headed for.

On the other hand, if you are presenting a sketch in a worship service and it falls between the hymn and the prayer time, you might not choose to gallop through the sanctuary in bright colors and silly hats. (You can, . . . but do you really want to?)

WHAT'S THE SITUATION?

What's your situation? Write down the factors you need to consider. Here's a list to help you start:

◆ audience size
◆ audience age
◆ audience ethnic and cultural backgrounds
◆ audience familiarity with elements of popular culture
◆ audience expectations (would it be really new for them to laugh in this situation?)
◆ actors and other personnel available
◆ time to rehearse and prepare
◆ availability of sets, props and costumes
◆ sound equipment and capability
◆ performance space size and configuration
◆ performance space sightlines
◆ acoustics
◆ special problems or obstructions (a pole blocking people's view, overwhelming heat or cold, lack of sound reinforcement, ambient noise, etc.)
◆ time allotted for sketch; total time for event
◆ position of sketch in the lineup of other elements
◆ particularities of what comes before and after the sketch (mood, content, etc.)
◆ time to prepare stage, or opportunity to set up ahead of the event
◆ mood of overall event
◆ complexity of overall event
◆ amount of writing and preparation time before event

Take inventory, then look at the rest of the chapters in this section for help getting words on paper.

11 SKETCHING LIFE

Alison Siewert

Many of the things we eat are cooked over a gas stove, but there is no taste of gas in the food.

THORNTON WILDER

A sketch does not have to be a complete statement—it's a sketch. It is by nature not complete. It's a suggestion, an impression, a glance, a moment in which we reflect the beauty or mystery or trouble of the whole. It does not have to teach, preach, explain, exhort, introduce, correct or push. It might do one or more of these things, but it should do them by effect and not design.

In this book we use the term *skit* to denote something not quite a sketch. Skits are not as designed to evoke, nor are they necessarily invitations to experience. A skit is something else, entirely valid in the right context, aimed at making or having fun, getting people to do something or to enjoy a particular group of people (e.g., skits made up by youth group members for "talent night"). Even though we've had fun with them, skits are not what we're talking about here. Our focus is on sketches—pieces of theatrical art we can use in worship and other settings to evoke.

THE ECONOMY OF LANGUAGE

Sketches are similar to poems. They are language distilled, compressed and focused in order to evoke an image or experience. Like poetry, they are not usually literal. They don't have to show us the practical details or the beginning-to-end process. Poetry is " 'like a finger pointing to the moon.' . . . To equate the finger with the moon, or to acknowledge the finger and not perceive the moon is to miss the point. Poetry invites, but does not compel, insight."[1]

When you write or choose sketches for your context, try for scripts that use language well. You can do a lot with just a few lines if the script carries rich, dense images. Sketches have to economize language for the sake of time. You don't want too much detail anyway. All you need is a sketch. If you have copious information to communicate, it may be wiser to give a talk.

PART OF A WHOLE

You don't need to preach: the preacher can get up and preach, and people will appreciate how the truth of God's Word interprets and responds to the truth of what they saw on stage. A dramatic sketch should do the same thing as a pen-and-ink sketch. It gives the shape, shows an idea. It invites people to look more deeply. Visual artists often sketch what they eventually fill out in paint or clay.

In a meeting or service, a sketch can create space to be filled out by the whole experience.

Sketches rarely stand completely alone. They're not long enough to warrant seating an audience just for one dramatic piece. So at the very least, a sketch will appear with other sketches or elements that round out the gathering.

Since sketches don't stand alone, we don't have to make them speak alone. They don't need to say everything. In fact, if they try to say too much, they get overwhelmed. It's like a donkey trying to carry a 747. Not gonna happen. The load of meaning needs to fit the size of the delivery vehicle. We think of sketches as part of mosaic, or aggregate, communication—one piece of many that make up a whole picture. They are micronarratives that tell part of the overall story, or metanarrative. These pieces might not go in linear order, but together they make an impression and they communicate.

A PICTURE OF TRUTH

If you design a sketch to push an agenda, the audience—even if they are sympathetic to that agenda—will push right back. People will not receive what is pushed on them. They know propaganda when they see it. On the other hand, if you design a sketch to explore what's true, the audience will receive it, think about it, relate to it and expand their view of the world. Give audiences a choice to hear and see your insight, and they likely will.

Sketches are great because they allow the audience to project their own experience onto the stage. If you want folks to engage with a story, let them into it. And when we're dealing with the stories of God and his people—well, the point is for us to be in the stories. One of the most important things Christian communities do is draw us into the story of God and train us to see salvation history in the Bible and in our own lives. That's why we recite creeds, sing hymns and share Communion. These communal expressions are ways to say, "This is our story, and as we give ourselves to it we find God ever more fascinating, compelling and convincing." This is where sketches fit.

A sketch exegetes the story and invites us to

participate in it by reflecting on our own lives A good sketch well performed creates space for the audience members' projection of themselves into the picture. It also alters their perspective by presenting the story differently, in our case Christianly, according to the met-anarrative of God's story. A sketch invites projection; it offers to adjust our view. A sketch can point to the moon so that we look up and see it where we might have ignored it before. And that is exactly what we hope: that people will see because we have helped them to look.

12 BUILDING A WRITING TEAM

Lisa Harper

For me writing for the theatre is never a lonely activity, it is a practical activity that takes place with the actors.

JATINDER VERMA

A leader from my church called to ask if I would write a dramatic piece for an upcoming Sunday service. I was part of their writing team: a writer they could call to create new work. I had been feeling unconnected, so I saw this as a good opportunity to invest. When I got the call, I immediately went to my computer and, in isolation, wrote away. I came up with a five-minute monologue that captured the theme of the service. I sent it to the worship leaders, who asked if I would perform it the following Sunday. I was excited to be involved with its development. In the past when I'd written, the scripts were passed on to other actors, and rather than seeing the art take shape, I only saw the finished product in worship.

I arrived Sunday morning, ready to per-form. I'd spent hours the day before honing and memorizing the piece and preparing to perform it. It wasn't until I arrived at the church that I found out that they had asked several people to write pieces for that same Sunday and my piece was being cut because the pastor decided at the last minute that there wasn't enough time in the schedule.

Has this sort of thing ever happened to you? When I think about my experience that day, I realize that much of my own struggle has been rooted in the isolation out of which I've expected myself to contribute to a community.

Often we assume that because writing is a solitary act, it should be done in isolation. Yet even in the professional theater, where playwrights can become individually famous for their plays, there is a balance. The fruitful writer usually has a writing community where he or she receives feedback, development and encouragement on a regular basis. Then, once the work reaches the stage where other artists become a part of the development process (actors, directors, designers), the writer is often on hand, taking their feedback and continuing to develop the work.

WRITING IN COMMUNITY

I've discovered that I'm happier, more fruitful and a better writer when I work with others. I spent two days with some friends, developing a play we planned to perform. As I looked back over our two days, I could honestly say they had been the most creative, most fun, most affirming in recent memory. We wrote from 10 a.m. to 10 p.m., parting, each to our own laptop, to work on segments, then regrouping to hear from one another, writing and rewriting as a group.

We warmed up together, acted together, improvised scenes together. We danced together, laughed together, ate together, prayed together and even cried together as God used the very art we were creating to raise issues and bring healing to our souls. And in the end, we created a play together.

In graduate school I wrote drafts of plays alone at my computer, but I was surrounded by community at various intervals in the creative process. I had readings of the play where actors took parts, sat in a circle in my apartment and read out loud so that I could hear it and receive their feedback. I brought scenes into class where other students would take turns reading each other's scenes. Next we held staged readings of the play: a chance for the writer to get the play on its feet—to see actors move on the stage. It's an opportunity to see what works and what doesn't, and to begin to open up the creative process to actors and a small audience. From staged readings came more inspiration. I went back and wrote still more drafts.

HOW DOES THE WRITER WRITE?

Christian communities often think in terms of gifts. If someone has a talent, then they should use it to serve the body. If a person can sing, they might be asked to lead worship. If a person can preach, they might be asked to preach on Sunday mornings. If they can teach, they might be asked to teach Bible studies on Wednesday nights. In most of these ministry settings, we have teams or groups working together in various capacities. Preachers have pastoral staff meetings, musicians are most often grouped in worship teams or choir, and Bible studies usually create a communal environment in which teachers lead. These groups of people nurture leaders as they serve the community. We can do a lot to bless writers by giving them opportunities to work in teams of writers, or as members of larger ministry teams.

The process of creating drama needs to be communal. A writer in isolation will dry up over time. Writers are charged with the task of creating something out of nothing: a story from a blank page. But we are not wells of endless creativity. We are like buckets that need to be creatively, relationally and spiritually poured into so that we can continue to pour out.

BETTER, DEEPER ART

Really good drama happens when we make time and resources available to creative teams. It's not unusual for one person to write a single draft of a sketch, on their own, for use in a service or event. It's tempting to make the creative process quick and efficient; but if we go for speed we're likely to sell ourselves short. Often we're left with a dry point made rather than the beautiful, transformative, powerful experience of the dramatic piece that has been properly developed and pulses with the life of the creative community who offers it.

Now, obviously, most situations aren't theater grad school, and most of our communities lack piles of people with theatrical expertise waiting to meet and process our art. We also don't usually have the time to spend a year developing one piece. But there's still a way to build functional, nurturing writing communities in our contexts.

DEVELOPING TEAMS

I led a new drama writing team that we started in a workshop format. We gathered actors and writers who wanted to develop their gifts to enhance the drama we were using in evangelistic events. Most of the team had limited acting and writing experience but exhibited enough talent and motivation to grow. We spent a year meeting two Saturdays per month. Most of the team participated in acting workshops for the first part of the day. Even the writers benefited from exploring acting and often developed ideas that emerged through improvisation during the acting sessions. After a break, a smaller group would stay to work on writing for the last couple of hours.

From that year of development, a group of actors and writers was formed that continues to create new work in community. We've gathered throughout the years to create new pieces for ministry, including a small touring ensemble.

Our commitment to creating in community does several things to develop our art and us:

◆ It gives us accountability to write, while at the same time providing a motivating environment within which to work.

◆ It gives us a venue to receive through other people's art.

◆ It gives us a place of connection with like-minded creative partners. The freedom to share in a nurturing environment helps us reach new depths.

God strengthens us and builds our character as we serve. He also gave us our talent to bless the body. When we withhold our art, the body misses an opportunity to have their souls opened and to experience God through our gifts. We can help writers to offer their best when we support the development of teams.

LEADING THE TEAM

So, we're in the middle of working on an improvisational exercise that will evolve into a written scene, when the writer, watching the actors, begins to cry. The scene is hitting close to home. It mirrors a real experience she's recently been through. We stop, gather around her and pray. God meets her, assuring her that he is in this situation and wants to do a work of healing. We started the session in project mode; but the important task in that moment was pastoral, not theatrical.

We've found that in our ensemble there are three categories of leadership we need to be mindful of at all times: project leadership, skill leadership and people leadership.

In order to build with quality, we need a skilled, organized, resourceful, networking, visionary project leader. In order to bring out the best work in our actors and writers, we need skilled direction, writer coaching and actor coaching to guide us through the creative process. In order to meet people's spiritual needs along the way, we need a pastor. Our team leaders can identify their strongest gifts; but we must also switch in and out of roles according to need.

It may seem new to think so strongly in terms of leadership skill. But to create an environment that's free, and the sense of safety the actors and writers need to be able to let go and create, leaders need to build security and hope. Actors and writers need leadership to make space for them and set a framework in these areas: projects, skills and people. They need courage to enter the vulnerable creative process. Skilled leadership serves the people on the team and fosters creative reflection on the gospel—so in the end it serves the whole fellowship.

13 TELLING THE WHOLE STORY

Susi Jensen

I saw a strange sight. I stumbled upon a story most strange, like nothing in my life, my street sense, my sly tongue had ever prepared me for.

WALTER WANGERIN JR.

All writers and most artists involved in your dramatic endeavors should know what makes a story great. Books on this subject line a number of shelves at your local bookstore. One of my favorites is *Story, Substance, Structure, Style, and the Principles of Screenwriting* by Robert McKee.[1] This book is a great read for anyone writing for the stage or screen.

How important is it to plot out a story when writing a dramatic piece? Is it possible to compel your audience with a few interesting characters engaging in witty dialogue without a plot to hang it all together?

GOT STORY?

Hollywood producers pay millions of dollars for the rights of a book or a screenplay that tells a good story, and advertisers certainly know the importance of story. The creative writers behind the "Got milk?" ads have become wealthy with a very simple plot repeated in different scenarios on TV. A protagonist (the central character around whom the story revolves) eats a favorite food, like a just-baked chocolate chip cookie. He walks to the refrigerator, eager to pour himself a glass of cold milk. You, the viewer, empathize with the character and can almost taste the cookie. You know what it's like to have a warm cookie in your mouth, mingled with melting chocolate chips. Next, the protagonist opens the door of the refrigerator. You see the milk carton. It's the one ingredient that's missing from this delectable food experience. The protagonist reaches for and grabs the carton. His face falls. He shakes the milk carton desperately, opens the spout and pours two drops of white liquid into his glass. Suddenly this beautiful moment has turned into a tragedy. You feel his anguish and vow to never let the milk supply get that low in your house.

This basic plot contains in it all the elements of a good story. The next time you watch TV, grab a pad of paper and pay attention to the ads. Scribble down their plot lines and see how selling a product or an idea takes place in the context of story.

Hollywood is not the only community sold on story. Christian thinkers and leaders, in response to a culture shift from modern to postmodern, write and talk about story. Postmoderns, they say, respond more to storytelling than didactic teaching.

Any child of Sunday school can tell you that the Bible is filled with fantastic stories. The heroes are grand, yet flawed. The battles and banquets and travels are colorful. The failures are devastating, and God is right there in the mix.

So how much is Christianity rooted in storytelling? The gospel writers chose to record the historical life of Jesus in a narrative style. Moreover, Jesus himself communicated about the kingdom of God most often through stories or parables, even a short parable: "The kingdom of heaven is like treasure hidden in a field. When a man found it, he hid it again, and then in his joy went and sold all he had and bought that field" (Matthew 13:44 NIV). Amazingly this parable contains the making of a drama in two sentences. We see a protagonist, someone not unlike ourselves, stumbling upon a treasure. This encounter changes his life. He can no longer go about his business knowing what he knows. He will turn his life upside down in order to purchase this field. If he is married or has friends, these are secondary characters he will need to convince that this crazy selling spree is worth it. What conflicts will arise around him? The story ends with the final choice of our protagonist . . . to sell all he has, to gain the field and thereby gain the treasure he most desires.

THE ELEMENTS OF A GREAT STORY

If stories are so important, how do we make them great? How do we plot them out?

Protagonist. When you write a story, choose a protagonist based on who your audience will be. You may want your protagonist to be similar to your audience. Jesus' protagonists were often Jewish farmers, fishermen, wives, mothers, fathers, sons, laborers, hosts, guests, masters and servants. His protagonists were not astounding superheroes. Jesus' first-century audience could relate to these people.

If the protagonist you put on stage is unlike your audience, you must find a way to make your audience empathize with him or her. For example, if your audience is twenty-something students and your protagonist is a forty-year-old banker, you will need to find a way to help your audience relate to this character.

Consider the diversity of your audience and make your protagonist someone of color. People of color in our culture are used to viewing the white male protagonist in film and television. In fact, Hollywood has a preference for this type of hero and often casts the minority as the villain. It will be refreshing for your audience to see a woman or a person of color as the protagonist of your story.

You will most likely choose one protagonist. There are exceptions, but be forewarned: writing about multiple protagonists means taking on an extensive writing project in order to develop each character well. For most of our applications (like sketches), one protagonist is plenty.

Setting. In the parable, Jesus offers enough information to give his listeners a sense of where the story takes place. In drama, much of this can be shown with a few props and some well-chosen lines. Another aspect of setting is showing the equilibrium of the protagonist's world, the everyday life that will soon be disrupted. The man walking in the field moves through his day as if it is any other day, except on this day he stumbles upon something.

In the bang-up opening scene of the Lawrence Kasdan's Western *Silverado*,[2] the protagonist, Emmet, has just been released from prison. He sleeps peacefully until he realizes a number of gun-wielding men are creeping outside his hut, preparing to ambush him. Emmet's and the audience's equilibriums have been destroyed. Kasdan will spend the next two hours showing how Emmet tries again and again to regain his equilibrium. Eventually he must face his arch nemesis (a storytelling must in Westerns).

Inciting incident. In a good story, something always disrupts the life of the protagonist: the empty milk carton in the "Got Milk?" ad or the treasure that trips the man as he saunters through a field. These external incidents bring tension into the life of the protagonist, giving the writer a reason to tell the story and the opportunity to develop the protagonist and any secondary characters. In all great stories something happens, usually a problem or a conflict, to move the story along and give the characters something to do. This happening is called the inciting incident, because it incites the story—it gets it going.

Villains and antagonists. Choosing a smart villain, or villains, will lend any dramatic piece excitement and brilliance. In great stories, smart villains can steal the stage. For example, in the movie *Superman*, Lex Luther has a more colorful personality and more witty lines than our hero, Superman.[3] (Most comic books rely on their villain to build a great story.)

The villain is not necessarily external to the protagonist. The villain may lie within the psyche of the protagonist himself or can be more of a concept. For example, time could be the antagonist in a story that highlights the life of a stressed-out college student who is trying to work two jobs, study and hang onto her long-distance boyfriend. However, personifying the villain, even in the story I've outlined above, is a strategic way to show what lies within the psyche of the protagonist. In order to show the true villain, the college student may have a roommate who takes on the voice of her inner conscience, enabling the writer to reveal the protagonist's shadow side.

Action. If there is a golden rule of theater and film writing, it is *Show, don't tell.* In order to do this, you must trust the audience to be wry observers. They will get the subtleties. If your protagonist is a perfectionist, you don't have to have his girlfriend exclaim in dialogue, "Look, here comes my perfectionist boyfriend!" Instead, while your protagonist brings his girlfriend to see his parents for the first time, show him obsessively flicking the lint from her black blazer. Show her getting annoyed with his constant pawing over her appearance. Not only will the audience pick up the fact that your protagonist is a perfectionist,

they will also enjoy the humor of the scene and learn something about this relationship.

The climax. The climax of a story is the protagonist's final and most important choice about how far she will go to achieve what she desires. This choice reveals the character and moral courage of the hero. The climax is the payoff you give your audience. If you've done a good job drawing them into the life of your protagonist, they are invested in the culmination of this character's growth.

In the parable of the treasure in the field, the climax follows the moment when the man hears the price of the field and realizes he must sell everything in order to afford the property. His choice to sell all reveals how much he values the treasure and how far he is willing to go to get it. He not only decides to sell all his possessions, but also does so, Jesus tells his hearers, with joy.

In Lucas's *Star Wars* trilogy, storytelling climaxes reach greatness with Luke's need to confront the dark powers of the Empire. In *Star Wars*[4] he confronts the Death Star, the evil supership that has the power to destroy planets. In *The Empire Strikes Back*[5] he faces off with Darth Vader in revenge for the murder of his mentor, Obi-Wan Kenobi, and the suffering of his friends. The twist in the tale takes on epic proportions when Vader reveals the fact that he is Anakin Skywalker, Luke's father. In *Return of the Jedi*[6] Luke must confront his father and the evil potential within himself.

What are Luke's important choices in each of these confrontations? In *Star Wars* he chooses to confront the Empire; moreover he chooses to trust the Force more than his piloting skills and more than the technology of his fighter jet in destroying the Death Star. In *Empire* Luke confronts Vader with wrath. His subsequent confusion over his identity nearly overwhelms him. His ultimate choice is to hang on and not follow the path of his father. In *Return of the Jedi* Luke's choice is faith in his father's compassion. He chooses against revenge but hopes for his father's conversion, so much so that he is willing to give his life to win him.

Unifying idea. Many fiction writers diagram stories by using an arc. The arc gives the visual of beginning, middle and end—with the rise in action, tension and meaning increasing to the climax of the story, then decreasing in the final scenes that show regained equilibrium. The arc is simplistic, but it's useful for the discussion of the unifying idea. The unifying idea is the spine of the story. It is the reason you are telling the story and can be reduced to a sentence. Any great play or movie hangs together by its overarching, unifying idea.

As you plot out your story and discover the climax, the unifying idea will become clear. The unifying idea of *Star Wars* is "Goodness overcomes evil when the courageous and faithful stand up and fight." The unifying idea of *Empire* is "Hatred taints the hearts of people—even good people." The unifying idea in *Return of the Jedi* is "Goodness overcomes evil when the courageous and faithful stand up and love."

The unifying idea in the parable of the treasure in the field is "When a treasure is found, the possession of it is worth everything you have." That sounds like a sermon title, doesn't it? Yet Jesus, instead of preaching a sermon on the value of the kingdom of God, tells two little stories, the parables of the treasure and the pearl. Do you begin to see how powerful the medium of storytelling can be?

Subplots. Subplots are the various stories of secondary characters woven in with the story of the protagonist and main plot. Subplots have the potential to enrich all aspects of your story, not the least of which is to lend humor to a serious-toned drama. Shakespeare was the master of this. Falstaff was one of his most beloved fools. Read or watch *Henry IV, Part I* and *Part II* and see how essential the Falstaff character is to fun and laughs, but on a more serious note, to the ultimate choice that the young prince Hal will need to make between immoral, rowdy living and that of a responsible leader.

The writer. If you study great fiction in film, theater or literature, you'll discover the secrets of how to compose a great story. A good writer will have some instinct about what works as story. A great writer will work hard to incorporate the elements of a good story into every scene. When you find talented writers in your fellowship, encourage them to spend time and money developing their craft. Sponsor them to take a class, see movies and read scripts. As your writers develop, you will have great drama, because great drama begins with a great script. A great script begins with a great story. A great story is conceived in the mind of the writer.

14 CONTEXT ISN'T EVERYTHING, BUT IT SURE IS A LOT

Alison Siewert

Even if you had a quick eye for things it would have taken time to see and understand all that was going on if you went into a Dutch room in the seventeenth century.

H. R. ROOKMAAKER

David Mamet says, "The audience will teach you how to act and the audience will teach you how to write and to direct."[1] The audience represents your context. The people sitting in the chairs carry with them the attitudes, assumptions and hit songs of the day. They live daily in culture. When we write and perform drama, it's our job to grasp the context. Even if you live in the same culture as your audience, it's wise to take frequent trips around the cultural block, to keep up on what's happening out there, in order to enliven your language and pictures and hone your onstage choices so that they make sense to the audience. The audience will teach you—if you ask and if you pay attention.

Think about your context. If you've ever watched TV in another country or culture, you know what I mean. Both dramatic and comedic theater are rooted in culture. Drama can usually make the translation from one cultural context to another, because it tends to rely on natural dialogue and deals with universal subject matter. But chauffeuring comedy over a border is quite difficult, because it relies not on presenting what's universal but rather on turning the specifics of a moment, culture or event so that we see them from a different angle. Something we thought of as normal suddenly has its absurdity exposed. If you weren't there for the event or don't know the specifics of the moment or culture, you don't get the joke.

WORD USAGE

We must also pay attention to word usage, which changes over time and by culture. Dorothy Sayers, in her 1939 play *He That Should Come*,[2] has Joseph and Mary arrive in Bethlehem in need of housing. The centurion, trying to keep governmental peace, and the landlord (innkeeper), trying to help the young couple, speak this exchange:

CENTURION: How about the stables? Is there any room there?

LANDLORD: Well, I dunno about that. Let me see now—it means getting their ass in as well. *[to Mary]* Could you lie along of the ass, mistress?

I think we all see the problem here. Check the words.

GENERATIONS AND THEIR CULTURES

We must also pay attention to the generation, the day-to-day verbal, social and visual culture of the specific group for which we're performing. This may be the most treacherous path of all, because youth cultures in particular are accustomed to marketing that knows and understands their needs, wants and preferences—right down to the color of their shoelaces. And marketers don't just know what people want—they actively shape it.

If you want to create a character who's a current high school student interested in tattoos, weird hair and the latest retro-punk clothing, you'd better either be one of those people, know one well or do very good research. What you don't want to do is try for such a character and fall short (the "wrong" kind of tattoo, outdated blue hair and so on), because that will produce laughter, but in ridicule rather than identification. You can write wild characters if you work hard, test them on people who know better than you, and listen humbly to feedback and critique, which will help you get it right.

The same goes for writing dialogue. The humor predominant in Christian theater writing is what we might call boomer-oriented. That is, it's written toward the culture of baby boomers—people born between about 1940 and 1960. Postmoderns (people born mostly after 1960), who can be divided into several cohorts and described many ways, generally respond more strongly to drier, subtler humor. As a generation we've been marketed to from before speech (know any one-year-olds who can identify certain fast food by its arches?), so we become cynical toward staged communication. There's a sort of low retaining wall that we always suspect people are trying to jump—with a big, stylish jump—in order to sell us on what will make them rich.

The movie *Mystery Men* is a flawed but effective illustration of the Zeitgeist of this generation and its departure from "boomerness." Captain Amazing, who is (of course) amazing, handsome and outfitted in his corporate-sponsor-covered uniform, is kidnapped by the evil Casanova Frankenstein, who, having been released from a criminal asylum, wants to take over (of course) the world. Meanwhile,

a motley group of superhero wannabes has been auditioning more superhero wannabes to join them in their vague fight for good. The group includes Mr. Furious (his superpower? Rage!), the Spleen (don't ask), the Bowler (carries her unjustly murdered father's skull, encased in a bowling ball, which is deadly accurate when bowled at bad guys), the Blue Rajah (knife-throws his mother's forks), the Sphinx (imparts non sequitur proverbs) and Invisible Boy (has never actually become invisible but would like to).

There's a traditional good-versus-bad conflict raging through the entire movie. All the while, the sub-superheroes strive just to find their footing. In the process they inadvertently toast Captain Amazing, fall apart, slam into their own self-doubt and nearly lose Mr. Furious altogether . . . but (of course) win in the end. Their back-story is about living at home with your parents, not having enough income, getting stuck with unresolved family issues and trying but never quite reaching the standard-issue American Dream. They are superheroes for a post-superhero generation. Which is to say they are not really superheroes at all but a struggling, shoe-on-the-wrong-foot community of friends that sticks together and somehow makes it through. That's our context.

If you want to communicate to rising generations, understatement is a good place to start. Write for underplay rather than for big, stagey acting. We tend to distrust anything that tries too hard. We're used to seeing television; not that many young adults go to theater regularly. So we're trained on intimate, underplayed acting that can be seen on a screen. The transmitter is not the actor but the camera. While we may not always project theatrical communication onto a screen, all theater needs a foundational understanding of understatement in order to work well. Off screen, actors will likely play things bigger than they would if they were playing to a lens, but they should not play to the back of the house. Scripts, likewise, need to play to understatement rather than the back of the house.

A note: Once you have some practice with understatement, you can write satire and camp pieces. *Mystery Men* is a good example of how over-the-top humor can actually work in an understated way.

SELF-CONTAINMENT

In an understated script we trust the audience to get the point without having it explained. The sketch should be self-evident. This is most obvious in comedy: puns, clever rhymes (I almost said "Boomer humor," but . . .), big physical or slapstick jokes and cheez. Obvious, proclamatory humor won't work. If a sketch has to be explained, it probably hasn't sunk its roots deep enough into the soil of the context. A note to leaders and speakers sharing services and events with drama teams: If the art doesn't need to be explained, don't try to explain it. You will most likely ruin whatever the sketch did to evoke if you get up and decode it for us. To do well at contextualizing for coming generations, we have to be there and be listening.

Here's an example of what I mean. In this boomer-oriented sketch, the woman caught in adultery (John 8) is observed from the front porch by two other women from her village:

ETHEL: *[sitting down with her coffee]* Ach! Did they finally deal with that harlot?

MYRTLE: *[looking out]* Isaac said they're about to bring her into the square now. They want to consult this new Rabbi.

ETHEL: Jesus of Nazareth?

MYRTLE: Yes. Oh, look! There she is.

The action unfolds, as people demand a stoning, hear from Jesus and then are dismissed by him. We skip ahead to the end of the sketch . . .

ETHEL: Look! The rabbi is talking to . . . to her?

MYRTLE: She's talking, too! That tramp. She ought to be ashamed of herself.

ETHEL: Well, do you think he knows?

MYRTLE: About her? What kind of—man—would that make him? I thought he was a rabbi, and a rabbi is supposed to be—

ETHEL: Wait.

MYRTLE: Ethel?

ETHEL: She's . . . Is she? She's crying.

MYRTLE: Are you sure she's not trying for a sympathy hug?

ETHEL: No, she seems deeply moved.

MYRTLE: *[leaning for a better view]* I'll say.

ETHEL: Wow. She's all worked up. Do you think she's scared? Or devastated?

MYRTLE: She seems more . . . stunned.

The device of this sketch (the scene described by characters observing) is clever and could be effective. But the dialogue is overstated for a postmodern audience; you can have someone show, be or hint at "deeply moved," but you don't want it described by anyone on stage. It's too much. It doesn't evoke, it announces. Some folks won't mind that, but young adults generally won't go for it.

A monologue of the woman at the well, written by Carey Cecil, shows a similar kind of woman: a frustrated, lonely figure, folding her laundry away from the chattering church ladies who have annoyed and humiliated her. She mutters to herself:

MARA: Religious ladies . . . with their lives so . . . perfect . . . *[sarcastic]* so together . . . *[pause]* I only . . . *[glancing back behind her toward the ladies]* Well, who needs it? [3]

The monologue implicitly sketches the life of this woman. We know that she has interacted, even if from a distance, with people who have made their disapproval of her quite clear and that this has left her angry, resentful and alone. We don't need to hear the whole of the conversation because from our own experience we know what she's talking about. The audience is trusted to get the gist and to connect the storyline from there. In the context of a young adult crowd, that's all you need.

STEREOTYPE

One last contextual issue we need to stay aware of is the potential for drama to devolve into stereotype. A *stereotype* was an early French printing machine. Now it's a way of looking at people that enunciates only one or two predominant characteristics about them: "They have blonde hair" becomes "They're a blonde," and draws its conclusions from that limited characteristic: "Blondes are dumb" or "Blondes have all the fun." Usually stereotypes relate to physical attributes, origin or culture, and occupation. So we get the impression that Californians are airheaded surfers likely to be high on pot or carrot juice in between trips to the gym; Asians are wise, quiet, eat rice daily and need us to talk loudly and slowly so they can understand our language; football players are loud, loutish, unintelligent; and so on.

Be careful. It's nearly impossible not to be influenced by stereotypes, but it's our responsibility to become aware of them and avoid falling into them. We create drama in order to reach people; stereotypes cut people off by assuming we know who they are. When we allow stereotypes, we communicate that we don't even care to listen to a person, let alone talk deeply with them about the meaning of the gospel in their lives.

Be very aware of language choices, accents and mannerisms when you are creating sketches that involve strongly cultured characters. Are you making the women's lines catty or gushing? Are your men large, tool-laden and emotionless? Are you asking African American characters to "be more black"? Do your high school kids all hate their parents and hang out at the mall every day? Are the British people always more intellectual? Are the Southern people ever intellectual? What we ought to do is dismantle stereotypes for the sake of seeing and sharing the true identity and the full beauty of people who were created by God.

15 WRITING DIALOGUE

Alison Siewert

I found the theater such an exciting experience that one day I went home to try. I had one character say to the other guy, "Hey man, what's happening?" And the other guy said, "Nothing." I sat there for twenty minutes and neither of my guys would talk.

AUGUST WILSON

How do people really talk? Unless you are writing a highly stylized script that requires its speeches to rhyme or has a character not from this world, your dialogue needs to reflect how people—your characters—really talk. You have to become a student of the speaking world.

This presents an interesting problem for anyone who lives or works in a Christian cultural milieu. Take worship songs, for example: despite the growing number of songs being written with vernacular lyrics, lots of them speak in Christian lingo. A musician I know said, "Think about that lyric 'Your Name is like honey on my lips.' What does that mean? I don't even say that to my wife."

True, most of us don't speak in psalms. The poetry of our everyday language is simpler and more practical than the grand analogies of the Scripture.

Part of our problem rests in the peculiarities of the Bible and its translations. Sometimes when we're trying to make a biblical point or sketch a biblical character, we just keep the biblical language. Perhaps because it seems important to stay true to the Word, or perhaps because it can be scary to paraphrase—*Will people be offended? Will I get it right?* We can get stuck when we try to make formal language and terms sound natural and colloquial.

Now, if you want to do formal language—say, Shakespeare—you can do it. Pick material that's well written and actors with major chops, and go for it. Then again, that may be a problem, as most of us aren't swamped with actors who were trained at the Royal Shakespeare Company. Or who are accustomed to thine formal speech.

If you're not going with Will, then you have other work to do. Two characters need to have a conversation. How do people really talk? Listen. Listen to people talk. When you're in line for cafeteria mystery lunch or at the bookstore reading the latest *Insect Journal* or in the produce aisle examining zucchini, listen. Sometimes hearing people outside your own head helps you get past your own presuppositions about conversation. Sometimes it's really funny. Sometimes you hear whole stories.

This is not the same as eavesdropping. You are not after information. Sometimes, to be fair, a talker will distribute information you didn't ask for. While waiting at my favorite airport, I heard the entire story of how a lady bought a bracelet for her stepdaughter's graduation, only to find the girl's mother had bought the same bracelet and what were they going to do about that because after all she didn't want to be rude. The whole story. All the details. At a zillion decibels. The woman was at least fifty feet from me. I wasn't trying to listen, I promise—neither were the other hundred people waiting in the terminal. She was just . . . so . . . loud!

You can pick up peculiarities such as accents, local colloquialisms and exclamatory expressions. It can be fascinating to observe modes of interaction in other cultures too. Though I would never presume through brief observation to know a culture well enough to base a sketch in it, I do see new ways of relating. For example, when I did mission work in England, I noticed that British people not only tend to speak more quietly and with less gesticulation than Americans but also take up less sidewalk space when they walk. Americans tend to use a lot of space-per-person as they walk. We almost swagger. You could see English people having discreet conversations along the street, while American Lou yelled to Tina, "Tina! Hey, Tina! I'll meet youze over there on that little . . . what's that red box? The telephone thing! I'll meet youze there in an hour!" I learned about my own culture by being in a different one. And listening.

SCRIPTING THE STORY

As you listen, you will develop an ear for dialogue. You will also develop an ear for subtext. Subtext is what isn't said. For instance, the lady who bought her stepdaughter the bracelet was probably experiencing some anxiety about her role in the girl's life. Was it appropriate for her to give the bracelet? Or was it better for her to step aside and let the girl's mother give it to her? From her tone and volume, it was clear this was a difficult situation for her. But this was all below the surface of her words. She didn't actually say, "Gee, I don't know what's most appropriate here. And this brings up painful questions about my role in Susie's life." That was the subtext. We all have them, so it's important for our characters—especially in more fully developed sketches—to have them, too. Subtext reveals as much, and sometimes more than, the words.

Look at your storyline and begin to write the conversation that comes to mind for your characters. (This is a highly intuitive process; just jump in and try it.) For example, if you want to create a conversation in which two characters are having a big fight, you need to think about how people really sound when they're fighting. If you're going for comedy, you will likely exaggerate:

MABEL: You are so—

ANGUS: I'm so what?

MABEL: You're a slob!

ANGUS: I'm a slob?

MABEL: Do you know where your project files are? No! Because they're all over your house! You can never find anything because you always leave piles all over the place! And when you lost the conference registrations last year? I found them under your bed with a MilliVanilli CD and a dog food sample! You are a slob!

ANGUS: Oh yeah? Well you always leave your sweaty socks on the couch after *ER!*

MABEL: Do not!

ANGUS: Do too! *[picking his nose]* And you get moody when you don't eat breakfast. And you listen to country music in the car. And you always have to have coffee! What is it with the coffee? You're a total coffee addict. Coffee! Coffee! Coffee! It's a bad habit and, frankly, it makes you smell!

MABEL: Makes me smell?! How can you tell how things smell when your finger is always up your nose?

ANGUS: *[removing finger]* My finger is not always up my nose.

MABEL: Oh, okay.

ANGUS: You know . . . it's amazing, you are such a . . .

MABEL: What? What am I?

If you're writing a serious sketch, you should not exaggerate. Keep things understated, for underplay. In serious or difficult situations, most of us try not to say too much. The drama is as present in what is not said as it is in the words. I sometimes imagine what the characters are thinking, then think about where they would cut themselves off. What are they thinking but not saying? The dialogue reflects the subtext of their conversation as well as what's actually exchanged.

MAN: I'm gonna miss you.

WOMAN: Me too.

MAN: Really, I mean . . . this has been great. I mean, really.

WOMAN: I know what you mean. It's been really fun. I wish we had—*[interrupted]*

MAN: *[interrupting]*—I wish we had more time. To be together.

WOMAN: *[sighing]* Yeah. That would be really great.

MAN: But *[with Woman]* you gotta go.

WOMAN: *[with Man]* I gotta go.

MAN: Yeah. I know. I mean, this is a big life thing.

WOMAN: Yeah, it's kind of a big thing. *[Pause]*

MAN: What time's your plane? Again? *[laughing nervously]* I keep forgetting the time.

WOMAN: Yeah. I'm trying to forget, I think.

MAN: Can you check?

WOMAN: Eight . . . *[checking ticket]* Eight fifty-five.

MAN: Yeah . . . *[checking watch]* Eight fifty-five.

In emotionally difficult situations—when we don't know what to say—we generally try to say what feels normal in order to defend against what doesn't. So we talk about the weather, the time. If we refer to our feelings, it is often in circumlocution, talking around issues, or in subtext, admitting our feelings below the surface of what we're really saying.

In this clip, the characters attempt to deal with their inevitable parting by focusing on other things. They check the time on her ticket and his watch as a way of expressing their anxiety that they don't have much time left. They attempt to steel themselves for what must come: her exit to the jetway and the airplane.

When we're sad or troubled, we have less energy to compose a long soliloquy about why we're sad or troubled. Our energy is wrapped up not in why we're troubled or how we feel but rather in how we can escape our trouble, alleviate our discomfort or deny our pain. We spend a great deal more energy not saying things than saying them. Fragments of our true feelings may pop to the surface occasionally, but most of us don't dwell there. If we did, the dialogue might start out something like this:

MAN: I don't want you to leave! I'm gonna miss you. Because we had such a great time working on this and becoming friends. I can remember so many really important moments along the way. This year together has been the most meaningful time I've ever had. We got to see people worship and come to know Jesus for the first time and commit to loving others around them. It was so wonderful in so many ways. Having you leave now makes me feel dismal about the future, because I'm afraid I won't be able to develop another friendship as good as ours. I fear the loss of you and the work we were engaged in—all at the same time. I'm not sure what my life will mean without you and the work. I mean, what will I do with all my spare time?

WOMAN: I don't want to get on that plane. I want to stay! I feel precisely the same way you do. I'll miss you. I agree with all you've said—this was a deep, amazing time for us. It seems like we'll be kind of afloat or something for a while. I have no clear destination except just to go and see what happens. That scares me. Because if things go well, I think I'll feel okay, and hopefully I'll make new friends, and of course we'll stay in touch by e-mail. But what if I go and I'm not okay? What if I'm really lonely? Or I can't find people who want to get deep, to know Jesus with me? What if it's just . . . a wasteland out there? I'm afraid, and I'm not sure how to handle this.

In high-stress situations, few people, if any, would speak so profusely. And if real people wouldn't say it, then neither should your script.

MOVING THE STORY

Finally, good dialogue must move the story forward. I've written plenty of lines that I've later cut because they didn't contribute to the plot. Dialogue must make the plot keep happening. The story in a play is told through the dialogue. So when you're choosing to keep or toss, make that one of your evaluative categories. It's not good enough for the talking to be good; it has to be meaningful to the story. Even the couple at the airport, though not making a huge point, is talking about the point of the story and moving things ahead. Departure time is on its way. Their words attempt to forestall the inevitable, deny the pain of leaving, make sense of something that . . . doesn't. That's what the story is about. Even though they could have launched on a discussion about what they had been doing (the project they refer to), they don't. The immediate story is about leaving.

Writing good dialogue takes practice. Sometimes you'll think it's going to work. Then you hear a couple of actors read it and realize it doesn't work. Keep at it. Because at some point along the way, being a student of talking humans will pay off and your dialogue will tell amazing stories.

16 WRITING FUNNY

Alison Siewert

Obvious Rule No. 1

Never look down on comedy or regard it as the poor cousin of drama.

ALAN AYCKBOURN

If you've ever watched *Saturday Night Live*, *Mad TV* or any other sketch comedy show, you know it can be pretty difficult to write funny sketches—and have them turn out truly funny. TV shows have the highest-paid, best-supported writing staffs anywhere and should therefore (you'd think) be able to come up with awesome comedy. But quite often it deteriorates to the lowest common denominators of our culture: the crude and the lewd. It's not easy to write funny, relevant stuff. But it is possible.

KNOW YOUR CONTEXT

In comedy, context is almost everything. Humor is deeply rooted in culture. What strikes Europeans as funny might seem intellectual and, at best, droll to Americans. What makes one culture crack up can make another one walk away puzzled.

Figure out what's funny in your community. Listen to people telling stories, making jokes, throwing off sarcastic comments. Watch what they are watching on TV—even if you don't like it—so you understand what is in people's ears. Check out shows and comedians, and study how they make people laugh. At what are they laughing? And why are they *really* laughing?

LOOK FOR TRUTH

Humor can help a theatrical moment to sneak in and make an impact. When people are busy laughing, they let their guard down. And that's when a sketch can assert its true moment and catch people's attention, affection and curiosity. That's the moment when your characters can express what's really happening to them. What they couldn't say at the beginning of the conversation they now can say, because the audience has reached a level of trust and connection with the characters. The hearers are ready to identify.

In *Ed and Laura's Seriously Scary Conversation*, based on Jesus' parable of "clean evil" in Luke 11, I wanted to illustrate how easy it is for us to be aloof to true evil. Jesus says that things can look clean—but underneath be death-dealing (Luke 11:24-26, 37-44). Our culture is fascinated with pretending evil but often doesn't rightly see its own real-life complicity with the enemy. That's a heavy topic. I could've used a heavy sketch, but I decided it would be better to develop something funny that would trace our culture's glib acceptance of evil from a couple of different angles. Ed, therefore, is excited about an over-the-top horror flick; Laura is concerned by news of real evil she has just read.

ED: *[describing a movie]* So anyway . . . then the Devil Dog, it like runs really, really fast up to the poor innocent farmer-girl, and it like jumps up and it doesn't bite or anything, it just howls this hellish howl, and so the farmer-girl, she just like . . . dies. Right there.

LAURA: *[looking up from the newspaper she's been reading]* Did you hear about what's going on at factories overseas, like in Indonesia?

ED: Just dies. *[imitating fainting]* Right then, from the bark alone. Dude, it was so completely scary. 'Cause it's not actually the bite that kills people with the Devil Dog—it's the bark. Ya know?

LAURA: Yeah, uh-huh. At these factories, the rumor is, at least, that if you ask for a raise, you disappear.

ED: And the Devil Dog, it's like running around the countryside and pretty soon it starts breeding with other dogs, like, ya know, regular, innocent dogs, and then there's a whole new breed of Devil Dogs. It's really scary.

LAURA: Like, if you ask for a raise, some overlord or boss or whatever, they take you out.

ED: And then, I hear that in the next one, I think it's called *Devil Dog Six: Revenge of the Bloodhound*, they're gonna have the Devil Dog like take over a whole village, or maybe a state. In the English part of . . . England.

Sneaking in humor can make people pay attention to things they'd normally avoid thinking about. I mean, I don't like to think about the fact that my shoes may have been made by the hands of a virtual slave either. But when it's presented across from something as silly as *Devil Dog: Hound of Hell*, we find ourselves and the audience hearing the real, more significant issue before we know it's hit us.

Explaining comedy is sort of like defining the color chartreuse. You know it when you see it; you know what it's not; but it's pretty hard to explain. I'll try, though, and you can let me know if any of this is helpful.

KINDS OF FUNNY

◆ Exaggeration—"They're gonna have the Devil Dog like take over a whole village, or maybe a state."

◆ Bathos, or understatement—This is key for postmodern audiences:

MARK: Hey, Kent!
MARK'S INTERNAL VOICE: *[offstage]* Nice shirt. Wish I had a shirt like that.

◆ Incongruity—Ed talks about *Devil Dog* movies; Laura talks about injustice.

◆ Contrast—An extremely loud, extroverted person talking wildly to an extremely quiet, introverted person who is nonresponsive.

◆ Running gag—*Saturday Night Live*'s famous Hans and Franz characters, who weren't that funny until they kept repeating their "pump you up" line. Over and over. (David Letterman is also fond of this device.)

◆ Blended words—Nastiferous, skankweed, stumiliating, ubiquiBob and their friends.

◆ Gentle absurdity—Characters named "Rila: Love Warrior" and "Bible Power Princess Claire." Anything involving "Action Moses" and "a burning bush playset" (sold separately). Also, capybaras engaging in discourse about the virtues of watermelon.

◆ Metaphor (use sparingly)— "As attractive as standing beneath a steady drizzle of dead cats."[1]

◆ Rant—"Why does it always sound like a flannelboard story? Jesus is this flat, white, figure with dippy hair and a lamb. I don't get it. Jesus said stuff like, 'I came to bring fire to the earth, and I wish it would start already.' Dippy hair and a lamb?"

◆ Repartee—Quick, witty banter, usually challenging or insulting:

JACK: You . . . you broke my chopstick.
JANE: It's just a chopstick, Jack. It was cheap . . . free with your food.
JACK: It's my cheap chopstick, Jane.[2]

◆ Physical recovery—Tim does a spectacular triple trip down the stairs, slides across the floor and twirls, landing on one knee, with his shirt turned backward. But he has not dropped his Bible, which, after clearing his throat, he nonchalantly opens to read.

◆ Misunderstanding—A guy thinks Hawaii

and Alaska are within a few miles of each other because "they're always together on the map, aren't they?"

And here, for your further pleasure, are some "rules"—the best I can come up with—for writing funny sketches.

RULES FOR WRITING FUNNY

◆ Don't write more than you need. Once people are laughing, move on to set up the next joke. Don't kill a joke by telling it again. We already heard it, so we don't really need to hear it again. If you say it again, it kind of gets . . .

◆ Don't write more than you need. The pieces of the picture must be close enough together for the audience to follow.

◆ Let it explain itself (if it refuses, kick it out). If it's not funny on its own, explaining it won't make it funny.

◆ Check to make sure it's funny. Ask someone besides your mom.

◆ Hold off on the punch line as long as you can. Delay creates suspense, suspense creates expectation, and if people expect to laugh, they probably will.

◆ Make a U-turn. It can be funny—and fun, for that matter, to make a sudden switch of direction. Just when everyone thought they had the sketch figured out.

◆ Have a really good time. If you have fun, and if you have friends, you will figure out how to write funny. Situations will happen (like the guy who thought Hawaii and Alaska were next-door neighbors—that's true, I'm not kidding) in your lives. These situations will make you think of other things that will make you laugh, which you, in turn, will write down for us. Then *we* will laugh. The kingdom of God will be a place of great laughter . . . let's start practicing.

17 WRITING MONOLOGUES

Alison Siewert

There are no *ordinary* people.

C. S. LEWIS

MARY *sits in a big chair. She is visibly pregnant. She speaks as though to a supportive counselor.*

MARY: It's . . . it's been really hard around home. I mean, my parents are great and everything but this . . . they're having a hard time. I mean, they don't believe me. They think I must have gotten drunk or whatever and like blew it with some guy. But I didn't. It wasn't like that. I was walking back from my cousin's house . . . and this, [*pausing, uncomfortable, trying to find a word*] this, this wind—I mean, I guess it was like a wind. I don't know what to call it. This wind hit me right here [*touching her right cheek].* It was warm, and . . . and I just kind of . . . I knew. I knew it was something. And it blew around me—the wind—and then I just felt like I was supposed to kneel down, like it was God. And it was . . . *[pausing, then quietly continuing]* God. He asked me, he asked me if I would do it, if I would carry the baby, if I could carry the baby to term and not get scared and back out and . . . *[pause taking a deep breath]* So I said, "Yes . . . okay. I will."

WHO IS THIS PERSON?

Arthur Miller said, "The sheer presence of a living person is always stronger than his image."[1] Mary shows up quite often in Christian drama: she is an image. How many little girls vie to play her part in the Christmas pageant? But when we look past the image at the real Mary, we recognize that her life experience was not always crowned with a halo, and her pregnancy was not always understood as the blessed event. In fact, Mary's life was a scandal. She became pregnant through mysterious circumstances—usually we call it "fooling around"—at a very young age, before she was married. In first-century Palestinian family life, Mary was waaay out of line.

So when I made a monologue of her experience, I wanted it to sound like the gritty life it was. It struck me over and over as I wrote, *Nobody knew.* No one understood what was happening here. A high school freshman was carrying the Savior of the universe and no one got it. How could they have grasped this? It's not a category—becoming pregnant through supernatural circumstances. Having God's baby who is God himself incarnate—it's a little much for a theologian, let alone a morning-sick high school kid.

MAKING THE PERSON A STORY

Monologues can be difficult to write for a couple of reasons. First, with just one person onstage, there's no inherent conflict. You have to find a reason for the person to tell her story,

then sink the reason deep into the speech. The character may not be able to say, with any naturalness, why she is suddenly showing up and telling you about herself. Your first problem to solve is, what sparks the person to talk? In Mary's case, it is the continuing crisis of being pregnant, of being in the middle of the story, still trying to understand what is happening to her. She needs to talk it out.

The second problem in monologue writing is that the character has no one onstage to whom he speaks; therefore he must talk to an imaginary person (as I have Mary do here) or directly to the audience. One way to understand the difference in the effect of these two approaches is to consider a basic view of a fourth wall. The fourth wall is the imaginary wall between the actors onstage and the audience in representational theater. When the play happens behind the fourth wall, the idea is that, in our imaginations, we consider the play to be self-contained on the stage. As with Mary here, the audience observes, but is not part of, the action. By contrast, presentational theater functions without a fourth wall: the actors include the audience in their interactions. The stage is imagined as having only three walls, with the fourth side open, and the audience is in it with the actors. For a monologue, you can use either device—they are only devices—depending on what best fits the kind of character you're writing.

The first thing Mary does in this monologue is exposition. No, she doesn't expose herself exactly—although, she kind of does. She lets the audience in on her predicament. They come to understand who she is, what she's up against, how she's feeling. She introduces herself, and they decide to get to know her. You want your audience to like and be interested in the character, so the actor needs to involve them from the start. Have the character tell them enough so they know what's up, but not so much they're overwhelmed with detail.

MARY: That was the beginning of . . . things being hard. I felt kind of sick, but I couldn't tell anyone, so I had to, you know . . . I mean, I had to pretend everything was normal. And my fiancé, Joey, he was really nice because he thought I had like mono or something, I was so tired. But then . . . [pause] . . . then I started, you know, showing, looking like I was gaining weight, and then all of a sudden it's huge, my middle is huge. And everyone's talking. And Joey—everyone thinks he's such a nice guy, and his dad's a pastor, so they believed him when he said, "Hey, it wasn't me." But they didn't believe what I said . . . "Who'd she—?" "Whose baby?" "Why did she go an' blow such a nice engagement? Think of how her parents must feel." "That Joey's such a sweet boy and she's just a tramp."

Now the conflict intensifies. Keep the telling lively. We need enough detail to keep it colorful, not clinical. And the story must stay in the character's voice. You can probably gauge Mary's voice quite rapidly in this piece. She talks with teenage insecurity, a girl making the transition to young woman under very difficult circumstances. She trying to find her footing through the whole thing. In this case, I asked the actor not to be timid, but to use a *sotto voce* ("half voice") and to observe the ellipses and interruptions in the script, which reflect a person who is searching for what she really wants to say.

Keep in mind, too, what the character does not say, what she tries not to say. This is as important as what she does say. Every story has a subtext—something going on below the surface of the story. Look for what the character would prefer not to talk about, what she's trying to hold in, because it's too painful, or might imperil her, or feels embarrassing. You can probably locate a subtext in your own life if you review your last few conversations and ask yourself, What was I trying not to say? Mary does not complain. She doesn't theologize. She doesn't give a chirpy "It's been hard, but good" summary to her experience. Because she's telling us how she got to where she is, but she's not telling us how she's getting to the next thing. She doesn't know. And

her not knowing, and struggling to be okay with not knowing, is the subtext of her story.

Writing Mary made me think of the many interactions I've had with teenage mothers and birthmothers. My kids are adopted; I have deep respect for the young women who carried them to term when the very carrying broke apart so much of the rest of their worlds. Mary sits in exquisite tension—perceived by her own family as a tramp (they did, after all, pack her off to a faraway cousin to spare everyone the embarrassment) and perceived by God as a major player in salvation history. It's the space between what Mary tells us and what she keeps to herself that defines her voice. That is where her heart sits—in the middle of the struggle.

MARY: A couple of nights ago—maybe it was last night, I can't remember—Joey came over while I was in class and talked to my mom and dad. . . . Then when I got home, they all told me to sit down and they told me the wedding was off. My mom made this big show of taking the dress—the wedding dress she bought me—and putting it away in a bag. My dad said how they were so disappointed in me, and how they hoped I'd figure out a way to make something better of myself, and how sad it was for me to lose such a nice man like Joey. And then Joey left, without even talking to me . . . [pause] He just walked away, down the street, and didn't say anything. Not even goodbye.

Now Mary faces the great cost of her "yes" to God. She has lost her status, her engagement, her fiancé, her parents' approval—and, in a crushing, material symbol—her wedding gown. Any woman in the audience old enough to think seriously about marriage will get this. Having your mom, in disappointment and grief, pack up the wedding gown you shopped for together . . . well, that's more than most of us would bear. The putting away of the gown is the final statement to Mary that her life as she's known it is done. From her family's perspective, her irresponsible behavior made her unworthy and changed everything. From her perspective, it is God's decision that changed everything. But who's going to believe that?

Not Joey. He doesn't get it. But how could he? He simply leaves, packs himself up like the wedding gown and goes away. I had him remain silent because in Luke's Gospel he doesn't even show up, and in Matthew's he chooses to remain silent, to do what's most honorable for Mary, until God speaks to him through an angel in a dream (Matthew 1:19-23). Joey needed to reflect a man who was willing, even in great sadness, to depart quietly. The world applies all its pressure.

MARY: So . . . now it's just me and . . . the baby. I'm moving out this weekend—I think to my aunt Liz's, a couple of towns over, where people don't know me.

Now we relax the tension a bit. Notice it doesn't get all worked out. Mary is still very pregnant and still lives without any certainty of how or whether it will all turn out. She can't know—she can only trust. And trust carries a certain amount of risk and therefore tension. We don't want to wrap it up prematurely. Give people time to sit in the character's trouble. That was why I wrote this, remember? Mary's life was difficult.

She has just lost all her life plans, her hopes, her fiancé. Her beautiful gown is now folded up in a bag—she may never wear it, never get to be the bride, never regain her reputation. That's her reality.

[Pause]
MARY: *[touching her cheek]* That wind—did you feel that, just now? *[looking above the crowd]*

This line worked because our actor understated it. It will not work if an actor enunciates it too broadly, making it very dramatic—"That wind!!" She should not sound like Jo from *Little Women*, all eagerness and ingénue. Be careful! Ending a monologue before the charac-

ter's story ends is kind of difficult. You need to leave the tension tense but release the audience to respond. It's hard to make that happen without cheez. Cheez happens when we try too hard to make it happy or conclusive or even theological. When we used this sketch in the worship service I wrote it for, we brought in music right after Mary's last line. I had her, like a young woman, kind of sway to the music a little as we brought backlights up and houselights down. She sat in silhouette as the song began, and exited as we prayed.

You might be wondering, did we make Mary look pregnant? Yep. The old pillow worked (make sure it sits well and is completely covered by loose clothing). She dressed in normal clothes, a loose sweater—kind of teenage shabby chic. Mary likely looked like any other high school girl, except for the pregnant-with-Messiah detail. And perhaps you're thinking, *Wedding gown? Did they have those?* Well, they likely had wedding clothes, but talking about "your bridal toe ring" (or whatever) doesn't carry much emotional weight for a contemporary audience. This is a good example of a way to connect the now with the then. The meaning of Mary's loss is communicated in the thought of packing up a wedding gown. We understand the weight of your mother putting your gown away. It's a cultural cue that makes an otherwise inaccessible experience tangible.

GETTING STARTED
◆ Choose a character you like, or invent one. I enjoy writing biblical characters, because they so often get left in the dust of the familiar. But you can also imagine a character you'd like to work with.
◆ Figure him or her out. Who is he? Where is she from? What does he want? What's keeping her from what she wants? Many of the questions we ask at this stage are the same ones actors ask when they're developing a character.
◆ Decide whom the character will talk to.
◆ Find a voice for this person. Look for the ten-

sion and texture, but also for age, style, and so on.

◆ Expose the character with detail, situation and conflict. Give the person enough color to be attractive.

◆ Incite the character to talk. Give her a reason to talk with an imaginary other (a representational view, behind the fourth wall) or with the audience (a presentational approach). What does she really want to tell us?

◆ Get him to tell us about the conflict he's in. How has he felt about it? What scares him? Gives him hope? Fill out the person's experience. And finish telling the story.

◆ Hold the character back. What doesn't the person want to tell us? The tension between what the character wants to tell us and what he or she holds back creates the texture and voice of the character.

◆ Bring things to a close. Where do you want the character to be when the audience leaves? The character will sit in our minds in the position and with the attitude exhibited in his or her last line. How does that look and sound? Remember, if the character's story isn't over, be brave and let it hang in the air. Find the entire script for this monologue on page 190.

18 CREATING COLLAGES

Alison Siewert

Metaphorical language can communicate more powerfully and imaginatively than abstract language.

JOHN DRIVER

When I started building a new worship service for a church, I wanted to introduce drama but didn't have much of a team. I barely had a worship team! The people were inexperienced, but they were game to try just about anything. One of the ways I dealt with our uninitiated enthusiasm was to build collages—groups of very short dramatic material, layered or spliced or successive. What I discovered has become one of my favorite forms.

One reason I like the collage form is that lots of relatively inexperienced people can partici-

pate in it and still have it turn out well. I remember when Gloria, a member of my first college creative ministry team and a dancer, created a "movement piece" from Hebrews 11. She grouped people across the large dais area and assigned them group movements. One group did the waves of the flood for Noah, another looked forward to the city by stepping forward one step, and so on. Now, if you had told me about this, I might have cringed a little: We all know the potential for dance-oriented things to be remembered for their "weird ladies waving scarves" look. But she had a whole row of football players out there being waves! It worked because Gloria had the eye for it and enough people were willing to work hard to make a beautiful, tangible picture of the passage. The fellowship loved it— it became a legendary worship experience.

I wrote a sketch called *Help!*[1] in which three different live scenes play along with a video clip of a distressed, insane guy who hears a man yelling for help for his wounded son inside an abandoned building. The crazy guy repeats the father's plea over and over to an empty city street, "Help! Help, help. In the building . . ." The live scenes are very simple: a person asking another for help with a ladder, being refused and sent to yet another friend for help; a person asking another person for help with a stuck zipper; and a single person asking, "Where is God?" I call for each scene to play on its own, then the video starts and all the scenes play together several times through with increasing speed and volume. The end of the video is the end of the sketch, and it can be followed by Scripture. This sketch, one of the first we did with the enthusiastic but inexperienced church I described above, really worked. It gave us a clear picture of the main idea, reinforced that idea (we need help) and expanded the idea (we need help from God). The cumulative effect of going from the scenes on their own to faster and faster replays along with the video also built tension into the experience—without any one actor having to pull off major dramatic effort.

Collages work for another reason: they are how much of our communication happens. MTV and advertisements use this form all the time. You see a picture of Susi Star singing on the beach, then—without view of her transport—in a garage, then back to the beach, then in an evening gown at the prom. You don't see how or why she is in those places; sometimes the places have nothing at all to do with the song. You might be able to string together a story, but is formed in your own head rather than on the screen. It's a way to build trust with an audience, to suggest that "you know what I mean; I don't need to explain it to you."

This is aggregate communication. It's like a mosaic. It doesn't rely on overtly created, linear, rational connections to make its point, but rather suggests connections and lets the audience do the connecting. It's common in postmodern art and advertising.

We can use aggregate communication in the whole of an event (see "Theater and Worship"), but we can also use it as a medium for sketches. For example, if you want to make a sketch of Jesus' call to the disciples, you could have one person calling for his kid or dog or turtle at downstage right. Another person could walk down the center aisle, reading the story from the Scripture loudly enough to be heard, but casually, as though reading it to herself. Three other people could walk onstage from different entrances, carrying huge armloads of work-related things—one a set of tools, one a big fishing net, and one a laptop and newspaper. You could have each of them drop their items as they scour the horizon for something unnamed. When the person reading the Scripture gets to the front, the actors freeze where they are, you bring down the lights, and the sketch is over. The whole point has been, Jesus calls. He is out looking, calling us by name. Those who hear the voice and respond to it— by dropping their stuff—become his disciples.

You can also sketch the meaning of a story in collage. For example, in *Zacchaeus Was a Wee Little Man* I explored one of Zacchaeus's major issues: shame. He is unwanted and, based on the text, never considers whether Jesus might have something to say to him directly. He knows deep down that he is a fraud and has wronged his own people for his self-centered gain.

But isn't that the basic issue of sin? We all stand ashamed before God, not because God shames us but because we know there's a chasm between who we say we are (life professionals) and who we really are (incompetent managers of our lives and the world). The gap of awareness is shame.

Rather than starting with Zacchaeus, I decided to start at the root of the problem with Adam and God (here ELO, for Elohim), when they're supposed to meet in the garden in the cool of the day (in this case, for a run).

ADAM: Shoot! Here he comes. *[to himself]* Hide, Adam, hide! D'oh!

ELO: Yo! Adam! Where are you? Adam! Hey—don't you wanna go for a run, dude? Come on!

ADAM: *[to himself]* Geez. Ok. Here goes. *[to* ELO*]* Over *[resigned pause]* here.

ELO: What? Where?!

ADAM: Here. Right here.

The second movement of the collage focuses on the fame factor surrounding Jesus. But it's offset to something more immediate to our experience: the fame of a rock star. Dave Matthews had recently been in town with his band, which is why I wrote him into this sketch. The other two characters, Stan and Fran, are officemates.

STAN: D'you hear Dave Matthews is coming to town today?

FRAN: Uh-huh.

STAN: They blocked off Main all the way up to Union. Dave Matthews. Can you believe it?

FRAN: What? Here? Why? Oh—wait, I know—*[sarcastically]* He collects Moravian Love Feast memorabilia, right?[2] I'm so sure, Dave Matthews coming to Bethlehem. Nice try, joker man.

STAN: Doubt me if you must, but just wait . . .

Finally we introduce Zoe, a character who has wrecked her social life by writing a letter to the deeply disdained Parking Authority. She, like Zacchaeus, has betrayed her friends to the bad guy and now feels cast out.

ZOE: *[on the phone]* Yeah, I would love to go to your brother's party, but all those people hate me. *[pause]* No, not that—Remember that letter to the editor I wrote a couple of weeks ago? Yeah, the one they printed? Yeah. The one I wrote that they printed. About how we just need to love and respect the Bethlehem Parking Authority more and more?

These three conversations are woven together not to tell Zacchaeus's story directly but to explore its meaning and contours of it. The collage gets at what it feels like to be ashamed, to want to hide—both Adam and Zoe try not to be seen. And Stan and Fran want to see this really famous person who came into town. First-century Palestinians knew what it meant to climb up a tree in order to get a glimpse of someone. We don't do that much tree climbing, but some people will work pretty hard to get where they think a celebrity is going to show up.

The sketch didn't tell the whole story, but the preacher did. The sketch allowed us to think about parts of Zacchaeus's story without overstating it in either the sketch or the whole of the service.

To write an effective collage requires thinking outside the box. If you aren't an intuitive person, start with one of the other types of writing first. But if you're intuitive, you might enjoy this form. You get to play with more angles and options than you do in a linear storytelling setup. And you can use music, video clips, funny and serious dialogue, poetry, dances—all in one piece. Make sure people can follow the basic ideas of the sketch. It's fine if they don't all fit together directly, but folks should be able, at least in retrospect, to understand what it was about.

For a sample collage, see *Zacchaeus Was a Wee Little Man* on page 200.

19 BRINGING THE WORD TO LIFE

Bruce Kuhn and Nina Thiel

Words and silence; a marvelous medium.

ARTHUR MILLER

Jesus came into a city called Nain . . . and behold, a dead man was being carried out" How would an eyewitness tell this story? Probably not like a church reading. It would be alive with the details, the passion, the awe of seeing a dead man brought back to life by the carpenter of Nazareth. The story would smell of truth because the teller was there.

Imagine the power of that first telling. To perform Scripture drama is to present the stories of the Bible the way they were first presented: as well-told stories. With a lot of work, we can come close to recreating that. We can know and speak the Word with the same honesty, naturalness and simplicity as the first eyewitnesses. We can become like them and tell the stories as they did, having seen them through their own eyes. That means memorizing their words, but not in the traditional "rote" method of repeating something until it is drilled into the memory and all life drilled out of it. Recreating the memories through a natural method will be richer and truer, though it will take more time—up to two hours per finished minute of text.

HOW DO WE DO IT?

The first, vital question is the magic If. To recreate an eyewitness account, we must ask, *What if I was there?* Other questions naturally follow: *What did I see? Why did he say that?*

How did he say it? Already you will have started the process that Bible scholars call *exegesis* and actors call *text analysis*.

The storyteller is not an actor in the traditional sense: you are playing yourself, not some other person. You will borrow an actor's tools, however, to create the artificial memories required to give an imaginary eyewitness account. Think of how you remember a story that actually happened to you: the specific images, how you imitate Aunt Lucy's strident tone or George's faint sneer. Most important is the intimate knowledge you have of what happened in those moments of reality.

One of the ways actors break down an event is by figuring out motives: What does each character want? What are their objectives: in life? in five years? in the next ten minutes? What are the obstacles to each character reaching those objectives? What actions do they take to get around the obstacles? Those actions—how they interplay and conflict—are what life is made of and what make stories interesting.

A famous actor and teacher named Uta Hagen wrote ten starter questions for approaching narratives. Answer these questions thoroughly, and you will have the groundwork for telling the story:

1. Who (character biographies)?

2. What time is it (century, year, season, day, minute)?

3. Where (place, country, city)?

4. What is physically present (animate and inanimate objects)?

5. What are the given circumstances (past, present, future)?

6. What are the relationships?

7. What does each character want (overall and immediate objectives)?

8. What are the obstacles in the way of those wants (find the conflict)?

SCRIPTURE FOR SCREENAGERS
Nina Thiel

Our conference speaker wasn't a bad speaker at all. In fact, she did a great job. I say this so you'll know what I saw happen wasn't her fault. She, like many savvy communicators, made excellent use of video clips to introduce each of her four teaching sessions. We saw long, wonderful moments from As Good as It Gets *and* Dead Man Walking. *Our speaker talked about the clips with us, drawing out principles of relating to others and being the kinds of people who change the world. And the students would nod and laugh and gasp and bury their faces in their hands, responding to the truth they were hearing. But then she said, "This reminds me of a situation that Jesus was in. Please open your Bibles and read with me . . ." And it happened. I saw them getting out their Bibles. I saw them opening their Bibles. And I watched the energy drain from the room. Glazed and heavily lidded eyes drooped down to the words on half-opened pages as the stories of Jesus were read.*

I couldn't believe it: Sean Penn holds our attention better than Jesus? I tell you, I don't even remember what the passages were. And I thought to myself, This is wrong.

Fast forward to our next year's conference. A colleague and I had studied Scripture drama with Bruce Kuhn over the summer. We decided then and there to perform the passages from which our speaker for the conference would be teaching. One of our passages was John 9, the healing of the man born blind. As I brought this story to life before them, the students nodded and laughed and gasped and buried their faces in their hands, responding to the truth they were experiencing. Someone turned to their pastor and asked, "Is this in the Bible?"

One writer said, "The Word became flesh, said St. John, and the church has turned the flesh back into words."[2] Scripture drama works because these stories happened (flesh); they were told before they were ever written (flesh); their messages were intended to be lived out (flesh); and if we tell them, if we show them, if the Word becomes flesh in us onstage, it has its perfect medium, God's Word incarnate in someone he has redeemed.

When audiences respond to Scripture drama (and they really do respond!), it's because they've encountered the Living Word.

9. What actions will be taken to get around obstacles to get objectives?

10. What is the story about?[1]

Each of these elements might profoundly affect the story. For example, in the story of Jesus telling Peter to cast out his nets (Luke 5), the time of day has everything to do with what happens. It is early morning; they have been fishing all night and caught nothing. If it had been evening, then Peter would have said, "Sure, we were going out anyway." That one small element of *when* means they are exhausted, that no other fishing boats are out, that they risk humiliation to fish in daylight when everyone else fishes at night by torchlight. It all weaves together.

You might be amazed to learn how much is communicated when you know something deeply. First come the facts ("They had been fishing all night"), and then come the inferences ("They are probably exhausted and not eager to throw out nets they had nearly finished cleaning . . ."). From there, picturing the event gets easier. The more specific the images, the sharper your created memory; and the sharper the memories, the truer the telling. Everything comes out of this deep knowledge. If you are concerned with inflection, then you're focused on technique instead of reality. What happened, why is it important, and how do you feel about it?

Try paraphrasing the story in your own words and in the first person (remember, you were there . . .). Include all the research in the telling and all your motivation theory—why you think these people are doing and responding as they are—as if you were explaining it to foreigners (which all of us are to that first-century Middle Eastern culture). If done well, this paraphrase monologue might be stage worthy in itself. There is a power and authenticity in telling the words of the Word, however. The last step of squeezing all that work and theory back into the original words of the eyewitness is well worth it.

Of course, no one will know all the details of your research, all the great stuff you found and figured out; that is for another medium called The Sermon. You may be amazed, however, how much can be communicated by your knowing the story deeply. For example, in your study of Jesus raising a widow's son from the dead, you might recollect that Elijah also raised a widow's dead son, hundreds of years before Jesus. Every Jew knew the story. Perhaps as they spread this story of Jesus, they said, "A great prophet is risen among us!" as in, "This Jesus is not just any old prophet; he's up there with the greats!" instead of merely, "A great prophet has risen among us." It is such a small thing that, if you include it in your script, only a few, if any, will notice, let alone understand. That sort of detail, however, is the stuff of reality: there is always more meaning than words express. Those reality details subtly change and enrich our human speech and relations. Without the details, we are left to using artificial technique to grope for attention and meaning. And the danger of relying solely on technique is sounding like the radio ad with its forced inflection or the flight attendant trying to make seatbelts sound interesting.

Like praying and learning languages, mastering an art form comes from doing. The doing cannot be isolated. It needs the presence of others who do it better. At the very least, find friends to tell you, "It doesn't sound like you talking . . ." or "I don't quite believe you were there." Better yet, take some acting classes, or find a theater coach. For starters, try something simple like Blind Bartimaeus (Mark 10:46). It is only two minutes long, very straightforward and full of good images. And it really happened. What if you were there?

20 SCRIPTING SCRIPTURE

Alison Siewert

The prophets knew how to use words memorably . . . with great artistry. . . . They knew their contemporary culture and they knew how to speak words which would plunge like shafts of steel into the hardest of hearts or would reach with loving sympathy into the most desolate of predicaments.

PAUL BURBRIDGE AND MURRAY WATTS

Like most church kids, I studied the Bible growing up, and I was pretty sure I understood it. Then in college I started studying Mark's Gospel inductively—what InterVarsity calls a "Mark Study." We'd sit around a table for two hours a week, poring over pages of typed-out Scripture, trying to figure out what Mark was saying to his original, intended audience. *What is this about? Sure, it's the story of Jesus, but why in this order? Why with these details? Who's Abiathar, and why is his bread illegal?* It was like trying to determine the use of some foreign object, with only the object to study. What is this thing?

Around that table I came to understand a couple of things that have changed and shaped my life ever since: First, Jesus demands response. In fact, if we hear Jesus' words and don't respond, it would be better if we had not heard them at all. Hearing and telling the story is serious business, and I realized that communicating Jesus' words in a way people could understand and respond to them was not just a fun idea—it was an essential response to Jesus. The second thing I learned in that Mark study is that the Gospels and the Bible in general must be understood as crosscultural—they're from a time and place distant from our own. And if

we're working crossculturally, then we must translate the Scripture much as we do in a study, to make its language and context accessible.

Scripted Scripture is different from narrative evangelism. Rather than relating the Scripture directly—in its own words and nuanced by our study of it—a script of a passage incorporates what we learn through study and reflection into the actual dialogue or monologue. Rather than having the details and history affect the story, we include them directly in what we speak.

CALL AND RESPONSE

Here's an example of how we do not understand things as the original hearers understood them: At the beginning of Mark we see Jesus call Simon, Andrew, James and John away from their boats and their fishing to become fishers of people. It's obvious this is a big move. And it's clear that Jesus calls the men to something that promises to be better, or at least more fascinating: people instead of fish.

It's harder for us, however, to grasp that fishing was their life. We think of career choice being the result of natural inclination, the influence of a good teacher or a degree program we completed. But in the Zebedees' world, fishing was it. Fishing was what they did. It was who they were. They had succeeded at it too: they had their own boats and nets and hired crews. Their dad was in the business along with them and spent nights fishing with them the same way his dad had fished with him from about elementary school on. They were fishermen—not guys who fished. When Jesus calls them away from fish and into people, it changes everything.

How can we get a better view of the fishermen's reality? Well, Mark swings the camera back to the house where Simon's mother-in-law, who probably lived with his family, was ill. If you got sick in first-century Palestine, well that was just sad. There were no antibiotics, no well-developed painkillers . . . not much of anything that'd make you feel better. (Except Jesus. But hang on, that part's coming.) Mark includes a little story about how, right after Simon begins to follow, Jesus heals his mother-in-law: "As soon as they left the synagogue, they entered the house of Simon and Andrew, with James and John. Now Simon's mother-in-law was in bed with a fever, and they told him about her at once. He came and took her by the hand and lifted her up. Then the fever left her, and she began to serve them" (Mark 1:29-31).

Let's think about this from Simon's wife's perspective. (Since Simon had a mother-in-law, he likely also had a wife.) Here she is, at home with the kids all day. Her mom usually helps out, but she's been sick. So things are hectic, and she's worried about her mom. And now Peter comes home with some big religious experience and wants to follow this teacher around. Usually Simon works all night but is home during the day; now all of a sudden he's not fishing. *And he's not home. (By the way, do you have a plan for how we're gonna eat? And make the payments on the nets you're not using? Just wondering. . . . This is so confusing. What are you thinking?)*

We just imagined what it must have been like for Mrs. Simon. Do we know for certain? No. But can we understand the principle point of the text, which is that Simon's shift from

fisher-dude to Jesus follower has caused major disruption in his life and the lives of those closest to him? Yep.

PETER'S WIFE: Well now, I was at home trying to juggle our life—my mom was sick, and the kids were running around—and Simon came home from the boat saying, "Oh, honey, I met this great teacher—I'm going to follow him immediately!" I said, "Oh, great, Simon! My mom is ill. . . . He said, "I know exactly what to do." And he left.

Half an hour later he came back with a whole crew, mostly his fishing partners, and this "Teacher" they were all so excited about. They wanted him to see my mom. And Jesus, they said his name was, he took her hand and sat her up."[1]

By bouncing this story from its inconspicuous spot in Mark's opening chapter, we get to see someone who was there, but whose life rarely gets highlighted. Mark did include the story—and for Mark, who is the briefest of the Gospel authors, that's saying something. If you're in, you're important. Mark does not flower about with extra thoughts.

MOSES AND MIRIAM

The Old Testament stories are even further from our culture and experience. But since they are equally important to our faith, we need to work at making them accessible. Here's the start of *lifeDesign*, a sketched conversation between Moses and Miriam:

MOSES: My older sister grabbed me one day and she said, she said, "Come here. I need to talk to you."

MIRIAM: Moses, we have to talk.

MOSES: She said, "Moses, you are not them. You are us."

MIRIAM: You're one of us. You are not from them.

MOSES: I . . . am . . . not them?

MIRIAM: You're us. You're one of us.

MOSES: You are not them.

MIRIAM: You are one of us. Look! See the design of your skin, your hair—

MOSES: What? . . . I didn't know what to think, to say. I'm not Egyptian. I'm not—

MIRIAM: You are not them.

In just ten lines we are dealing with Moses' ethnic identity, his confusion about where and to whom he belongs. Moses and his contemporaries did not think in terms of modern psychology. But Moses clearly struggled early in his life to clarify his identity, to understand that he was called by Yahweh. As the dialogue continues, we hear the intractable pain of injustice and oppression, and the confusion this pain creates for Moses—a person of power in an abusive power system—begins to surface.

MOSES: The people of God are slaves.

MIRIAM: We don't really know who we are.

MOSES: Egypt is built on slavery.

MIRIAM: We are oppressed.

MOSES: I saw an Egyptian beating a man into the ground.

MIRIAM: We are beaten.

MOSES: I hated him . . . I hated the Egyptian. I hated Egypt.

MIRIAM: It has been so long . . .

MOSES: Israel has been oppressed here for so long.

MIRIAM: We don't know what it means to belong God anymore.

Then the sketch picks up as both Moses and Miriam come to terms each with the way their life's experience has shaped them, in their solitary space but next to one another, contrasting two separate but related lives in Egypt.

MOSES: I didn't even know his name.

MIRIAM: We don't know them and we don't know why.

MOSES: Some overseer, a low-level manager. I didn't know him.

MIRIAM: They come and take the boys.

MOSES: I saw him, and then I grabbed him by the throat.

MIRIAM: They come and take them away.

MOSES: And threw him on the ground.

MIRIAM: And throw them in the river.

MOSES: And beat him.

MIRIAM: They throw them in the river.

MOSES: And beat him.

MIRIAM: You can hear them for a moment.

MOSES: And beat him.

MIRIAM: They cry as they're thrown.

MOSES: Until there was blood on my hands.

MIRIAM: And then you hear the thudding splash.

MOSES: And then . . .

MIRIAM: And then . . .

MOSES: Then he wasn't resisting anymore.

MIRIAM: Then it's very quiet.

I had studied Exodus inductively many times. But distilling the story in compressed language gave me a totally new understanding, especially of the personal dynamics of Moses' life. Moses is one of those biblical characters who are so well known that they're hardly known. It was exciting to hear this sketch performed and to see Moses rise from his flat life on the flannel board.

THE PROCESS: FROM SCRIPTURE TO SCRIPT

The potential in using drama to communicate Scripture is endless. We've just looked at two case studies—one from the New Testament and one from the Old—where drama was used to present the truths of the Bible in visual and provocative new ways. But how does a writer get from the Scripture to the script? If you want to try writing Scripture into scripts, here's how to start:

Study the script together. If Scripture is crosscultural, then we must approach it with the humility of knowing we don't know. The only way to come to know is through careful study and prayer—and, I would add, not just study, but communal study and prayer. The Bible was written by a community and for a community. We edge toward a certain cultural arrogance to think that we can just haul off, open it up and understand it deeply all on our own. If you've never studied Scripture communally, try it—and see what happens. When a group of people comes at a text from different angles, they explore questions that never would have been raised in one individual's own mind. The depth and texture that come from such study provide fuel for good script writing (and life too).

Find the point. Biblical writers were writing for specific audiences in specific situations and with the hope of communicating clearly. At some level, we must believe they were able to achieve their intent and get their point across. If they hadn't been able to do that in their time, they probably wouldn't be thought of as great leaders, and their work probably wouldn't be sitting on your desk wrapped in leather and gold. What is the main thing the author is trying to say? This is the key question in inductive study and the key question for a scriptwriter. You have to find out what the author is doing and go with it. Even when scripts don't use the traditional translation, they are, in effect, translations—into our time and place—of what the authors meant.

Explore the landing. How did this story sound to its original hearers? That's a question we can apply to any passage of Scripture. Take the parable of the sower, for example. Jesus is talking about a guy sowing seeds. The seeds land in different soils. Some of the seeds grow. Some of the seeds don't grow. What is this like? It's as if Jesus were saying, "Sometimes when you go to the grocery store, you buy groceries." Now, of course the parable has nothing to do with the grocery store. I'm not talking about the point of the story, but about the way it must have landed in people's ears. The story, in Jesus' time, sounded so elementary and obvious that only a few people pursued further understanding. Remember that part? The disciples and a few others come to Jesus afterward asking, "So . . . what's up with the seed thing?" They were the ones who got it, but they got it because they asked about something most people thought was obvious. The "landing" question allows us to explore how things sounded—which is an important part of scripting.

Find a voice. Who will tell this story? How might we approach it? From what perspective will characters speak? You have an idea of what the author is saying (the point), and how their words come across in our cultural terms (the landing). Now, how do you put those together? In *lifeDesign* I created a conversation between Moses and Miriam in order to incorporate Miriam's perspective. She allows us to see what Egypt feels like to a Hebrew living in the *middle* of it. Moses' perspective is *above* it, because he sees the problems but isn't required to live in them (until, of course, he chooses to). The juxtaposition of their two perspectives creates immediate tension: though they're linked by their heritage, their lives are at odds. This gives the sketch its voice—the way the story is told. You can see the contrast between this voice and the telling of the healing at Simon's house.

Keep the tension. Eager to ensure everyone knows everything came out all right, or wanting to be theologically thorough, writers will sometimes beat the tension right out of the story. Remember—the landing—the people in the stories really experienced them. It's unkind and inaccurate of us to play their stories glibly. Every character must want something from someone else in the story. That's how stories work. No character gets to know in advance (in the script) how the story turns out. The tension of a sketch happens when, because we allow the process to unfold, we see characters trying to figure it out, exerting themselves to convince or challenge someone, or struggling to do what God has for them to do. In *lifeDesign* both characters want something to change. Miriam wants to get Moses on

Israel's side. The tension hangs as Moses considers the two sides of his own story and must choose with whom to side. He wants an end to the oppression he sees, but doesn't know how to make that happen.

End well. We don't have to know the whole rest of the story—it's in the Bible if people want to check it out after the sketch is over. If you're writing for worship, the preacher can address a great deal more, including the end, in the sermon. Your job is to get us thinking, give us a fresh view, a sense of what's going on here that we can't get from someone reading the passage straight out.

Endings need to slow the action, but they don't necessarily imply the story is over. The resolution in *lifeDesign* hints at Moses' upcoming commitment to lead Israel out of Egypt, but it doesn't try to tie it up.

Why not tie it up? Because that's a whole 'nother story (see Exodus 3—40). It's okay to let it hang a little. We say nearly as much by what we don't say as by what we do. If we lose that, we lose much of the power of drama.

You can find *lifeDesign* on page 219. For another example of scripted Scripture, see *Hebrews 11: Pretty Much the Whole Thing* on page 193.

PART 3

ACTING

21 ABOUT ACTING

Alison Siewert

Acting is the furthest thing from lying that I have encountered. It is the furthest thing from make-believe. It is the furthest thing from pretending. It is a search for the authentic by using the fictional as a frame, a house in which the authentic can live. For a moment.

ANNA DEVEARE SMITH

Actors receive a lot of attention in our culture. Acting looks magical, glamorous and only distantly possible. People are more likely to know who played the president's deputy communications director than to know who actually does that job in real life.[1] Actors are presented to us in one of the few pieces of our communal culture almost universally seen: filmed drama in movies and on TV. But acting is not really about gilded talent or cameras or acting school or even looking good.

Acting is about doing the sketch. Actors help tell stories by playing them onstage. They do not make the stories. They do not become the characters in the stories. What they do is simpler and more accessible than celebrity culture would lead us to believe. It's also harder work. There are some disciplines to the work of acting, and if your team can do them regularly, over time they will become able to do all you could ask for, and probably more.

Actors need to use their bodies, their voices and their imaginations. Some people do this more easily than others—and this ease is often labeled "talent." But even people who don't deal easily can still learn to deal.

BODY

An actor's body does the action, which is at the root of acting. Most everything we ever do onstage has a physical quality to it, even if that quality is sitting, relaxed, in that chair. We are always doing something when we act. Your team needs to learn how to think about what they are doing even when they are standing still. Nothing you do onstage is neutral—the audience's attention goes wherever the actors' attention goes, whether focused or wandering. If you are standing, stand firm and do not shuffle between feet. If you are sitting, sit because that is what you want to do. Everything you do onstage is part of the story you tell.

You will need to be in reasonable shape and be able to use your body if you want to act. If this is new to you, try a gentle exercise class, such as Pilates or stretch-and-strengthen, to help you get limber. And do some aerobic work, too, so you'll have energy for lengthy rehearsals where physicality will be important. (Also see chapter thirty-one, "Freeing Up Your Body.")

VOICE

Besides your body, your voice is the most significant equipment for playing the story. It used to be said, when someone went to the theater, they were going to hear a play. A choreographer might envision a dance and translate the vision into choreographic notation for dancers; a playwright imagines a story and puts it down in lines and stage directions for actors. The whole thing is set down in words, and most of the time you will have words to speak from the stage. The characters' conversations tell the story. So it must be heard.

Consider taking a voice class or voice les-

sons. Singing study is helpful, but it will also be important to learn about spoken diction, articulation and inflection. Some directors like to work on these disciplines with their teams, but you can also check with local colleges to see if they offer group lessons or classes in vocal technique. (Also see chapter twenty-nine, "Using Your Voice.")

IMAGINATION
One of the bad ideas I picked up from wherever we pick these things up was that actors are supposed to become the character. Now, I'm

JESUS LOOKS MAHVELOUS
Alison Siewert

How do we portray Jesus in sketches? I mean, Jesus is the most fully human person that ever lived. He's God. How do you do that in a sketch? We often see Jesus portrayed as a little mysterious, a bit overserious—a philosophy major who hopes one day to become a seminary professor. When I see Jesus portrayed in films, I'm often struck by the thought that I'm not sure people would really like him if he acted that way. He seems to be regarded as sort of odd, kinda nerdy and strangely retiring—unless you were a demon or a Pharisee. I love it when Jesus heals people in movies: His (blue) eyes bulge, his hand quivers, and the weird music kicks in. But Jesus doesn't come across as someone you'd put at the top of your blowout party weekend invite list, BYOB.

However—thankfully—the quivery nerd doesn't match the biblical picture. Perhaps we've underestimated Jesus' personal presence, his sense of humor and his ability to do normal social stuff (tell a joke, play a board game). He can't have been that weird. I mean, Mark says John the Baptist was the weird guy. Jesus, by contrast, comes off as approachable and likeable, affable and genuine, and he possesses the major social bonus of not eating bugs. Profound and prophetic, yes; coming to judge the earth, sure. But a great party guest all the same.

Maybe the way out of the bad pictures and the way into knowing and portraying Jesus is to do what Jesus did. Jesus was fascinated with people. He loved being with people and reveled in spending time with those who were furthest from him in social and religious terms. The Gospel stories show Jesus being invited to parties early on in his ministry, and he was still being not sure what I thought that meant or whether anyone ever really knew what it meant—but under no circumstances, except grave mental illness, can you become a character.[2] The guy playing Jesus is no more Jesus than you or I. He is only playing Jesus. And even though we may be dealing with historical, true, real characters, we never become them. (Come to think of it, it would be pretty disconcerting if you were, say, the apostle Peter and suddenly Bob Potato took over being you! Actually, that's the basic concept behind a very disturbing movie called *Being John Malkovich*.)

The character is an imaginary construct that is part of the imagined story called the sketch. The character doesn't really exist—at least not in the building at the moment. So your task is really to build the picture of the character in the context of the story, which is where it really matters for the acting. In other words, of course Jesus matters all the time, and of course we can know him, even quite well. But in the sketch, the character of Jesus says and does a limited amount. We are not trying in five minutes to show the audience all of Jesus. We're just sketching one story

invited to them late in the game. Can you imagine the number of extremely long stories he must've sat listening to? The Gospel writers mention a few: the bleeding woman, the man at the pool in Bethsaida, Zacchaeus. There were probably many more.

Jesus knew people. He knew the specific people he was talking to, and he knew people in universal terms. He understood sin and sickness and hope and happiness. And he got people's attention. Frederick Buechner says,

> He does not speak of a reorganization of society as a political possibility or of the doctrine of salvation as a doctrine. . . . He suggests rather than spells out. He evokes rather than explains. He catches by surprise. He doesn't let the homiletic seams show. He is sometimes cryptic, sometimes obscure, sometimes irreverent, always provocative. He tells stories. He speaks in parables, and though we have approached these parables reverentially all these many years and have heard them expounded as grave and reverent vehicles of holy truth, I suspect that many if not all of them were originally not grave at all but were antic, comic, often more than just a little shocking.[3]

Jesus is a great model for dramatists, in art and in life. We may not be Jesus in our ability to gauge who people are and how to connect with them, but we can give ourselves to partnership with Jesus by listening, learning and extending ourselves to the people around us. We won't be fully like Jesus—yet—but the more we reflect him in day-to-day life, the more our words sound like his and our attention is focused like his on others, the better portrait we'll paint onstage. Our hope is to see God for ourselves and to invite others to see him with us and, in drama, through us. Which is precisely what Jesus makes happen when he's in the sketch.

from his life, and you (if you're playing Jesus) are sketching Jesus in that one story for today's performance. You only have to figure out what Jesus is doing in this sketch. What would Jesus do in any other instance is a great question for a novel (*In His Steps*) or a youth group retreat, but it's not salient to your sketch.

THE JOB OF THE ACTOR

Your job in the sketch is to

◆ learn the lines

◆ understand the lines

◆ figure out how to do what the character is doing

Learn your lines by memory unless you have agreed as a team that this will be a reading performance, in which case you should still know your lines so well that they are nearly memorized. This will mostly come by going over them. A lot.

Understand what the lines mean in the context of the sketch. The line "Whoever comes to me, I will never drive away" can mean many different things, depending on its inflection. Figuring out which thing it means and how to inflect it is a function of the context. (See the sidebar on inflection on page 100.) So first we ask the question, What does the character do in this sketch? But since what the character is doing—say, sitting alone on a couch—can have myriad meanings, we need another step, another layer.

The most useful way to understand the context and the lines is to ask the question, What does the character want? What is the character trying to do or get? Is Andrea sitting on the couch because she wants Michael to join her there? Or is she sitting on the couch because she is despondent and wants to swallow that bottle of pills next to her? Or is Andrea sitting on the couch because she's waiting for her sister Amy to pick her up for a shopping trip? What does Andrea want?

You can find the want of the character in

the script. Let's look at an interaction:

[MICHAEL *enters.*]

ANDREA: [*sitting on couch, alone*] Hi.

MICHAEL: [*turning to see her*] Oh, hi. I didn't realize you were home.

ANDREA: Yeah. I've been home all day.

MICHAEL: By yourself?

ANDREA: Yeah.

MICHAEL: Is that why you look a little down?

ANDREA: I guess.

MICHAEL: You wanna—

ANDREA: I've been thinking—

[*They laugh.*]

MICHAEL: You first.

ANDREA: [*patting couch*] I've been thinking . . . Can we talk?

MICHAEL: [*moving toward couch*] Sure.

Andrea might want to feel better, but how would the audience know that? She can want Michael to come sit next to her. Now, that might be actable. What might she do to get Michael to sit with her? She could ask. She could gesture to him, patting the couch next to her. An even stronger choice than wanting to get Michael to sit with her, however, is wanting to get Michael to sit with her so they can talk. She wants to talk to Michael about something.

Every time you take the stage, you have to want something. This is usually called the *objective* of the character. Every character must have one. The objective is something you can do: it is attainable. Even a character who appears not to want is wanting—probably to attain something they can only get if they look like they don't want it. An aloof teenage character might appear nonchalant in order to get his parents to spring for a dicey activity that a more passionate approach would betray.

In every sketch, in every part, actors must ask, *What do I want?* Then find actable wants. Actable wants are "commonplace, gutsy activities that an ordinary person could put his shoulder behind and push hard for ten minutes."[4] We are looking for verbs we can do, not merely think about. Physical verbs are best. And they need to be verbs we can do for at least five minutes (since sketches are usually shorter than that), if not ten. For a long time I had trouble with a spot in a play where my character was supposed to more or less disintegrate. I kept thinking about how to disintegrate—which is unactable. What I needed to want was not to disintegrate—or, more actably, to hold together in the face of pressure. My character wanted to hold on physically (which also happened to be emotionally). An objective is a sustainable action that you can do and the audience can perceive onstage.

In *Chopsticks* Jack has just finished explaining to someone on the phone about how a policeman stopped him for speeding but forgave him the offense. Jack is thrilled to have escaped a ticket. Jane enters with an objective: she wants to get Jack to forgive her. Jack wants to make Jane see what a jerk she is for breaking his chopstick.

JANE: *[quickly spilling it as she pulls out the broken chopstick]* One of them broke—I don't know when, I don't know how . . . I'm really sorry, and I'll get you a new one. Sorry.

JACK: What?

JANE: *[holding up chopstick]* One of them broke. I'm sorry.

JACK: Wait. I—it sounded like . . . You're saying you broke one of my chopsticks?

JANE: Uh-huh.

JACK: Oh. My. Gosh.

JANE: I'm sorr—

JACK: *[interrupting]* You just broke one.

JANE: I don't think I actually broke it.

JACK: Well then who did, huh? Santa Claus? King Kong? Who did it?

JANE: I dunno. It was just like this—I went to gather them up to bring them back, all nice and washed, and this one was just . . . broken.

JACK: I can't believe this.

JANE: I'm so sorry. But it's just a take-out from the restaurant, right? I mean, we can get more for free, even . . .

JACK: You wounded it. You . . . you hurt my chopstick.

JANE: Will you forgive me?

JACK: Forgive you? You want me to forgive you?

JANE: Yeah.

JACK: What is wrong with you?

JANE: I—I—

JACK: What?! What is your problem? You waltz in here breaking my things and you think I'm just gonna forgive you? Well you've got another think coming, honey. Forgive you my a—

JANE: But Jack, it's a chop—

JACK: It was my chopstick. And you broke it!

This sketch is fun to play because it's ridiculous and because the two characters' wants are so opposed. There's a lot to push on here. Everything Jane does is focused on getting Jack to forgive her. Everything Jack does is aimed at proving to Jane what a jerk she is.[5]

22 IS IT OKAY FOR CHRISTIANS TO ACT?

A conversation with Scott Brill, Daniel Jones, Susi Jensen, Jason Gaboury, Bruce Kuhn, Alison Siewert, Nina Thiel and Lisa Harper

Is it okay for Christians to act?

Scott: Why not? We all do it. Constantly. With each other, God and ourselves. Good drama helps expose our acts and pretensions.

Daniel: What we are doing is telling a story. The audience doesn't walk into the room thinking the characters are real people. They know they are actors who will engage them in an exploration of life for a time.

Susi: We would be fools to give up the stage given its potential for powerful proclamation of truth.

Jason: Back in the first century, actors were not allowed to remain actors if they converted to Christianity, but that had more to do with the idolatrous nature of the theater of the time (in honor of the gods) and the licentiousness of the theater experience (often combined with drunkenness and orgies).

All: Hmmmm.

Jason: In the theater there is a willing suspension of disbelief. Essentially this means that everybody (actors, audience, playwright, stage crew) knows that the actors are pretending. Actors embody (flesh out) characters the same way singers place and shape notes, or dancers embody a series of movements.

Isn't the whole idea of staging plays and sketches tantamount to lying?

Jason: Is writing poetry tantamount to lying? Is telling stories tantamount to lying?

Bruce: Would anyone call Jesus a liar upon discovering the Lost Son wasn't a real person, but a fiction? Can it still be true even if it did not really happen?! Yes, Christians can tell stories that did not happen and play people they are not in real life.

Alison: Yeah. Anna Deveare Smith says, "Perhaps these fictions are the clothing for greater truths."[1]

Daniel: I remember having an acting coach once who made the argument that acting is essentially all about telling a lie. I struggled with that. While on one hand you are trying to make something believable—which would imply that it currently is not believable—that's not the same as telling a lie.

Lisa: I believe the stage is meant by God to be a sacred space where truth is told and beauty is experienced . . . and God speaks to the souls of those with ears to hear. The stage offers a heightened experience of life.

Scott: Actors are only lying if they portray something that is false to the human experience as those who are made in the image of God. As

I'm writing this, I'm listening to my three daughters playing. Are they "lying" because they're pretending to be people they're not? I don't think so—I think they're being good drama writers! I see them expressing themselves and their developing souls through their games in a way that's deep and meaningful.

Jason: Actors are playing parts written for them by someone else for the purpose of telling a story. Everyone involved knows this, and there's no intention to deceive. Instead, everyone is invited to "pretend" along with the actors. God has given us language, story, poetry, hyperbole, imagery and drama as gifts. To suggest that these things are lies because they are not mathematically or propositionally true owes more to Platonic philosophy than to the scriptural worldview.

Lisa: Drama is the communicating of truth through imaginary circumstances. The actor and the dramatist are not liars. They are better described as prophets. Like when God commands Ezekiel to build a set representing Jerusalem and to act out its destruction. (Ezekiel 4) Ezekiel was to act out the drama of Jerusalem being besieged as a warning to the people. God called a prophet to become an actor. Was Ezekiel really besieging Jerusalem? No. He was destroying a miniature set of Jerusalem. God's point was for Ezekiel, through the art of acting, to communicate truth to the people.

What parts are okay, and which ones aren't? Can a Christian play an evil character?

Bruce: We are sinners; we should play them better than anyone! I have never murdered anyone, but I hope I can still play Macbeth.

Nina: Sean Penn's redemption in *Dead Man Walking* was only sweet to the extent that we believed how vile he was on his way there.

Daniel: My general rule is that taking on an evil part is fine if the evil gets exposed for what it is. Over the years I've played some nasty characters, but in the end what was evil about them was brought to light. And the evil was neither glorified nor, I hope, attractive.

Susi: The holiest gift actors give us is the ability to step into someone else's shoes, something Christ wanted for his followers. This is an act of human compassion, when seen in light of the gospel. A great actor finds the human core and frailty even in a hateful criminal and thus reveals the truth about our humanity. Human beings are made in the image of God, yet we all have the potential to choose evil instead of good. Acting, in its essence, explores this theological truth.

Lisa: Inherent in the medium of the drama is the need for two sides—for conflict.

Alison: If you read Dante's *Divine Comedy*, you'll notice that "Inferno" is the most interesting, followed by "Purgatorio" and, finally, "Paradiso." Why? Because there's no conflict in Paradise. It's the blandest of Dante's realms. C. S. Lewis figured out a way to create conflict in heaven, but he had to bring in a bus full of visitors from Somewhere Else to do it. Conflict is not only what motivates drama but what calls us to life itself. We don't always think of day-to-day life as conflictual, but it is. We have conflict with our bodies about getting up, with the traffic about getting where we're going. Dropping kids off at school creates the conflict of being happy to have a break and being sad to leave them out of our sight. We call this state of mind and heart conflicted. It happens all the time. And it's the fuel of drama. No bad guy, no drama. No good guy, no drama. Gotta have both.

Lisa: Think of some great films. They all contain some content that is in itself morally questionable or, in some cases, downright evil. Yet if that content were removed, those films would tell less of the truth about the human condition. In order to tell that truth, they have to be truthful in the way they portray their characters.

Nina: Yes. Someone has to play the bad guy in our stories. And be a convincing bad guy (including the language and activity that befits his state of mind). Otherwise we won't believe it.

Alison: We won't believe either the bad guy or the story.

Daniel: Because the reality is, we all engage in evil, and God is all about redeeming us. We need to see that played out on the stage. If everyone we portrayed were perfect and shiny and pure, I suspect we would have a pretty unrealistic portrait of our world.

Alison: Because we know that's not how it really is. We'd lose any ability to explore the world through art because we'd predispose ourselves to lying about the state of that world.

Lisa: So for us to understand the magnitude of our redemption, we must first understand the magnitude of our depravity. If I'm afraid to venture into showing the depravity of human-

kind, then I have given up the power of my message.

Alison: And then there's the practical question for actors: Which roles will I do?

Nina: My question now is, As I audition for roles in community theater, would I do a show that I wouldn't allow my children to come and see? My older kids have flipped out seeing me in *pas de deux* moments with a male dancer. This takes the discussion into a whole other ethical realm, but it presses it for me.

Lisa: I must ask the question, Do I have the spiritual maturity to play the role of a character whose worldview is different from my own or who is immoral, and maintain my own convictions and spiritual health? If, after seeking counsel from mentors and praying in community, I

WORKING WITH WORDS
Alison Siewert

Look through the script. Once you've read it, highlight your lines. Leave stage directions unlit or highlight them in a different color, so you aren't tempted to read them aloud.

Listen carefully to the first reading. Listen to the other actors and take in what they are saying. Even though you will be following your script closely, listen. This will be the way your audience hears the sketch. Get a feel for the initial impact—how it sounds. This will give you a sense, as you rehearse, of where you're headed.

From the very first reading, work at understanding the language of the scene. Make sure you know what all the words mean—not just alone, but in their context. Prepare your script by noting any new words. Check pronunciation. If there are multiple options or regional accents possible, iron them out together before you get far into rehearsal. It sounds strange if one person says "offen" and the other says "often" (with the T pronounced). Unify!

Look at rhythms. How does the language fit together? What is the overall sound of the sketch? I sometimes write in musical rhythms. Some writers make very short sentences or use repetitive language for emphasis. Some sketches are narrative, like storytelling. Familiarize yourself and, if you're directing, your team with the tone and quality of the language.

Figure out where to break. If you've ever sung in a choir, you know how important it is to breathe can answer that question with a "yes," then I think it's fine to accept that kind of a role.

Jason: A few years ago, I played a character that had premarital sex. I was a Christian at the time. As I thought about the role, it struck me that the play was not promoting premarital sex. It also struck me that many people I know (even in the church) had, or struggled not to have, sex before marriage. Because I was doing the play, I had the opportunity to explore the consequences of premarital sex (in the case of the play, an unplanned pregnancy) and be a part of a story that as a whole was redemptive.

Daniel: We need to think through what kind of evil is being represented. Often we just think in terms of swearing or drinking or sex—but we need to stop and think about more subtle evil.

Like, does the character objectify and use people, and does it seem okay in the context of the play? Or, do the play and the character give the audience an approving, agreeable picture of things we think we're entitled to—money or power or prestige? Or, does the play dwell on stereotypes and inappropriate pictures of people without exposing them to critique and change? These are some of the things that concern me. We need to ask better questions about the more subtle, clean evil that can be represented and encouraged in characters and plays.

Alison: It seems to me that these questions, and even our need to answer them in a book like this, are rooted in a fear of dealing with sin face-to-face. Putting evil onstage can be risky business. But if we do not play the story for all

---

together. You won't usually have to do that in sketches, but you will need to attend to where the breaks, pauses, "beats" (used sometimes to mean very short pauses) and other shifts come.

Check your pace. Many, many, many sketches are ruined by s l o w pace. Badly paced drama feels awkward and disjointed. The words have to come out at a fairly natural speed. Spoken too slowly, words start sounding distended, and the audience will start to focus on the sound and speed of the words rather than their meaning. (I know this sounds odd, but it's true!)

Check your diction. Though you will be speaking fast—perhaps faster than in real life—you must speak very clearly. Your words should sound crisp as a fresh bag of chips (minus the crunch).

Be careful about starting or ending phrases with little grunts, puffs of air, under-breath chuckles and ums. Think of your lines as a relationship and make the commitment to them. Once you start a line, just keep going. It's okay if it came out botched—if you keep going, you're likely to carry through the meaning of the line even if the words are mangled, and the audience will follow.

If you keep getting stuck on a word or phrase—a common occurrence—break it up one time by inserting something that means the same thing. Then go back to the script. Or take a quick break, then turn to the script and think through the line. What does it mean? Say it just in your head. Try again.

Memorize your lines "flat"—without much inflection—so you avoid "line readings" that sound tired and rote in performance.

it's worth, if we do not tell the gospel vividly and truthfully—as though it had something to do with the reality most unbelievers, and we, face every day—then we have made the God of the gospel into nothing more than a lovely hand-painted decorative accessory. Here's how Dorothy Sayers prefaces her play on Jesus:

> God was executed by people painfully like us, in a society very similar to our own—in the over-ripeness of the most splendid and sophisticated Empire the world has ever seen. In a nation famous for its religious genius and under a government renowned for its efficiency, He was executed by a corrupt church, a timid politician, and a fickle proletariat led by professional agitators. His executioners made vulgar jokes about Him, called Him filthy names, taunted Him, smacked Him in the face, flogged Him with the cat, and hanged Him on the common gibbet—a bloody, dusty, sweaty, and sordid business. If you show people that, they are shocked. So they should be. If that does not shock them, nothing can. . . . It is curious that people who are filled with horrified indignation whenever a cat kills a sparrow can hear that story of the killing of God told Sunday after Sunday and not experience any shock at all.[2]

23 CHARACTER AND CARICATURE

Jenny Vaughn Hall and Daniel Jones

The person you are is a thousand times more interesting than the best actor you could ever hope to be.

KONSTANTIN STANISLAVSKY

From the actor's point of view, drama is an adventure. Through drama we have the opportunity to explore life from another being's point of view. There we discover pieces of ourselves and allow those pieces to be magnified through the expression of the characters. We come to understand other human beings and why they do the things they do. We suspend judgment on their behavior, because our goal is to understand what motivated the behavior in the first place. We want to paint the fullest, most believable picture of character and see what makes each person tick.

For this reason the process of playing a character happens from the inside out. It is an inductive process. We begin by making observations in the script. The writer has done most of the defining work for us: we notice how the character responds and reacts to other people and circumstances. From there the actor begins to ask why, what and want questions.

Why does she decide to throw the birthday party even though her husband is cheating on her? What is she thinking as she bakes the cake? Why does she get all dressed up? What does she want from her husband? What does she want for herself? Human beings never do anything without a reason. Even if we aren't conscious of it, there is always a reason why we do what we do. Something propels us to step into the next part of our lives. This is as true for the characters on the stage as it is for all of us every day.

Now that you have questions on the table, you can begin the art of answering them. This is where the rubber meets the road. The choice you make is what puts the flesh and bones on the character, what makes them believable, what gives the character on the stage dimension and depth. It's at this point, when the character is being realized, that you create someone the audience can connect with.

CARICATURES ARE NOT PRETTY

It's difficult to develop a character in this thoughtful, disciplined way. But what happens if you skip the process? You have a caricature and a cliché. Have you ever had a caricature done of yourself? You know, where an artist draws an exaggerated picture of you? It can be a bit humbling.

I (Jenny) had one done years back, and when I look at it I still feel a pang of self-consciousness. The nose resembles my real nose but protrudes far from my face. My smile is big, like it is in real life, but it takes up half the picture. (Remind me why I paid money for this!) I mean, if that's how I really looked I would be freaky! Here's what's scarier: as I looked at the finished product and compared it to all of the artist's sample drawings, I found that we (his clients) all ended up looking pretty much the same. Save for a few details, every drawing appeared to come from the same freak

family! The bulbous nose, the gigantic teeth—honestly, I felt a little cheated.

Caricatures exaggerate reality. They are broad strokes of what makes up a person's true countenance, but they lack the fine details that make a face unique and distinct from all other faces. They may be fun and funny, but they don't move us deeply. "Oh, I love how you captured the essence with that enormous nose!" No. Not happening.

WHO IS THIS GUY ANYWAY?

If an actor avoids the hard work of finding and painting in the details of the character, then what you end up with is a caricature of someone, too exaggerated to resemble real life. In high school, I (Daniel) played Peter's father, Mr. Van Daan, in *The Diary of Anne Frank*. If you've seen the play or the movie—the older version with Shelley Winters—you know that Mr. Van Daan is a large personality, middle-aged, a bit self-centered. Keep in mind I was in high school and a scrawny seventeen. To make this character believable would be a stretch for me now—and nothing short of a miracle for a high school kid. Well, I stretched as far as I could possibly stretch, and I couldn't make him much more than a caricature.

I had never been a middle-aged man seeking refuge in an attic with my wife and teenage son. I was a teenager myself. So, for starters, I was drawing on zero personal experience. The best I could do was grasp ideas of what I thought this guy would be like. Mr. Van Daan became a flat, one-dimensional representation. While it's arguable whether a high school student could ever do justice to this character, I might've done better if I'd known how to ask the script questions about him and think through his actions. Then I could have combed my life to see if it offered me anything I could pull into this character. I managed a tiny glimpse of the events of the story but not a very full picture of Mr. Van Daan.

This is a problem not just for full-length

plays but for sketches, too. Sometimes we assume in doing a sketch that it's passable not to discern a character. But when we perform sketches, we need to fill out as much as we can. The point of doing a sketch is often to raise questions that relate to our lives. As actors, if we don't give the audience a window into the character's life, we don't help them into the sketch to ask the questions. We're not trying to lay down a big ol' guilt trip here, but taking the time to do a little work in thinking about character goes a long way in serving the audience.

BUILDING A CHARACTER

Once you've considered these questions, choose two or three ways the character could work, and take them to rehearsal. For example, you might say, "Hey Derek, I'm considering playing Flo, the former steelworker with a hoarse voice and a slight limp who loves her dog, Precious, a little too much." This leaves room for your team and director to collaborate with you. And your director will stop you

immediately (I hope) if your initial explorations will not work. If they give you the go-ahead, you've got something to work with. Recognize that you are in a process. You have the option, along with your director, of keeping or discarding what works and what doesn't at this point.

You and the director have to figure out whether the character works as you imagine him or her. It's important to make these decisions based on what the script dictates. Playing Hamlet's father as a young dude with a cocky swagger may be a fun experiment but probably won't serve the play. Honor the writer: make solid, clear choices that match up with the script and with the script's interpretation of your character.

You must also evaluate whether or not you can perform the character in the way you've imagined. For example, if you want to make the character Southern, ask the questions, *Am I able to pull the accent off? Can I master it well enough to avoid stereotype?* While it's fun to ex-

BUILDING A CHARACTER
Daniel Jones and Jenny Vaughn Hall

Here are some questions to help you build a character. Looking carefully at the script, ask yourself,

* *What is the sketch's main plot?*

* *What is my character doing in the story? What does he or she want?*

* *What is my character's relationship to other characters?*

* *What specific, physical goal is my character pursuing?*

* *What is the action like to me? (Find a personal connection to the action being played in the scene.)*

* *How do I imagine the character? What does he or she look like? Wear?*

* *How does my character move and walk?*

* *How does my character speak?*

plore, we've all seen the result of actors using bad accents (Kevin Costner as Robin Hood: "Look! Mistleto-oowah!" his Southern California accent overpowering his not-so-good attempt at a British thing). In one sketch, *The Tale of the Shrewd Manager*, I (Daniel) used an overly theatrical British accent. The sketch was a comedic take on a *Masterpiece Theater*-style telling of the story. The script satirized a particular theater style, which made it appropriate to do the hyperbolic accent.

Let your character live in the moment of the scene. Once you've done the groundwork and get into rehearsal, get free with your character—according to the choices of your action and the intent of the author, of course. Allow yourself to react impulsively to the other actors in the scene. During a scene study of Shakespeare's *Troilus and Cressida*, the actor playing Cressida instinctually felt the need to move in close to me (Daniel) and begin to circle me as she was revealing Cressida's romantic feelings. She took a risk in her character choice, which mirrored the risk Cressida was taking in the scene. The element of surprise for me as the actor, not knowing Zoe was going to make this choice, mirrored the element of surprise Troilus experiences as Cressida's true feelings are revealed. It created good, spontaneous tension that served the scene. Had both of us not been free to live in that moment (e.g., if I had freaked out or she had been too nervous to try it), we would have missed learning something new about our characters and how to tell the story in a crisp way. Some of the best moments can come from knowing your character well and then responding freely as the character. Take a risk; see what happens.

A MAN, A RAT AND HIS LICORICE

One of my (Daniel) best experiences developing character was in a production of *Etta Jenks*, a postmodern play about the fall of a young woman who moves to Hollywood seeking fame and fortune. Along the way she gets ac-

quainted with a number of shady characters that prey on her and attempt to bring her down. (Right—not your laugh-a-minute, light-hearted fare.)

My character was James, a speed (amphetamine) addict who preys on Etta and later becomes prey himself. I had some help from the script and quickly found that there was more to him when I started asking questions. Putting him together was a work of art. As I worked on building him, I found a wiry heap of contradictions—true of real people I've encountered.

One of the initial directions our director gave was to go to the zoo, observe animals and choose one that is most like your character. Since the characters in the play are all animalistic, preying on Etta, this made a lot of sense. While in the rodent house, I decided James was like a rat. I noticed the rat's quick, jerking, gnawing movements, and it reminded me of someone who would be using speed or had about nine cups of coffee. I also remembered hearing a story about the rat in the Chinese calendar who won the race against all the other animals (each representing a year) because he was shrewd. He climbed in the ear of the fastest animal and then, just as the other animal was about to cross the finish line, jumped out and won the race. This was James! Manipulative, shrewd, cunning, small and rodentlike: more choices to tuck in my belt. I thought of all the ways I could play a ratlike dude and then began to hone in on him.

I noticed some striking things about the evolution of my character. As I incorporated quick, jerky movements, my voice changed. I was speaking more quickly and rhythmically, sometimes breathlessly. Then I incorporated gnawing. I decided James would always be chewing on something, generally black licorice. This affected my voice even more. I had to be aware of enunciation and pace, but James was becoming less like Daniel and more like, well, a rat.

I thought about manipulation, shrewdness, cunning. What was James's status like in relation to other characters in the play? How would he interact in order to manipulate? Where would he feel confident to rise above someone else, or where might he have to lower

THE COST OF EXCELLENCE
Bruce Kuhn

In the midst of storytelling training for college ministry staff, someone asked me to help with a "model worship" demonstration. They had a student-written monologue they wanted performed, but needed a "regular person" to do it (one of my storytelling students), not a professionally trained actor. "This is for students," he said, "and we want to give new staff the confidence that they can do this for themselves, with the resources and people on hand." That made sense.

We worked together several times in the writing, rehearsing and polishing, for perhaps six hours total. The actor put another four hours into rehearsal on her own, exploring, testing the reality of the experience and experimenting with the images that would trigger honest emotional response. She did amazingly well the first time she performed it for an audience, getting eighty percent of her rehearsed work onstage. I promised her later that the second performance would be better, and that after the third it might even be out of previews and ready for a real audience. Unlike painting, film or writing, theater is not what it is until it happens onstage with an audience, and it grows with the contact (hopefully). Everyone was rightfully impressed with the performance. "That was great!" someone said in feedback and asked, "How long did that take you?" Her answer surprised everyone. The room got still for a moment. Someone said, "Ten hours of work for just five minutes onstage?!"

"My students can't put in that kind of time for a skit," said someone else.

No one would dare play the violin in public without training and rehearsal. Theater is more forgiving, of course, or can be. It can be fun to play music or do sketches within a loving, forgiving community. Expectations are lower. The standard is entirely different. However, if that community wants to present art that affects an outside culture, especially one so media savvy, the cost in time and investment is high.

Before I get too dizzy from standing on this pedestal of Righteous Artistic Integrity, let me confess that God does not need our artistic excellence to do his work. I am scandalized to admit that God can use the worst street-corner gospel skits to glorify himself. To paraphrase Paul, "If God works through our weakness, should we then do bad art to glorify God?" (2 Corinthians 12:9). Of course not. Can we do the best we can with what we have, while being ruthless with our mediocrity?

his posture to get what he wanted? I decided when he was around someone who he felt was lower, he was more aggressive, "in your face" and bold. When he was threatened or needed something from someone more powerful, he was more subtly manipulative, his voice softer and more oily.

As I made specific choices, I got to know James inside and out, and other decisions fell into place. What he would wear: a stylish wardrobe, dark, rumpled and dirty. His hair was unkempt and greasy, but with a trendy cut. The James I ended up playing was not just the words in the script but the sum of many choices. Asking questions and exploring his "world" allowed me to engage with the other actors and respond to the choices they were making for their characters.

A CARICATURE-FREE ZONE

Making specific choices creates a clearer, more accessible character on stage. Vagueness leaves room for caricature to rear its bulbous-nosed, smiley-faced head. You don't necessarily need a trip to the zoo for a short sketch, but you do need to be specific about voice, movement, wants and desires. The better we know the lives of the characters we are portraying, the more comfortable we are on stage. Our hard work creates interest and identification for the audience so they can engage the questions our sketches explore.

24 USING YOUR VOICE

Daniel Jones

The voice is in itself an instrument on which you must learn to play.

UTA HAGEN

I'm driving down the road with my tape series of Edith Skinner's *The Seven Points for Good Speech in Classic Plays* cranked up. Edith's perfectly crisp and well-enunciated voice booms loud, "Correct: Caah-rry [pronounced with a slightly affected, but pleasant, ring]. Incorrect: Caaaae-rry [pronounced with an exaggerated nasal quality]," followed by Edith's assessment of the incorrect option, "That's atrocious!"

We are not all going to be James Earl Jones, but learning to speak clearly and correctly on stage is a mighty handy tool. I could fill volumes rambling on about great vocal exercises and techniques that probably wouldn't be helpful. Besides, there are several great books on the subject. You may want to caah-rry one or two out at your local library. What I *can* do here is offer some practical ways of thinking about our voices on stage.

Some technique will be useful, but I want to focus on how we think about our voices on stage, what we need to keep in mind in relation to the audience, and how to let the words that come from our mouths tell the story and clearly invite those in earshot into the story we are telling them.

TALKING CAN BE A CHALLENGE

You think at first, *Well, it's just talking. I mean, how hard can that be? I do it all the time.* But when we hop on stage, it is rarely as simple as letting the sound fall out of our mouths. It is challenging to juggle all the things we need to think about and make it look like we're not juggling. One of the biggest challenges I've experienced to date in using my voice onstage is in a play that covers nearly the entire gospel in two hours—performed by two actors. Yep, just the two of us. All alone. On the stage. With all those characters. Needless to say, taking on the challenge of playing multiple characters is an exercise in using your voice creatively and effectively—a concern for any actor all the time.

YOUR VOICE AS AN INSTRUMENT

Uta Hagen talks about our voice being like an instrument, which we need to learn to play. Yes! The voice is an instrument that takes time to understand and nurture. When

HOW THE VOICE WORKS
Alison Siewert

Your voice makes sound when you push air through the vocal folds (they're not really "cords"), which send their vibration up into your resonating chamber (mouth and throat). You change the sound of your voice by adjusting the amount of air flowing through it, the tension in the vocal folds (like guitar strings, the tighter or thinner they're pulled, the higher the sound), and the shape and capacity of the resonating chamber.

Our body condition affects our speaking. If you slouch, you limit the amount of air space available to your lungs. Your lung capacity is increased when you expand your diaphragm and stretch out your intercostal muscles (between the ribs). Some musicians call this "diacostal" breathing (diaphragm and intercostal). If you are breathing correctly, your shoulders should not rise. What should rise? Your tummy area. When your dad's asleep on the couch, his book resting on his stomach and rising like a little boat on the ocean, he's breathing correctly. All his muscles are relaxed, and his body is able to take lots of air. He's not in a rush, looking around or holding his breath.

Warm It Up

You can do this standing up, though it might be easier to discover by first lying down. Once you stand, look at yourself in a mirror. Put your hand just below your ribs and cough. You

we work at it, we improve; and when we slack, we begin to lose what we've gained. But it is important to keep our voices tuned and be aware of what we are communicating through inflection, tempo, pitch and other vocal nuances.

The voice is a complex, delicate instrument. Notice that it's located right in the middle of life's functions: talking, eating, breathing, snoring (sleeping). When you feel upset, what happens physically? Your voice probably feels it first—you "choke up." It's instructive that God located our primary means of communication and so many other functions in one small area of the body.

YOUR VOICE AND BODY

How we speak affects the rest of our body. In *The Voice Book*, Michael McCallion says,

You cannot separate your voice from the rest of you. The impulse to communicate vocally comes from and uses your whole person, not merely your vocal organs. And your whole person is affected in a mechanical or physical way by such things as your environment, your relationship with yourself and other people and your intention of the moment. And however your mechanical use is affected, so is your voice, which is an ex-

---

should be able to feel your breathing muscles contract in the cough. Now that you've found them, watch yourself take a deep, slow breath. Are your shoulders moving? Are you trying to hold your stomach in? Exhale and start over. This time, stand on tiptoes and stretch your hands waaaay over your head. Feel the intercostal muscles stretch? Good. Now keep your hands where they are, but bring your heels slowly down. Keep the stretch. Now slowly bring your arms back to your sides. Keep the stretch. Relax your arms. Roll your shoulders back until they're comfortable. Keep the stretch. Put your hand back below your ribs and breathe. This will, believe it or not, become easier. When you're cleaning house or changing the oil in the car, prompt yourself to breathe correctly—deeply, with lots of room.

The amount of air and the quality of its movement over the vocal folds is called support. To have a supported voice means you are not making the muscles in your throat do all the work of producing sound. (Don't make them do all the work. They can become strained; it's happened to me and is not pleasant.) A supported voice has energy from the lungs to the mouth. You will want all the support you can get onstage. More support equals more energy; more energy equals more options and shapes your voice can take when you want it to.

Note: If you are congested or sore, do not use anesthetic cough drops of any kind. These will keep you from knowing when you are in pain, which will endanger your voice. Pain is your friend—it lets you know when you've spoken or sung too much or when you need to see a doctor. Also, remember that caffeine tends to dry your throat. If you're tired, take a nap instead of a cup of coffee; and if your throat is dry, try drops that include glycerin or slippery elm.

pression of yourself and what all of that self is doing.[1]

He challenges actors to think about what we're doing with our bodies before we begin to think about our voices: "Because for good or ill, that is the foundation upon which your voice use rests."

Before we begin anything else, we need to be aware that our physical state affects how we speak. This means when you are preparing to perform, get good rest, exercise, stretch, eat well, warm up your voice and know how you are doing physically. If you know what will be problematic, you know where to concentrate your attention. I suggest making corrective exercises and practice a regular part of your discipline.

YOUR VOICE COMMUNICATES

Our voices communicate our emotions, our thoughts, our stories. Our voices respond to other people's stories. How we choose to use our voices affects what emotions we express, how passionate or passive we seem about our thoughts and how our stories get told.

This is obviously true when we are on the stage. We don't just use our everyday indoor voices when we are performing. Remember that indoor voice your mom encouraged you to use in the house? Performing calls for a voice that projects and penetrates the room (sorry, moms). Tempo and pitch also reflect character and affect our communication.

Volume, projection, tempo and pitch: these

INFLECT CORRECT
Bruce Kuhn

Try speaking the following line, using the setup lines as guides for how to speak it. Hear the differences in meaning?

◆ *I don't care if you are a murderer or a saint,*
   Whoever *comes to me, I will never drive away.*

◆ *First and foremost, people have to come, give themselves to me, and*
   Whoever ***comes*** *to me, I will never drive away.*

◆ *Come to Caesar or wealth or even human relationship: they may drive you away.*
   Whoever comes to ***me,*** *I will never drive away.*

◆ *People come to me, and sometimes they drive themselves away, but*
   Whoever comes to me, ***I*** *will never drive away.*

◆ *I love people so much that*
   Whoever comes to me, I will ***never*** *drive away.*

◆ *Whoever comes to me, I will never hate, I will never demean.*
   Whoever comes to me, I will never ***drive away.***

all communicate something to the audience. They may not be sitting there consciously thinking, *Wow. Jane's voice is much higher than normal, and it sounds like she's quickened her speech. She must be trying to tell us something through her pitch and tempo.* But the choices you make will indeed tell the audience about your character and help them understand and enjoy the sketch.

WARMING UP

Keep your voice crystal clear and limber. Warming up your voice before you perform, even for sketches, will help you not to strain. Begin by stretching your body (see Jenny's exercises, page 108). Then warm up your voice. Start by vocalizing without specific pitch to get phlegm out of the way and get the air moving. When you sing notes, your voice works subconsciously to adjust. If it's phlegmy, it will work too hard under the weight and get strained. Eew. Once you've gotten warm, sing scales. Play or have someone play scales for you on the piano, and sing the progression of notes on vowel sounds. Repeat the exercise, changing the vowel each time.

In another exercise you throw your voice. Stand straight up with your feet firmly planted on the ground, then yell "Hey!" like the shout is coming from the your gut (check with your hand to make sure those breathing apparatuses are working) and "throw" your voice. To help you with the throwing part, pretend you are throwing a baseball at the same time you are throwing your voice. Imagine you are sending your voice to the same place you are sending the baseball. Keep it easy—not like you're throwing your voice at the ump's bad call, but like you're tossing the baseball back into the game.

Another simple exercise is to read poetry (out loud, of course). Concentrate on enunciation. Make your consonants come out crisp and your vowels sound slightly exaggerated. You will sound funny. Don't worry about it. It's for art. Most people slur words together, and

this will help you be cognizant of trouble spots before you perform.

VOLUME AND PROJECTION

In general, lean toward loud. You may think you sound too loud, but you probably don't—that is, literally, in your head. (We hear through the vibrations in our bones as well as through ambient sound.) Your director will give you the thumbs down if you are a booming foghorn that just needs to stop. Controlling your volume does not mean shouting out all your lines. You want to imitate everyday conversational style while making sure you are heard.

PITCH

This is the highness or lowness of the sound you produce. Be aware that when you change pitch, you will also be changing the volume of your voice. When you speak higher, you will become louder; and when you speak lower, you will quiet your voice. It can also work, though less naturally, the other way around; but remember, when you increase or decrease in volume, your pitch will change. Keep in mind that very high pitches are more difficult to understand (due to complex physics we will not attempt to explain here).

Pitch is a great way to add texture to your character. It certainly will make your characters more interesting—as opposed to a pitch-free (monotone) performance. Think about your character: Would they speak with a higher or lower pitch, or would they modulate more frequently?

Annette Bening is a master at using her voice. In *American Beauty* she demonstrates a complex characterization by the fluctuations in her pitch. When she is portraying the superficial, in-control-of-how-people-see-her side of Caroline, her pitch tends to be a bit higher and her voice becomes sing-songy. When we see the real, behind-closed-doors Caroline, her voice deepens in an almost guttural sadness. These are distinct vocal choices in pitch Annette makes to communicate the state of Caroline Burnham.

TEMPO

Tempo is the rate of speed at which you are speaking. Often, beginning actors will rush through their lines as if they can't wait to get them over with (which may actually be the case). But don't do that! People want to hear you. Don't rush. Gauge your tempo as you are practicing your lines. (It's also not uncommon for actors to speak too slowly, which can make things drag.) Ask your director to listen to you for tempo. Slowing down may feel funky at first, but you will serve the audience by allowing them to take in the words you are speaking.

When you've mastered the control of your tempo, you can then use it to your advantage. Similar to pitch and volume, the rate at which we speak communicates something about our character. When I played a speed addict (the kind on drugs, not a racer), it made sense to speak more quickly and rhythmically. I had to be aware of my clarity, but the speed helped the audience into the physical and emotional state of the character.

In another play, *Tartuffe*, I slowed down the tempo of Tartuffe's speech. He pretends to be someone he is not, duping a family out of control of their property. I decreased his tempo in order to give the sense that he was lulling the family into his deception. Where his true character is exposed in the play, I quickened the tempo to show the contrast of his duplicity.

ENUNCIATION AND ARTICULATION

To pronounce and speak distinctly and clearly is crucial. Form your words and sentences with an ear to crisp clarity. In American speech we often mushwordstogether as if speaking a sin-

STUMBLING INTO TRUTH
Jason Gaboury

One time onstage in a Christmas show, I was overwhelmed by emotion. We were doing a piece that was asking if "peace on earth" was viable. In the middle of the performance I started crying (not planned), my scene partners saw me, and they got choked up as well. Somehow we made it to the end of the piece, and there was a silence and stillness in the audience, a pause, and then thunderous applause. Why?

I think the reason was that, in the midst of doing the piece that day, the three of us had stumbled on something true. Suddenly I was really overwhelmed, my partners really choked up, and all of us (actors and audience) were caught by the irony of "peace on earth" in the midst of our experience of war and pain. It was not the emotion that was moving, but the truth of the situation, the question that was being exposed.

I think when drama works well it's because the scene is pointing to something true. When an audience is able to recognize the truth of a particular behavior, relationship, question or struggle, and can see themselves in that situation, that's drama.

gle run-on sentence. Clearly speak your consonants at the beginnings and ends of sentences. Don't let your S's hissss.

You may not have a problem with enunciation and articulation, but if you do, it can greatly affect your performance and what the audience is able to take in from you. After rehearsal, listen to yourself in the performance space. Every room has different acoustics. When Alison directed a play in a modern, stark, concrete building, the actors had trouble with articulation because there was so much echo. They worked and worked on it—so much that one night her roommate heard her say, in her sleep, "We need to hear your lines clearly and distinctly."

ACCENTS AND DIALECTS

Accents and dialects are a distinguishing manner of pronunciation. Some scripts may call for an accent or dialect. Make sure you are able to master it before you get on stage to perform it. It is sometimes better to forego the accent if it's not coming out right. We've all seen movies and plays where the accents don't work. All of a sudden, we are focused on the shabby accent more than on the story.

You can use accents to highlight. When I play blind Bartimaeus asking Jesus for his sight, I slide into a childlike British accent in the manner of Oliver Twist, and ask, "Please sir, could I receive my sight?" It's humorous, it recalls something familiar, and it highlights the point that Bart wants to see and is willing to ask Jesus for healing.

Be careful not to stereotype by using accents and dialects. And in any case, be sure of what you are doing before you dive into an accent. Know which dialect you are using, and make sure its usage is helpful in the context of the sketch.

POTENTIAL PITFALLS

Watch out for regional patterns of speech. In some parts of the country, folks inflect up at the ends of sentences; in others, they inflect down. And in still other areas, people inflect strongly at traditionally awkward points in the middle of the sentence. I wasn't aware of this problem until a director pointed out my tendency to inflect down at the end of sentences. When I was attempting Hamlet's "To be or not to be" speech for a class, I kept trailing off at the end of each line. This made the speech consistently undynamic and sucked the energy right out of it.

Speaking of energy, which is hard to describe, make sure you speak with energy. Sometimes when we adjust volume or tempo, our speech loses energy. Our voices become dull. It then sounds to the audience like we are bored by what we are doing. S-s-nore!

Confidence is key. Be confident in your vocal choices when you step onto the stage. Let your voice be strong and clear. Enter the stage knowing that people want to hear what you have to say. Don't hold back.

FAILURE HAPPENS

Allow yourself to mess up. That's how we learn, right? If you are confident, people will focus. You or your director will be aware of what works and what doesn't. And you can go from there. Risk and failure are part of the process. Interestingly enough, they also happen to be part of following Jesus. You've done the work; you've thought through the options. Go for it.

25 THE UNSELF-CONSCIOUS ARTIST

Jenny Vaughn Hall

In the midst of a leap, there are no guarantees. To leap can often cause acute embarrassment. Embarrassment is a partner in the creative act—a key collaborator. If your work does not sufficiently embarrass you, then very likely no one will be touched by it.

ANNE BOGART

Acting is half shame, half glory. Shame at exhibiting yourself, glory when you can forget yourself."[1] The most profound art comes from artists who are not self-conscious, but rather free to express themselves honestly before God and other people. The more you receive the kingdom of God like a child, the more unveiled and unabashed you will become as a human being and as an artist. King David is a perfect example of someone who lives in this reality. In 2 Samuel 6:16 we see David so overjoyed with God's goodness that he begins to leap and dance around to the sound of trumpets, in front of everyone is his kingdom. Imagine seeing George Bush do an interpretive worship dance to a bunch of trumpets on national TV! What would you be thinking about him as you watched?

In all honesty, I would be embarrassed for him and worried that he might seriously pull some kind of muscle, and I'd probably change the channel. This is exactly how some viewed David. His own wife was shamed and infuriated by David's creative and exuberant expression. How did all of this affect David's artistic expression? He couldn't care less. It didn't matter that he looked like a fool; it

didn't even matter that his own wife was ashamed of him. He was being a child of God in the fullest sense.

This spirit can infuse our art, allowing us to take risks in scripts we write and parts we play. The more we can let go of whatever brokenness keeps us insecure and self-conscious, the more this freedom will direct us and our art. I think it is incredible that the number one thing all artists are looking for, freedom and confidence to risk, is exactly what following Jesus brings into a person's life.

How about you? To what extent do you carry yourself as a child before God? How free are you to creatively express yourself before him and other people with all of your might? Personally, I am still journeying into this freedom. However, in just my ten years of following Jesus, the reality of "receiving the kingdom like a child" (Mark 10:15) has already revolutionized my life and my art.

I have always been a very expressive person. In fact, when I got back a series of candid photos recently, I was shocked by the crazy expressions I had on my face in each shot! I have also never been someone who felt particularly reigned in by social codes of how one is supposed to act in public. I went to a performing arts school where creative personalities, expressive clothes and assorted ways of being were encouraged. However, during my first two years in a college theater department, I found myself terribly self-conscious. During rehearsals for shows, half of my mind was always wondering what everyone thought of my acting or singing. During my acting classes I found it hard to let go of control and cut loose like a lot of the other students could. It wasn't fun. In fact it was burdensome, and it was burning me out. So, I decided for the next two years of my college career to take a break from theater and explore what the kingdom of God had to offer me.

I dove into Bible studies and learned how to apply the Scriptures and relationally invest my life in other people. I asked God to shape and change me, and he did not disappoint. It was during those two years that God showed me how much my sense of value had rested in being a good singer, dancer and actor. I began to see how much I depended on those things to feel important. During that two-year break, God began to strip away the superficial things I had put my value in. Through prayer and tears he replaced that brokenness with the wonderful knowledge that I was his child and I was loved. End of story. Because of that, I had freedom in life to just be myself. That meant I had freedom to be good at things and freedom to be bad at things. It was the most liberating reality to know I wasn't valuable because of my talent.

FREEDOM TO RISK

How has this changed my art and me as an artist? I have a freedom to risk, to go for it in acting classes, rehearsals and performances. In a recent acting class we were required to act out something fantastical. I decided to be a superhero: tough and full of courage and adventure. So on the stage, in front of everyone, I jumped around on all the furniture, screaming things about the destiny of the world as we know it be-

ing at stake and then diffusing a bomb! It was so much fun to use my imagination before God and people with all my might.

On a different note, this freedom also allows me to dive into raw and emotional depths of characters and bring those inner realities to the surface. Allowing yourself to be expressive of painful or angry moments in a scene can feel vulnerable. But the more I understand what it means to be unguarded before God, the more I am able to let my guard down in characters that I play and let their humanity show through. This is what touches an audience and creates safety for them. The performer's freedom gives the audience freedom to look inside themselves and be honest with what they see. On top of all that, by being free, a performer wastes much less energy worrying about what everyone else is thinking and simply enjoys the creative process.

The key question for us to consider, to reflect on, is, How much has God healed you from the fear of what people will think of you? How much of your value rests on doing things well and being affirmed by people? How free are you to creatively express yourself before God and people with all of your might? How much do you carry yourself as a child before your Father? These are issues to be discussing and praying through with the Christian community you are a part of.

Clearly, the journey toward being an uninhibited person and artist begins inwardly. There is no formula when it comes to our healing and personal growth. However, we can exercise external disciplines that help us with internal realities. Acting exercises have helped me on the outward journey of becoming a more freed-up actor. It has been interesting to see how much the inward and outward journeys overlap. I find that working on a particular exercise brings up new insecurities and self-consciousness that I need to pray and work through. An acting coach said to me recently after a certain exercise, "Jenny, you have a lot of pleaser energy in you. You want to please people and are very focused on making them happy. You really need to work on that in life and on stage." WHOA! Hey now! He saw it! And I was glad he did, because he was right. He wasn't a Christian, but God sure was speaking through him! Acting—even in exercises—frequently magnifies the issues you deal with in normal life. So don't be surprised. Expect stuff to show up, work with it, and know that God will use it to heal you and change you if you let him.

26 ACTORS' EXERCISES

Daniel Jones

When my play . . . was put on for the first time . . . the set designer . . . was responsible for providing the $15,000 cash that one of the characters has stolen. There was no budget to speak of, so [he] made fake money by Xeroxing imitation $20 bills on sheets of greenish-yellow paper, and whenever he wasn't busy with something else, he sat on the steps in the theater in the dark, personally cutting out each bill with a pair of scissors until he had enough stacks of them to pass for $15,000. I'll never forget that, because it showed the difference between somebody who cares about his work and somebody who doesn't.

KENNETH LONERGAN

Here is a group of exercises that you can use to polish your acting skills.

EXERCISE 1: THREE-IN-ONE

Pick one movement from each of these three categories: the focus of your eyes, your arms and upper body, and your legs and lower body.

Then practice walking with the three movements together. So, for example, you might walk with an unfocused gaze, looking in multiple directions, never focusing on any one thing in particular. Meanwhile your upper body is wringing like a washing machine, and your lower body is strutting like you're the coolest kid in school! (Obviously you won't look too cool since the strut is combined with the unfocused eyes and the wringing.)

The point of this exercise is to make each of these movements looks natural, so that if you were walking down the street, people would not be able to tell that you are not your normal everyday you.

Category #1: The Focus of Your Eyes
Choose a level of focus:
◆ Focused: Your eyes are fixed to one object or are always looking straight ahead.
◆ Unfocused: Your eyes dart in every direction, never landing on one object in particular.

Category #2: Your Arms and Upper Body
Pick a movement, and move your upper body in the way the word sounds. Use your arms and waist.
◆ Jabbing
◆ Slashing
◆ Wringing
◆ Swishing
◆ Chopping

Category #3: Your Legs and Lower Body
Pick a movement, and move your lower body in the way the word sounds. Use your legs, feet and hips.
◆ Floating
◆ Gliding
◆ Bobbing
◆ Strutting
◆ Climbing
◆ Creeping

Feel free to make up your own movements if you think of other possibilities. My best experience using this exercise was walking around the streets of San Francisco. I walked around Union Square, in and out of stores—unfocused, slashing and gliding. I got plenty of stares and actually collided with a few people—*oops*—but this exercise gave me a real sense of how a character I might be playing, embodying this physicality, would interact in real life with real people.

EXERCISE 2: SOAP OPERA THEATER

This is a great exercise for beginning actors. It breaks the ice, is totally funny and helps you think through believability in a performance.

Simply read a sketch or scene—*any* sketch or scene—as if you were the worst actors on the worst soap opera ever. You can be as melodramatic, boring, sing-songy or monotone as you want. Encourage exaggeration and ridiculousness: it gets people out of their comfort zones without the threat of critique.

EXERCISE 3: AM I IN THE RIGHT ROOM?

This exercise helps with reaction believability. One actor goes outside of the room, shuts the door and then re-enters as if walking into a room he or she isn't supposed to be in. The actor needs to give an honest reaction and then leave and shut the door. You want the actors to experience walking in confidently and then realizing their mistake. Have them imagine going to a class at college or attending a meeting. When they arrive, no one is familiar.

Allow them to be free with their responses. In one class, responses ranged from horror, to sweetly apologetic, to apathetic. The most important element is that the responses are honest, not exaggerated or faked. You want them believable. You may have people try this exercise multiple times.

EXERCISE 4: MEMORIZATION HOT POTATO

Once your cast has learned their lines and time permits, have everyone stand in a circle. The person who begins the sketch begins the exercise. The actor holds a ball, says his or her line and then passes the ball to the person with the next line.

This exercise not only helps with memorization, but also helps everyone know who is speaking when. This should not be a slow-moving game. You want the actors to reach a point at which a swift rhythm is created. If they absolutely are not able to do this, have them go back and look over the sketch and the lines with the awareness of the other characters who are speaking before or after them. Then try it again.

27 FREEING UP YOUR BODY

Jenny Vaughn Hall

Control, apparently, is not the answer. People who need certainty in their lives are less likely to make art that is risky, subversive, complicated, iffy, suggestive, or spontaneous. What's really needed is nothing more than a broad sense of what you're looking for, some strategy for how to find it, and an overriding willingness to embrace mistakes and surprises along the way.

DAVID BAYLES AND TED ORLAND

Most people in the United States are uncomfortable with the movement of their own bodies. In many other countries this is not the case. My husband spent a summer in Ghana, where everyone dances all the time. It's a regular, daily part of life. People dance on the streets, dance their way up to the altar to put their money in the offering plate, dance all the time. Not us. We are not very free with movement and motion. Certain moves are acceptable if they happen at the right time and place, such as on basketball courts or in dance clubs, and if we think our bodies are "qualified" to be seen moving; but in day-to-day life we are very body-conscious people.

Because of this, I believe that a major factor in becoming uninhibited onstage is to explore and become comfortable with our physical reality. Your body is your instrument in acting. It is the source of all gestures, sounds and emotions. If your body is tense and nervous, your acting will be too. For this reason we must become good friends with our bodies and allow ourselves to take up the space that we need to express ourselves fully.

Now I will be honest with you: acting exercises can feel really weird. I remember thinking once during a college movement class, *My parents are paying $10,000 to have me roll around on the floor!* But as I matured a bit, I realized how much these exercises set a crucial foundation for any actor. In a sense, the goal of all the exercises is to strip away inhibitions and leave the actor free to be fully in the moment, focused on the present, unguarded and tapped into the subtext of what's happening in the scene. The exercises are also very helpful in teaching actors how to let go of control and be unveiled on the stage.

There are many exercises, so think of this as a start-up kit and have fun exploring and experimenting. Please note: It's a good idea to debrief each exercise right after you finish. Find out how it went for yourself and others, and what you learned; ask for feedback from those who were watching. This way everyone is always in learning posture, and we become comfortable with feedback from peers. Alrighty . . .

EXERCISE 1: IMPROVISATION

Improvisation helps get you out of your head, where you calculate and evaluate your responses, and into the present moment, where your impulses guide your words and your actions. In this space you feel little sense of control; there are no lines to protect you and no plot to tell you where you are headed. It is all made up in the moment, so you are forced to trust your knee-jerk response to things and you learn to just go with it. Improvisation is a very creative and cool experience.

What's wonderful about improvisation is that you have no time to get all perfectionistic and analytical about things. You have to accept what's on the table and make the best of it. The more you do it, the more free and uninhibited you will become.

Here are just a couple of helpful guidelines. First, it works best not to say "No" to whatever another actor brings to the table, especially in the beginning of a scene. Negative starts often end up going nowhere, which can make the whole exercise flop. The second guideline is that it's best to make observations rather than ask questions. So instead of saying, "Why are you burning the dog food?" say, "You're burning the dog food! I never understand why you do that!" It's also helpful to have a third party who is there to call "scene" when he or she thinks it's time for the actors to stop. This way the actors themselves don't have to worry about when they should end. Keep these guidelines in mind as you try the following two exercises.

♦ Two actors go onto the stage. Once they're there, other actors (in their seats) choose a word. The word can be anything: "frozen" or "aliens" or "frustrated." From there the two actors begin a scene that is catalyzed by the word. If the word was "aliens," for example, you might decide to be an alien trying to abduct a human. Perhaps you see an alien land in your back yard. Whatever! The point is, you run with the word they give you and see where it leads you.

♦ Two or more actors set up a scene where the characters and the conflict are stated but no lines or resolution are given. For example, I was once assigned this scene with a friend: A daughter is in a waiting room with her mom who is pressuring her into plastic surgery. That was all we were given, and we had to see where it would lead us. It was a very interesting improv that I later turned into a sketch. This exercise is good for freeing you up—and it can provide wonderful material to build sketches.

EXERCISE 2: MOVEMENT

In improvisation we get comfortable with being uncomfortable. But we can also get comfortable with moving—it helps a lot! Knowing where our arms and legs are, how they feel in relation to our head when we spin, how far we feel good bending our back—our sense of physical equilibrium, limberness and strength—helps us to move when and how we want to and gives us confidence.

♦ A really easy way to begin familiarizing yourself with your body is through some simple warm-up exercises. Begin with gentle head rolls to the right. After four or five rolls, begin to include the upper body and shoulders in the movement. After four of those, begin to include the entire upper torso so that by the end you are swinging your body around in large circles. Hands can fly free and go where they please. When you're ready to let loose, try adding a guttural "HUH!" as you swing down with each roll. This allows the voice and movement to be connected. End by doing a standing forward bend, with your arms hanging as low as they can toward your feet. Take several deep breaths and roll up. Then begin on the left side. Basic stretches (like the ones you would do in gym class) are also excellent for warming up the muscles and getting you in touch with what's going on in your body.

♦ After the warm-up you can move into an exercise we call High Space, Low Space, Middle Space for reasons which will be obvious in a minute. Actors begin moving counterclockwise, doing any kind of movement they like (run, skip, hop, crawl), but the rule is, they must explore using high space, middle space and low space. They do this until the leader yells, "Stop!" From here the leader needs to give direction, such as, "Imagine you are walking through thick, cool tar" or "You're in a two-foot-wide tunnel." The leader creates a scenario in which the actors must decide how to respond. This shouldn't last for more than a minute until the leader calls out again, "High space, middle space, low space!" and everyone resumes their own movement. You'll feel foolish doing this at first, but it is extremely liberating to explore movement and motion and will help you shed your inhibitions.

◆ One last exercise that is simple and can be done anywhere at any time is to observe other people's body movement, as well as your own, in daily life. Take note of how you use your hands as you talk to different people: a friend, for instance, versus a professor. What do you do with your hands while you are waiting for a friend at a bus stop or restaurant? Simply take note and then go home, look in a mirror, and explore what it's like to recreate those gestures. Apply the same exercise to others around you. How do young parents react physically when their baby cries loudly in a grocery store? What's in a businessman's body language as he talks to an attractive woman versus a homeless person in the street? Take mental notes, and again go home and experiment with those gestures in the mirror. This toolkit of observations will help you be more conscious of the physical nature of relationships and routines and will assist you as you work on different characters.

True, you risk embarrassment in all of this. But what you gain is immeasurably good. Not only will your own soul become more free and childlike before God, but you'll have the honor of seeing your own vulnerability affect and transform the lives of those around you.

28 REMAINING CALM

Nina Thiel

To make art is to sing with the human voice. To do this you must first learn that the only voice you need is the voice you already have. Artwork is ordinary work, but it takes courage to embrace that work, and wisdom to mediate the interplay of art and fear.

DAVID BAYLES AND TED ORLAND

You want ME to write a chapter called "Remaining Calm"? What, are you NUTS?! What makes you think I'm CALM before I perform?! Didn't you see Bruce practically have to slap me that last night of Urbana 2000 when we had a sudden change of plans to deal with and I TOTALLY FREAKED OUT?!

"Sure, Alison. I'd be happy to write a chapter on remaining calm."

I bet I know why I'm writing this chapter:

it's because I look calm. What a great actor— people can't even see the hysteria raging inside of me all the way up to the second my feet hit the stage. Let's just say, then, that what follows is what I know to do to keep my anxiety from being worse than it is. I mean, really, what is there to "remain calm" about? Just 20 or 200 or 20,000 people *all watching you*. Are you *kidding?*

Argh. Okay. Cleansing breath . . . in through the nose . . . out through the mouth. Let's begin.

The key to remaining calm is preparation, to have nothing to worry about so that you can be free to perform your best. In my mind (and life), potential worries fall into three categories: rehearsal issues, technical issues and physical/spiritual/emotional issues in performance situations. Here's what I do to minimize the anxiety in each category.

REHEARSAL

Rehearse—and don't merely rehearse; rehearse more than adequately. Last spring I performed a four-minute sketch with a theater student at a local postmodern church. We rehearsed twelve hours. Yep, that's about right. Bruce Kuhn plans three hours of rehearsal per finished minute of performance. For me, this is not only about the hard work of really getting the piece right, but about the piece being so much a part of me that I can trust my body, my mouth and my brain to know what to do when I'm up there. This isn't about repetitious rehearsal that leads to autopilot performances, but about getting the piece, the scene and the words all the way inside me so that they emerge effortlessly from within during a performance. And that takes a lot of rehearsal time.

Our rehearsal needs to be prayerful, too, with the foundation of trusting that God is at work in us and in the piece laid from the very beginning. I pray a lot as I rehearse my solo show on Jesus' encounters with women. I also pray as I rehearse for a dance that has nothing (overtly) to do with Jesus and as I rehearse for a play in which my character considers a pas-

tor her enemy. "God, help me to do my job well today. Help me to hear from you as I work on this. Help me to communicate your truth, your beauty, your heart."

TECHNICAL ISSUES

All you ever have to experience is a performance in sub-optimal conditions to understand how things like lights, sound, stage and costuming can affect your serenity. There was the time I performed *The Samaritan Woman* (John 4) at my church, with eighteen inches of stage depth (that is, unless I wanted to perform from atop the piano or the drum set). I was so worried about knocking something over behind me, or falling down the steps in front of me, that the passage suddenly became the least, versus the whole point, of my worries.

Then there was the performance with the dying wireless mic battery. And the performance when they couldn't find the wireless mic and thought it would work for me to have a chord running out the back of my pants to the PA system. And you expect me to remain calm under these conditions?!

Know what you need, and don't hesitate to ask for it. Make sure you'll be lit from the front, so the audience can see your face. Make sure the batteries are fresh and the mics are working. Always take the time for thorough sound and light checks. Make sure someone, if not you, has properly requested all the equipment you will need—well before you arrive to perform.

Do a little stage check too. Run through some of your piece on the actual stage. Walk it; see how it feels. (I decide what to wear on my feet in performance based on this run-through.) I have often been surprised by how a performance space feels once I've started to perform. Surprise isn't good when you're trying to remain calm.

And think about costuming: how will you keep your hair out of your face? (Hair in my face drives me *crazy* when I'm performing.) What kind of shirt works well with the mic you'll use? (Hint: not a flimsy or low-cut shirt that a mic will pull open every time you lean forward.) What kind of pants won't show off more flesh than called for by the script when you bend down to be Jesus writing on the ground? What clothes can you move in, do you feel comfortable in, are appropriate for the part, the setting? Lay them out the night before—no last-minute washing or ironing or even looking for your favorite black socks.

PERFORMANCE SITUATIONS

Prepare the instrument: your body and your voice. I always spend at least half an hour before a performance doing Pilates stretching and centering exercises (sort of like yoga). Then I warm up my face (mouth and eyes opened wide; tongue out to whole face, then pulled into my nose—*very attractive*) and my enunciation. I hum a lot too—it warms up the vocal cords. I take lots of sips of water while I'm warming up to stay hydrated. If my mouth or throat is dry, I suck on lozenges with glycerin or slippery elm. I use the bathroom about three times in the half hour before the show begins. All this helps me know my body and voice will be there for me when I need them, so I don't have to worry!

Prepare emotionally and spiritually: battle the voices. If you don't know the voices, you will. They say things like, "Why are you doing this? No one is going to like this. You're not a professionally trained actor anyway. What do you think you're doing here? Oh, look, someone is sleeping. Your performance must be really boring. Don't forget your next line, stupid. If you want to be taken seriously as an actor, it all depends on tonight. Gosh, what a small audience. Gosh, what a big audience . . ." You get the picture. The voices are straight from the pit of hell, and their goal is to get you so self-conscious, so self-focused, that you are not *in* the stories you're telling on stage, but more like hovering *above* yourself, watching. Here's what has helped me fight:

Prayer. Being prayed for by others and praying myself into the presence of God. If you need prayer, ask for it. If you need to get alone somewhere to pray, do it. God will meet you and fill you with what you need. Find a specific psalm or liturgical prayer or hymn you can memorize, and let it lead you to God.

Worship. I have my favorite worship CDs playing while I do my physical warm-ups, and I don't hesitate to sing along. There are certain songs that open up my soul and remind me of God's call to me in performing.

Time alone. Sometimes I just need to rest and read quietly in my room for a couple of hours the day of a performance. I'm an introvert, too, so that time is crucial to keep my personal batteries charged.

Time with people. Right before I perform, I want to be with people. Not everyone is like this, but I am. I call it staying relationally warm after I've warmed up everything else and have prayed and been prayed for. One of my favorite experiences was hanging out at the tech table last spring with the guys hired to do lights and sound at the university where I was performing. They were theater people, so they were great at encouraging me and joking with me. I found my pre-performance home with those guys! And I had great conversations with two of them about Jesus after my last performance at their school.

As you perform, you'll discover your own needs and develop your own routines for physical, emotional and spiritual preparation. Add to these thorough rehearsal and technical preparedness, and calmness is a real possibility!

So you're about to perform. House lights are going down. Inhale. Exhale. Shake the tension out of your hands. Offer yourself and your performance to God.

And, "Remember, concentrate on the moment. Feel, don't think. Trust your instincts."[1] Even better,

Be still, and know that I am God;
    I will be exalted among the nations,
    I will be exalted in the earth.
(Psalm 46:10 NIV)

PART 4

DIRECTING

29 THE SERVANT DIRECTOR

Alison Siewert

Can art be as basic a service as a cup of cold water? Definitely, yes! Because, depending on your condition, it may not be water that you need: you may need a hernia operation or financial assistance—or you may need the help of an artist.

CALVIN SEERVELD

Most of us are familiar with the title "director," but what exactly does a director do? The director leads the actors and other artistic crews in developing and presenting the drama. The director leads. The most significant leadership of the director is in relation to the actors. They are the primary focus of the director; everything the director does is measured against the goal of having the actors prepared and strengthened to offer art to audience.

DIRECTOR AS SERVANT

Let's break that description down. The director leads. The director is the person in charge of the art. There may be others working on various aspects of the project, but the director is the artistic leader of the team. In our context, the director is also a spiritual leader for the team. Directors must be servant leaders. That is, they must seek to lead their team by serving, blessing, listening and extending themselves for the good of team members as well as the project at hand.

Robert Greenleaf described servant leaders as people who can answer the question "What are you trying to do?" in such a way that they give "certainty and purpose to others who may have difficulty in achieving it for themselves." A servant leader creates an artic-

ulate vision and effectively points others toward it. But, Greenleaf says, this is "not just any goal and not just anybody stating it. The one who states the goal must elicit trust, especially if it is a high risk or visionary goal, because those who follow are asked to accept the risk along with the leader."[1] What a great description of drama! Risks we accept together . . . a goal we would have trouble finding without direction . . . a situation in which trust is most important.

A servant director cares for actors, encourages and uplifts them, listens to them, and prays with them. But a servant director also actively directs actors toward a goal. Actually, directors usually have multiple goals. There is a concrete, immediate goal of getting the sketch together for the service so that the audience will be able to see and receive from it. There is a longer-term goal of developing a team that responds to God by creating art and grows in its ability to effectively present that art.

TREADING A NEW PATH

Some directors in mass entertainment culture are famous for exerting their wills and getting their ways. Some scare, schmooze, badger or flatter their actors into performances. But "it shall not be so among you" (Mark 10:43 RSV). Servant leaders build relationships of trust and love with the people they lead, and lead strongly from the basis of those relationships. There is nothing wimpy about this sort of directing. But in the context of following Jesus, "a sustaining spirit that will support the tenacious pursuit of a goal" shapes our leadership.[2]

Look long and hard at your actors. They are doing something risky and vulnerable, and they will engage at the level of risk you help them into. Think about how things feel from the actors' perspective. William Ball, founder of American Conservatory Theater, says, "Fear is the primary enemy of creativity. . . . It is essential that the director be the actor's ally"[3] You must build a creative alliance with your team, so that everyone knows you're out for the same purpose, investing together in it and in one another for the sake of making good art and growing as believers.

Servant directors work not just to make the drama look good on the stage; we work to help the actors develop. We also receive in the process. We work toward win-win situations. We don't need actors; they are not resources to us. We, in fact, are called to be resources to them. And we don't use actors in the sense that we keep them around as long as they carry an important role and then discard them. We employ the skills, but we serve the person. This is the basis of our relationship: we want the actor to win deeper faith and artistic growth; we want the audience to win a beautiful sketch that will evoke truth.

BUILDING DIRECTOR-ACTOR RELATIONSHIPS

How do we build those relationships in the context of doing theater together? Here are some starting points:

Know your people. Learn about your actors: what are they excited about? afraid of? What is going on in their lives? How can you pray for them? encourage them? Hang with people; spend time with them—don't set yourself off in some rarified director's cloister.

Make yourself appropriately accessible.

Do your homework. Figure out what the specific goal is, and work out how to achieve it. Preparation is an act of love and indicates that you consider the team's work to be important.

Use time well. Figure out how much rehearsal time you need, and ask for it up front. Then use it well by preparing ahead of time and working for efficiency in rehearsals. Do not show contempt for actors by wasting their time.

Recognize what the actors are doing. Come to terms with how vulnerable you are asking people to be, what difficulty you are directing them to bear. If you've never acted, it might be good for you to take a class or act in a sketch directed by someone else.

Make other people look good. Serve people by making them look their best on stage and off. Take others' suggestions and ideas seriously, and lead so the team works together and to its highest capacity. When you use someone's idea, give him or her credit. When someone takes a risk on his or her own initiative, pay attention. Thank people. Praise everything you possibly can. Notice improvement. Cheer people on. And when their work is noticed by others, praise God and point back to how wonderfully he is growing your team.

Build a safe environment. Create rehearsal space that allows actors to work without fear of ridicule (by you or others), anger and humiliation. Acting can evoke deep emotions. You must make a place where people can "go there," protected, as they work. Exert patience. Set aside anger.

Exude love and care for your team. Affirm! Find at least one thing about each person that delights you, and make sure you communicate that delight. When someone does something right, tell them. Again and again and all the time. You may feel this goes overboard, but if you're thinking that, overboard is not likely your tendency.

Practice selective neglect. That is, figure out what you alone must be responsible for. Figure out what can be accomplished—maybe even better—by others. Then delegate. Cultivate trusty partners who will take responsibility and follow through. Then abandon yourself to the parts of the process that are uniquely yours to lead. This will keep you accessible to the actors, confident of various jobs getting done without exhausting yourself, and more able to be fully present in the artistic process.

Pay attention to your spiritual life. Spend time with God and get refreshed. Take sabbaths. If you tank, you will pull others under with you. If you are struggling, ask some mature, wise people to pray with you. God does not *need* you to do artwork. If you need help, take a break and get it. You will damage yourself and others if you attempt servant leadership without giving yourself to being served by God.

HAPPY SHEPHERDING

You work to give the actors all the information, encouragement, help and understanding they need to present the sketch for all it's worth. You are the actor's chief ally against the forces of fear, judgment, poor self-image, embarrassment, lack of knowledge and bad choices. You must be on the side of the actor—as Peter says, we must "tend the flock of God that is in your charge, exercising the oversight, not under compulsion but willingly, as God would have you do it—and not for sordid gain but eagerly. Do not lord it over those in your charge, but be examples to the flock" (1 Peter 5:2-3).

If you find yourself complaining about your team, secretly feeling disdain for an ac-

tor or building resentment about some part of the process, stop, repent and pray. And invite prayer from friends. You will need the help of being prayed for by others. The job you are doing is difficult. But the call is to lead "not under compulsion, but voluntarily." Our spirits must volunteer gladly for this work. If you find yourself not there, your next step is to get there. Take it before the next rehearsal.

One great practical reason to lead as servant is that you will sometimes face conflict in the artistic process. When those times come, you will be very happy to have the actors *with* you—working out problems together—rather than having them oppose you and find yourself forced to justify what you want them to do . . . which they then only do grudgingly, if at all. Most of us prefer mutuality in groups. It can feel awkward to be called the leader or director. Our mutuality onstage must come from the relationships of trust we build—because we cannot actually lead the process with everyone mutually and evenly heard and chosen. You will not in the end implement everyone's ideas. Every member of the team will not act the lead. There will be times you ask actors to do something they don't want to do, or say no to their suggestions.

It will happen. So from the start, cultivate the best relationships you can with your team. Beginning with a foundation of good relationships will serve you, the team and the audience who sees your work, because your drama will have been formed in an atmosphere of mutual love and trust, led by your firm direction and God's grace.

THE DIRECTOR PREPARES

Alison Siewert

I want an artistic explosion. Our high-technology lifestyle demands a theatre experience that cannot be satisfied by video and movie screens. I want acting that is poetic and personal, intimate and colossal. I want to encourage the kind of humanity on the stage that demands attention and that expresses who we are and suggests that life is bigger. . . . I want to find resonant shapes for our present ambiguities.

ANNE BOGART

Take the script in your hands and read it. Let yourself imagine; don't limit yourself to your venue, your actors, your budget or anything else. Just let it fly. Anne Bogart says, "If I adopt the attitude that the project is an adventure larger than anything I might imagine, an entity that will challenge me to find an instinctual path through it, the project will be allowed its proper magnitude."[1]

Now that you've let the pictures begin to form, you can begin to shape the piece to work in your space and with your people and resources. Read the script again; get it all the way into your head. You need to read the script over and over. Some directors think in terms of making a mental movie in their mind's eye. As you read, try to see how the script looks played out in your head. Where do characters come from? What do they sound like? What are they trying to get? Experiment with different angles. For example, you might imagine Alice entering stage right, on crutches and blowing her nose. Or what if (assuming the script allows it) she comes in dressed in a ball gown, with a slight limp from dancing in her fancy shoes? Think through the possibilities, and develop the ones you think will work.

Look at the script from a technical perspective. Do you need props? Special lighting or sound effects? Is there anything that presents a problem that can be worked on now, before rehearsal begins? Arrange any technical items you can before you work with the actors. This includes asking technical staff to be present at rehearsals if needed. Getting extra tech business underway now will serve to make rehearsal more efficient and you more ready to prepare the actors for their jobs.

BE A BLOCKHEAD

Think through blocking. (For more on this, see chapter thirty-nine, "Blocking," on page 131.) Make notes on your script according to your best mental movie about where the actors should be and what they should be doing. Consider the size and shape of the performance area, the furniture or other props you'll need, and your lighting and sound capacity. Draw a floor plan for the stage area, including set pieces (furniture, worship instruments, etc.) and obstacles (the random post or podium). Become very familiar with your blocking plan before rehearsal. You can't block by reading from your notes—you have to be free to point and gesture, explain and encourage. Know your plan well enough to use notes only for reminders. You will almost certainly make changes as you see the actors speak and move, but rehearsal will proceed more swiftly and happily to decision if you start with one thing and change it than if you start with nothing at all.

CONSIDER THE ACTORS

Think about your actors. Can you anticipate any problems they're likely to have with this script? Their roles? The pace, timing, blocking or any other element? If, for example, they were struggling just last week to break the habit of dropping the volume at the ends of sentences, remember that and pay close attention to their cadence this week. If your drama ministry is new or your fellowship isn't visibly responsive to sketches, you may need to prep the cast by reminding them not to seek energy from the audience but rather from their characters' wants and needs.

A good headlock on the script will allow you to work freely in rehearsal. And especially if you're working with inexperienced actors, having your hands free is important. I was directing a play that included three trained and two new actors. I hadn't spent enough time working out the script in my head, so my eyes were on the book. I didn't notice until two days before the first performance that one of the new actors was hamming it up frequently. He had only done a couple of high school musicals and didn't know how to respond onstage to the subtlety of our play. He mugged all the way through it. I was able to call him aside and work with him a bit, but I could have been more helpful to him and the play if I had noticed the problem earlier.

Another time I did better. A small group needed to rehearse for a set of sketches to be performed at a conference. From my study of the script, I knew that one sketch involving a pair of actors was going to be the most difficult of the five to prepare. I set up our rehearsals to

give me maximum time with that pair, while still making good use of the time with the rest of the group. It took some planning, and I was glad I had focused on the piece well enough to know that it would.

PRACTICE EFFECTS

Good script preparation allows you to identify technical needs before they become technical crises. Because I have worked in mostly non-theater settings and have rarely had good tech support, my capacity for dealing with tech issues is, frankly, less than I'd like. I have learned, but slowly. We did a play that begins with the Genesis account of creation. Where God breathes, the script calls for FX (special effect) of God's breath. "How 'bout some smoke?" the tech guy asked us. "It makes a cool sound too." "Sure," we said. Well, the smoke machine was mounted at the top of a rail about fifteen feet above the stage. And guess what? So were the smoke detectors. The sound sure was cool, until thirty buzzing smoke alarms sounded.

Yep. You gotta love catching those things at rehearsal rather than in performance. (Note: Never use any effect without rehearsing it—thoroughly—well ahead of time. The actors and you and the crew and even the building need practice and confidence.) The smoke machine had to be moved, in the end, to the floor—a delightful change which made the sound clearer and nearer to the audience and put the dancer right in the mist of creation. Cool, indeed.

PREPARATION IN THE BANK

Preparation is like having money in the bank when you're building a house. You know something is likely to go over budget. Something will go wrong. Hopefully a lot will go right, and you'll have cash left for a groovy vacation. But in the meantime, save up.

The youth choir I directed in college did a performance tour with a musical. One of the lead kids was a boy who, though a normally spunky kid, wasn't a troublemaker. A couple of the other boys were more . . . challenging. And one evening at our rehearsal they all got together.

While I was talking with a parent helper on the other side of the room, the guys decided to have a chicken fight. That actually went well (if it's possible, really, for a chicken fight to go well). What didn't go so well was the lead kid's dismount from the bigger kid's shoulders. He jumped off and landed on his rear and both hands. "No, I'm fine. Nothing's hurt," he said. But ten minutes later he was saying, "My stomach kind of hurts." *Oh no*, I thought, *he might be going into shock.*

After I called his parents, I made a splint out of paper plates and someone's suspenders. He called me later that night. "I broke both wrists." Yikes. Time to draw on the preparation account. Things actually ended up going fine. There was a scene in which the lead was supposed to "learn" how to snap in time with the music, and that couldn't happen any more. But everything else was well enough underway that we could approach the new reality of a two-casted lead player with calm resolve. The musical was awesome, and several of those kids, prepared by their experience together, eventually became worship artists themselves.

31 THE AUDIENCE

Alison Siewert

The director is the link between one world and the other; like a medium, the director is there to unblock all the channels and to imagine how one world (the audience) might be perceiving the other (the production). As if she were the captain of a spaceship landing on the earth from another planet, the director wonders: Who are they? Who are we? What have we got to tell them and how best can we express ourselves?

PHYLLIDIA LLOYD

One thing that makes drama stand out among other arts is its ability to draw us into the story live, on stage, in front of us at that moment. It can create an opportunity for community (though this is not automatic, just an opportunity) around the experience of our humanness, of the lives of people somehow like us. It evokes the universal by playing out a par-

ticular story. Theater puts everything right there in front of us. There is no mediator but our eyes and our distance from the stage, no limiting our view to only what fills the lens or sounds perfect in the recording studio.

Drama is all about doing stories. From our first neighborhood kids' shows (well, at least in my old neighborhood we did plenty) to the ministry we're doing right now, the goal is always to make a story pop off the stage in a way that makes it seem real. And all of that happens when, and to some extent because, the audience is present. When you play a story on the stage, the audience actually does part of the creative work with you. You cannot actually be a character. You can only play one. But the audience subconsciously makes you into the character. People project the missing pieces, fill in the cracks. The audience in the theater co-creates with the cast.

RELATING TO THE AUDIENCE

If you're doing theater ministry, you will be relating to an audience. They're your partners. Even if you never talked to people in your audience, you would have a relationship with them—because they are showing up at church or in your theater or wherever they come, in order to see and hear what you have made, and to work with you, even if they're not entirely aware they are working. They have chosen to spend time on your art. They want to receive something from you. That's why they're there.

So never talk down to them. Never talk down to an audience. They are at least your peers and, in our context, most likely your partners in the gospel—or potential partners in it. The first rule is to treat the audience with great respect. Magnanimity, even. Cultivate in yourself and your team a love for the audience. Find out, on a regular basis, how your performances have helped them. Ask them what's been useful, what they have liked, what delighted or encouraged them. Ask them what didn't work or what confused them. But ask. They are the people to whom you communicate, and this is a sacred call.

Sometimes ministry workers become disdainful of their audience. I was on a staff once that often spoke of how people in the congregation were too this, or too that, or didn't get it. Harrumph. Well, of course—people don't get

it any more instantaneously than you or I get it. No one's got it all together. We cannot afford, either spiritually or ethically, to view our audiences with any form of disdain. Even with a cranky, critical or unsympathetic audience, we must always keep grace about us. They are allowing us the privilege of sharing with them. We must maintain a servant attitude no matter what. "The audience is the most revered member of the theater. . . . They are our guests, fellow players, and the last spoke in the wheel which can then begin to roll."[1]

As part of our service, we recognize that audiences need to learn how to deal with theater. Most people don't get to attend high-quality live theater very often. Now, maybe that's reassuring to your young team, who knows it's not exactly at the "high quality" mark yet. But it also means that your audience may need some time and help learning how to respond, how to be a good audience for your work.

Though few people see much live theater, lots of people see lots of television. When you're watching TV, you've probably noticed that TV characters on your screen don't respond to you when you talk to them. Say something nice. They just continue with whatever they were doing before. Yell at them about how that foul should have been called (yes, some of you yell, and you know who you are). They don't even listen to your advice.

So people develop what I call "TV face." This is the unblinking, un—well, un-anything expression you've probably seen out there in response to some of your performances. People . . . just . . . sort of . . . stare . . . nonspecifically . . . (yawn). And you're supposed to perform to that? Yep. That's your job. So, the second rule of theater is, Do not plan to gain any performance energy from your audience, because they probably won't help you with that. In fact, if actors look out there for encouragement, they may end up more discouraged and de-energized. Energy must come from the performers.

TIPS FOR ENCOURAGING AUDIENCE GROWTH

Eventually the audience will develop much better response skills, and your team will sense their support and enthusiasm. When this happens, it's wonderful. In the meantime, there are some things you can teach and help the audience with as they grow.

Do something worthy of the audience's attention. "The audience will finally have the most direct experience of the breadth or lack of your interest. They will feel the truth about your intentions. . . . They will instinctively know what you are up to. It is all visible."[2]

Give them permission to respond. We never want to demand or manipulate response, but we must make space for it. You might actually need to get up and say, "It's all right to respond." Give people permission to laugh. If a sketch is supposed to be funny, don't precede it with a slow hymn in a minor key. And make the opening lines funny enough that people can't help laughing. Church is not a place we're accustomed to humor (it's sad, but true), so we have to build that category for people. And if the audience is likely to need a reflective moment after the sketch, plan it in. Offering process time builds the expectation that there is something to respond to.

Fan the flames of response. When people in the audience respond, try to follow up with them later. Especially if you know them, you can affirm their openness. This sounds small, but the overall effect—the audience learning how to receive drama—will expand faster than you'd imagine.

Perform material that addresses people's real lives. Who's out there? Collegians don't know much (yet) about how it feels to be juggling groceries and trying to find your house key before your toddler wets his pants. And families with four kids in tow might not relate so well to a sketch about the beer bash at the frat . . .

Work with your team to plow in, regardless of audience response. Help actors avoid the trap of siphoning energy from a reticent audience. Have actors practice finding their own source of strength and inspiration in the script and the vision, rather than the response.

Have fun. If you have fun, the audience will have fun. If you draw attention to it, the audience will pay attention to it. If you enjoy what God is doing, so will they. Enjoy.

32 DIRECTING REHEARSALS

Alison Siewert

I regard the theater as the greatest of all art forms, the most immediate way in which a human being can share with another the sense of what it is to be a human being. This supremacy of the theater derives from the fact that it is always "now" on the stage.

THORNTON WILDER

Directing a good rehearsal takes organization and preparation. The actors and crew rely on the director to set the pace, tone and vision for the work to be done. No one else will do this; *you* must. Now, even if you're not an organizer by nature, you can learn to run a rehearsal if you'll take a bit of time to think through it. What follows is a trek through the movements I use in rehearsing a sketch on a two-rehearsal timetable. If you have a bigger time frame, or are doing a longer work, of course you will have more time to work with. In those cases, you can extrapolate from this chapter and also look at some of the excellent directing texts available (see bibliography).

Here is a rough outline of a rehearsal schedule for a typical five-minute sketch to be performed in worship or a special event. Every team and director works differently. A common denominator in effective directors is that they help their teams use rehearsal time well by planning and executing a clear, concise process. From start to finish, the process I describe here could take as long (if you have it) as twelve hours over two weeks. If you can do it—and in some cases you really must—do. If you don't have a setup that allows for this, a sketch can be rehearsed in three to four hours. It's worth it to give yourselves adequate time to pursue excellence. But even in a short amount of time, a good director can lead a great rehearsal and produce a good, solid sketch.

PRAYER (10 MINUTES)

I like to start rehearsals with prayer because I know we are about to do something that will, if we engage it thoroughly, press us beyond our own resources. It will call on us to take risks. It will require us to be vulnerable. We will have to concentrate even when we are tired. And we don't know, and won't know until we get in front of the whole fellowship, whether it will really work or not. That seems like a good reason to go to God. God provides a deep reservoir for our work together—a reserve we do not and cannot possess in ourselves. So we pray.

WARM-UP (10-15 MINUTES)

Then we warm up. (See "Ten Best Warm-Ups We Ever Warmed Up With.")

THE FIRST REHEARSAL: READING (30 MINUTES)

Next, we begin to rehearse. I get scripts to the actors ahead of time so they can read through on their own and highlight their lines. We gather, sitting at a table or around a circle, and have people jump in and read the script only for the basic meaning of the text. We are not acting things out, working on characterization or developing blocking yet—just reading and listening. In this phase we are discovering the script. We are hearing it. "For a director, no reading of a play is as important as the first, because the experience will most closely mirror that of the average audience."[1] I want the cast to listen carefully, to take in the sketch this way because this is in large part what the audience will hear. The audience only gets to hear it once. It's important for the actors to have the experience of hearing first and once—to think, *How much did I get from that? What struck or interested or fascinated or annoyed me?* This piece of the process will help the actors do all the other work of rehearsal.

We read the script again, still not acting, but working to listen carefully to one another. Listening is an underrated skill in drama. For an actor to understand her part, she must apply the most acute listening skills as she takes in other actors' lines. The characters must respond to one another; they are not merely creations of the actor's mind. Characters are already drawn on paper by the sketchwright. In a good sketch, characters will be shaped by how they listen to one another—their listening is a major shaping force in characterization. When the barista hears the customer's request for a vanilla latte, her listening posture is affected by her knowledge that they are short on vanilla syrup.

If people have listened to each other reasonably well, we continue. If we are having trouble listening, I might ask the actors to read once more. Once we have established listening, we move on to interpreting.

FINDING THE CHARACTERS (45 MINUTES)

A well-written character should be interpreted primarily from his or her words. Especially given the brief nature of sketches, you shouldn't need a long description from the writer. The script offers us most of the knowledge we need to successfully draw our characters, and we proceed to flesh them out. I often have actors stand at this point and allow them to move a bit according to what feels natural. I might say, "We aren't yet blocking, but move if you like." That way people are forewarned that blocking is yet to come. You don't want people getting attached to their spot on the stage and then feeling resentful when you move them, so be clear at the beginning and save the process grief. But allowing actors the freedom to move may help some to explore how to say the character's words.

If we have more than one rehearsal available—which we often don't (see "Rehearsing When You Don't Have Time to Rehearse")—I do basic blocking in the first rehearsal so the actors have the best possible information to work with in practicing on their own. Blocking helps the process of memorization: Remember when you learned all those motion songs in first grade? Same principle—we remember what we say and do better than what we just say. Having a sense of movement also helps actors visualize their characters in parameters greater than words. Once the sketch is blocked, we run through it at least once—and preferably two or three more times—so the actors will remember their movements confidently.

THE SECOND REHEARSAL (PRAYER, WARM-UPS, PLUS 1 TO 1-1/2 HOURS)

Two rehearsals are better than one. In a second rehearsal, I ask actors to have memorized or reviewed (if not memorizing) their lines at home. It's great for actors to work on their lines on their own, but it's awful for them to work together in such a way that they start to direct one another. You don't want *Waiting for Guffman* happening on your team: Ron gives his wife Sheila two hours of notes on her part of their dialogue. (Though this scene is very funny in the movie, it would be appalling in real life!) Actors should never try to direct one another. The most they should do is run their lines—which means *only* running through them, without comment on one another. This will ensure two things: First, you, and only you, are the director. And second, the actors are not the director. One person leads the artistic process. Too many artists glop up the painting; and there is safety for the actors in knowing that only one person will be directing, that they can try new things without the articulated scrutiny of every other person in the room. You are the arbiter of relationships on the stage. You're the referee. You are the director.

The second rehearsal is the time to start working through the sketch a little at a time. Look for beats—natural shifts in the conversation and relationships.[2] For example, when a character shifts to the other side of the room as he ponders his decision; when someone gets up and storms out of the room; when a new character enters—these mark beats. They're important for establishing a sense of flow and rhythm in the sketch. They're also good places to divide the script for rehearsal. Take each beat, run it, stop, make adjustments and suggestions, and run it again. This gives us room to consider our options and make decisions. If you only always run the sketch from beginning to end, your actors will have difficulty keeping track of what decisions were made for which section, and they'll struggle to find the natural beats. Breaking it down helps us by dividing so we may conquer.

This is the time to look for fresh angles. The cast will (we hope) know their lines and movements well enough to explore the subtext of the script—the things people are saying without really saying them. Bruce explains, for example, that when he initially worked on the character of the righteous Pharisee in Jesus' parable of the Pharisee and the tax collector in Luke 18, he made the Pharisee a pompous, self-righteous jerk. In "the second rehearsal," Bruce was spurred to think more deeply about the Pharisee. He realized that this man might be more typical—more like a regular, self-righteous churchgoer. More like himself. So he worked to make the Pharisee closer to us, closer to the audience's experience of itself. In performance, the character is quite powerful

THE DIRECTOR IN THE SKETCH

But what if you have to be in the sketch? Try not to be in the sketch. If it must be so, however, take the smallest part you can possibly play. If you are writing or have access to the writer, you might request a smaller number of parts so you can avoid acting. It is quite difficult, especially when you are just learning, to direct when you're also playing a role. This might be your big chance to recruit a new actor—the tuba-player guy from Bible study or that lady by the cookie table who always wears a flowered hat or your college roommate. If you must do a part, keep it as simple and conventional as you can. Since you can't see yourself onstage, you're better off leaving experimental moments to other actors whom you can watch, so you can evaluate whether something is working or not.

precisely because he taps into the norm rather than the extreme.

The first few times through a script, we tend to take the obvious paths. But now it's time to look for the shadows in the characters' souls, the hidden processes, what they're trying not to say. This part of the rehearsal process is about deeper exploration.

It's also time for smoothing out movement, blocking, props and whatever else is wrinkled. Sometimes you discover a bit of funny business or an inflection or even a new or adjusted line that makes a piece work much better. Finding and securing these items early in the process will make them attainable.

Make arrangements to work as much as you can on the performance stage. Ask your tech crew to set up lights and sound reinforcement if you'll be using them. Let them know how they can help you to help the sketch go well. Actors, especially if they're new, need opportunity to see where things sit in relation to one another, to hear their voices in the acoustics of the hall and to figure out how it will feel to cross to one another during the scene. Check the relationship between the worship team's drum set and the actors' entrance on that side. This is the time to establish distances, make final decisions and settle down. You can't be changing and fixing things ten minutes before a performance, especially if that's time you're supposed to be in worship. It's at the second rehearsal that we tack down as much as possible, we pray and we go.

RUN-THROUGH (5 MINUTES)

Once you've worked through the beats, run all the way through the sketch at least twice, without stopping. This may seem frightening, and the cast may get snagged on a forgotten line or movement, but they must practice this way. This is the only way to settle into what you've decided along the way. Sometimes the pressure of a nonstop run causes great things to surface. If someone forgets a line, he or she has to muster the energy to come up with another one. The overall effect of a run-through will be energizing to the whole cast and to the work. It's a little foretaste of the kind of risk taking they'll be doing when they actually perform. Failing to run all the way through deprives the actors of an opportunity to see and connect to the whole—which they need for their own motivation and confidence.

GETTING THERE (1 HOUR, ON THE DAY OF THE PERFORMANCE)

Once the actors have arrived and we've prayed and warmed up, we run through the sketch on the stage. Actors must have time in the actual performance space on the day of the performance. Lance Armstrong doesn't ride tiny laps around his cul-de-sac to train for the Tour de France; don't ask your team to practice in the custodian's closet behind the choir robes before a performance. It's amazing how much people can forget, especially when they are nervous. I want actors to be as comfortable and secure as possible in an inherently uncomfortable and insecure situation. They need time to refresh their memories and to warm up before they play the sketch. This gives everyone a chance to clear their heads, focus once more on the task at hand and feel prepared.

THE MOMENT ARRIVES (15 MINUTES OR MORE)

Take a break before you perform. It's not good to go from rehearsal straight into worship or an event. Even if you only have fifteen minutes, encourage people to take a full break during that time. Tell them, "Take a break." Offer them food or drink if you can. Direct them to some quiet place where they can rest or pray. People should not still be running lines when the first song begins. They need to worship. What you have at the end of rehearsal is what you have, and it needs to be enough. If it's really not enough, then the sketch is not ready to be performed and five more minutes of sweat won't make it ready. If the team is really not ready—and we can all hope this is the rarest instance—you, as the director, must make that call and either cancel or postpone the sketch. The world will not end if you have to do this, but it will be important for you to examine why the team wasn't ready and work to correct the situation next time around.

End your preparation process by encouraging people. At this point, they don't need notes or reminders or instructions on how to add something in. Inexperienced performers (and their directors) should plan on operating at about forty percent of their best their first several times onstage. It's normal to lose some of what you found in rehearsal—the pressure and newness of getting up in front of people throws you for a loop. The best way to manage the on-stage stress is to do a solid and thorough rehearsal, then help everyone to relax physically and spiritually. We do a relaxation exercise, pray and give people time to focus. One of the best effects of rehearsal is that it creates space for the team to recognize our need for God and to see him come through.

33 WORKING WITH ACTORS

Alison Siewert

It doesn't matter how you say the lines. What matters is what you mean. What comes from the heart goes to the heart. The rest is Funny Voices.

DAVID MAMET

Actors want you to direct. Them. As a director who has had to act for the last two years, I've found out for myself: A good director is a blessed presence. Directors do some things for actors that actors cannot do for themselves. Directing is more than telling people where to go or how to stand. A good director keeps the vision of the art in front of everyone and helps them get there.

A CLEAR VISION

Why are we here? What are we trying to do? What is this piece about? How will it be used? These are questions of vision. If your team is typical, you probably have a mix of people to work with—some who need the big idea and some who are happy with the practical details. Hang a clearly articulated goal in front of the group like a window. Your team needs to know the meaning of their work. How does it fit into the big picture? That vision window is the frame you give them.

Talk with your team more than once during the rehearsal process about why you're doing this sketch and what you hope for. People need help to go for it, to be brave in offering themselves. The director is in charge of reiterating The Reason. Don't hope it will be obvious, because it likely won't. And don't hope someone else will bop by to explain, because that probably won't happen either. Give your team a reason to work hard, a sense of what they're contributing to the whole.

COLLABORATION AND COMMUNITY

Actors like to collaborate, to act with other people. Theater is perhaps the most overtly communal of all the arts. It requires a large number of people to communicate with each other directly and on the stage, as well as with a live audience. It's all about working together, bouncing off one another. So do that. As the director, you will come to the rehearsal process with ideas about what you want. They will be excellent ideas. But actors will probably come up with ideas, too, and part of your job is to listen to them.

Shape the sketch with your ideas, while allowing actors to offer their own ideas to the process. People must sense that they will be taken seriously and that their effort is part of the overall work of the group. So you must build a frame within which your work will take place, then make room for people to move around within it, to fill it out. This establishes safety and builds permission to try into the process. Acting requires great courage from the actors. You fortify them by affirming, calling them out, helping them stay in the process.

You create a set of boundaries within which the acting process will happen. You build a playing field on which people are allowed to try the game. Actors without freedom get bound up. They inevitably feel used, like puppets, for someone else's show. If you want actors to act and not just imitate, you have to give them some latitude to try a variety of objectives and work with you on choices. They need to know what they are trying to do, which in large part must come from their process and not just your instructions. Dorothy Sayers said if you are "the more liberal kind of creator, [you] will eagerly welcome—I will not say bad acting, which is altogether sinful and regrettable—but imaginative and free acting, and find an immensely increased satisfaction in the individual creativeness which the actor brings to his part."[1]

Please note: Inexperienced actors will need more direction and less roaming room than pros. Listen and watch for people who need more room and for those who seem lost trying to identify action and choose objectives. New folks need more help figuring out what to do. When your teacher assigned your first essay, he or she didn't just say, "Write an essay" and end the day. The teacher explained what an essay is, then had the class practice paragraphs—the building blocks of essays. After that, your teacher probably assigned a topic or range of topics. All this for one essay. But what would the essay have been without the process? A bunch of students randomly, confusedly expending their energy on a vague, and therefore untenable, goal. For new actors, give shape to the space. When they've done it enough, they too will be ready for some room to roam.

One of the ways we make a process collaborative is by asking questions. You can help actors figure out what to do, without telling them directly, by asking them questions. When you do this, you also communicate to the actors that their decisions about their parts really count, that you believe they will discover answers along with you. If your actors are trained, they will know this. New actors probably won't, but you can help them by asking questions too. It's like a good Bible study: we ask questions to uncover what's in the text, and we keep asking until we understand how to apply it.

The most important questions are (from the perspective of the character), "What do you want?" or "What are you trying to get?" and "What is in your way?" Whenever an actor looks unclear, stalls out or seems unanchored, these questions are the remedy. Sometimes I write, "What do you want?" at the top of my script to remind me to remind the actors to identify what they're after. If an actor cannot in every moment tell what he or she wants, they aren't yet focused enough. Help them.

On the other hand, help them to *own* their characters' wants. Daniel recalled a time when a director prescribed set-in-stone blocking on the first day of rehearsal, no questions allowed and no suggestions taken. He said, "I never really got to know the character because I never explored who he was. From the start I was never allowed to shape the character's movements." In the end, he says, the director's input was hard to hear: "What I was told to do and the character I saw didn't match up. I felt shaky because I didn't know the character and I didn't know myself in the situation. When that happens, rather than improving, I tense up, pull back and play it safe—because I know there's not really room to try." Actors want to give their best effort, but if you cut them off too early, they and the process will be truncated, rather than helped, by your control.

So collaboration works when you frame a vision, build a shape, set a standard and focus objectives (wants)—tasks that are uniquely the director's. The rest happens when you're together in the rehearsal room. And that's the really fun part. If you are willing to allow for experimentation, rehearsal can be a blast. For most actors, it's an adventure. And in the end, they own what they've discovered. It's very cool.

WORKING TOGETHER

Sometimes actors need to get their minds off what they're trying so hard to do in order to actually do it. Ultimately they have to get so accustomed to their words and movements that they cease thinking about them and focus instead on the other people in the scene. The more time you have to prepare, especially with new actors, the better they'll be able to do this. Try to give them adequate time to get relaxed. In addition, exercises based on the script at hand can help actors and directors explore, ask questions, keep things fresh.

At about midpoint (especially if you have more than two rehearsals), try this: have the actors close their eyes and imagine their character basically as they see him or her in the text, but doing something incongruent with that character such as chewing gum or searching for something in a briefcase or protesting a war. Then have them read the scene from that perspective. Right away have them close their eyes and reimagine the character, this time with something significant changed. (You can prescribe the change if you want—"Now your character is very, very insecure about X," or "Now your character really needs to go to the bathroom.") Have them read the scene again.

Or try having the players sing their dialogue to one another. No particular notes are necessary—just have them jump in and sing.

Doing these kinds of exercises two or three times will get things moving. We once worked on a sketch that consisted primarily of the lines,

Oh yeah? Well you're a—

Oh, is that what you think? Well I think you're—

Really? Whatever, because you are—

I'm a? You're a—

And so on. We read it first as angry, then as New York Italians (in honor of my grandparents), then flirtatious, then like an elderly Midwestern couple who are too tired of the same old argument to really care, and so on. We ran through it enough times to try lots of options. We had fun. We explored enough angles to choose one we really liked. This helped us to listen carefully to one another and to recognize some of our choices in dialogue.

Once you've let the team try several options, of course, you must settle on one. The director is in charge of pulling together what's happened so far and shaping a final draft. Keep reminding people even once you've decided, however, that listening to one another and operating based on character wants are central.

THE NOTES

Over the course of rehearsals you should give

the cast notes at the end of each run-through. Notes are your chance to address problems in the performance. Handled well, notes can energize collaboration and the actors' personal commitment. Handled badly, notes can be like a sledgehammer to actors' confidence and hope.

Start with notes for the whole cast first. Notes should be brief and focused. Choose the most important things first. No one will remember eighteen corrections to be made; if things are going that badly, perhaps you need another rehearsal. As the sketch runs (without stopping), watch for anything that trips up the action or the people. For example, if an actor's words don't match what she does (e.g., giving the line "I really love you" with arms folded and eyes closed), suggest a change. If a prop keeps landing on the floor, solve the problem. If an actor needs work on a long speech, request a few minutes at the end of rehearsal.

I usually give the actors most of their individual notes in the presence of the team.

However, if there's an embarrassing problem to be solved, give the note in private. As you get closer to the performance, the actors' sense of well-being becomes more important and more fragile all at the same time. So guard people's dignity. Distracting issues such as body odor, licorice stuck in the teeth and inappropriate clothing are all private notes material. I took a junior high choir on tour with a musical and had a boy who'd reached the life stage when deodorant starts to be a good idea. Someone had to tell him. In private.

As you put the pieces together, it's your directorial duty to make sure everyone looks good (unless a character is supposed to look bad, in which case by all means make sure they look good looking bad). The main way actors look good is by their focus on objectives. What does the character want? You must also scrutinize for seams—places where transitions aren't yet smooth. Notes should address these issues. Here are some other items to consider:

◆ Can you understand everything everyone says?

◆ Do actors know what they want, and are they playing to get it?

◆ How is the pace? Too slow a pace (more common than too fast) will kill a performance.

◆ Look at the blocking. Does it work? Fix what doesn't.

◆ Look at stage pictures. Do they show up?

◆ Is anyone hamming? Chewing scenery?

◆ Are some people so quiet and unconfident that they, or their lines, are lost?

◆ Check for happy feet, extra motions and bad habits such as nose picking and hair flipping.

Look carefully and make adjustments. If you have enough time, you'll be able to fix a lot. If you are very close to performance time, fix only the things that distract and detract the most. Look for what can actually be corrected in the timeframe available to you. If an actor doesn't understand his character, he is not going to get it and will likely be further destabilized by any attempt to make him get it at this point.

A collaborative approach makes nearly every task work better. When a director takes note of a problem and joins with the cast in reaching a solution, it takes pressure off individual actors. If there's a problem with a prop, it's not left to the actor just to figure it out or to get so frustrated he or she finally blows up. If we've set up a friendly atmosphere where we are coworkers, a problem can be solved quickly because we have lots of brilliant people ready and willing to work on it.

THE PERFORMANCE

Once you've done everything, you've done everything. But the actors are still your focus. What's left is for you to encourage the players and free them up to go for it. If rehearsal has been difficult or you feel shaky about the actors' readiness, don't complain about it at this point. You can always examine later what did and didn't go well. Right now the important thing is to get people on stage in good shape so they can do the work you've been preparing to do. Tell them they're great, remind them that God is at work in and through them, and encourage them to toss everything out there and see what happens. You can't hold onto it anyway, and if you try you'll become even more uptight. Just toss it. People will gladly catch what you have worked so hard to offer them.

34 BLOCKING

Alison Siewert

The purpose of physical action is to give you something more interesting, important, and fun to concentrate on than trying to believe the fiction of the script.

MELISSA BRUDER ET AL.

Blocking is the work we do once we understand the basics of the script and the basic action of the characters. Now we know what the characters are trying to do—what they want—and we must work out how to make that visible to the audience. Blocking is the arrangement of positions, actions and travel among the actors on the stage. Moving onstage is entirely different from dancing through your house or walking downtown or even going to the front of a room to give a presentation. Stage movement has its own economy, because every movement is visible and meaningful—whether we intend it to be or not. It's not hard to begin learning how to move well, especially if you're aware that this will be a new and different thing.

The director and all the actors need to learn the areas of the stage. The standard stage is divided into six major playing areas designated as upstage left, upstage center, and upstage right, and downstage left, downstage center, and downstage right. These areas are defined from the actor's perspective, so that stage left is to your left when you are standing onstage looking at the house, but it is to your right when you are standing in the house looking from the audience's perspective (see chart).

Start thinking about blocking as early as possible. I usually think through a basic plan and make notes—in pencil—in my script. That way I at least have a place to start. As the actors work, the blocking will need to be changed. It never fails. You just can't anticipate everything that will come up in rehearsal. Usually the changes are for the better, because an actor has chosen an action for his or her character that you hadn't even considered but which gives the whole sketch a new angle. If you can block ahead but then relax, you'll create an opportunity for collaboration.

When you block, you need to think about several issues:

◆ Actors need to be seen and heard by the audience.
◆ Every time actors move, they need to have a reason—a motive—for moving there.
◆ We can build and release tension through blocking.
◆ The stage has weak and strong areas, which we can use to create stage pictures that elucidate the meaning of the sketch.
◆ Actors can use blocking to help them clarify their characters' motives and to help them memorize their lines.

Ideally, blocking should reflect the script so strongly that if you took away the words of the script, you could still follow the basic action of the plot. Blocking makes the story visual and not just aural—which is why we're building sketches rather than just reading Scripture out loud or telling the story straight out. The impact and memory of your sketch will increase markedly when you develop effective blocking.

SEEN AND HEARD

Isn't it annoying to be in the audience and find yourself blocked by a post from seeing the action onstage? Or to hear someone speaking but, even given a long monologue, never figure out who it is and where they are?

Don't let this happen to your team! Blocking can't remove posts in the sanctuary or adjust vision to 20/20, but it can help alleviate major problems for your audience. Get to know your space—where the blind spots and sightlines are. Many church and school buildings have stage areas that are not raised high enough. You may need, for example, to find platforms, rehearsal boxes or a solid coffee table for actors to stand on.

If you're in a worship space, you'll also likely have other furniture to negotiate. You might end up with an entire choir for a backdrop! (By the way, make sure they know to direct their attention—all their attention—to the sketch while it is being performed.) Lecterns, chairs, microphone cords and plants may all be part of the landscape. Figure out ahead of time what's there, what will be there (no surprise baptismal fonts!), and what can be moved. If it's possible to move some things out of the way, be sure to figure out how long it will take and how smoothly it can be done so you don't disrupt worship or create an awkward pre-sketch pause.

Note: In our church plant we often *had* to move equipment around for the sketch. So we developed a Question of the Week to facilitate

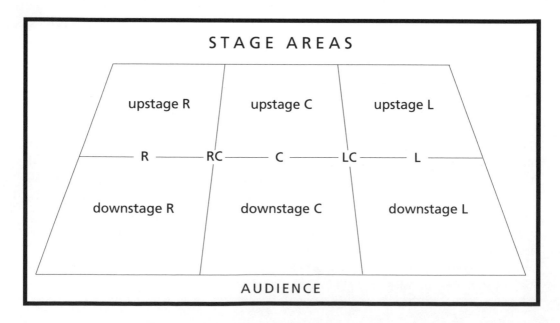

STAGE AREAS

| upstage R | upstage C | upstage L |

R ——— RC ——— C ——— LC ——— L

| downstage R | downstage C | downstage L |

AUDIENCE

the transition. Because we were serving post-moderns and unchurched folks, we didn't do the traditional meet-and-greet or pass-the-peace in our service. We used this time to ask people nonthreatening, lighthearted questions, such as, "Dogs or cats?" or "Why is it more fun to do the dishes at another person's house than at your own?" or "What's the coolest present anyone ever gave you?" We fully admitted this was sketch-preparation time, which fit the timbre of our meetings. I'd say, "Each week we ask ourselves a question—which you get to talk about while we set up the sketch." Once we had things set, the lights dimmed and the sketch started.

Once you've assessed the performance area, measure it (unless you also rehearse there) so you can mark the rehearsal floor with masking tape. This will allow the actors to work out their movements with the certainty that they know how long things take and which direction they go. It will also ensure you don't inadvertently plan the worship team's drum set into the sketch. Mark any blind spots or obstacles where people should not stand or sit. And gauge where the actors should stand to be heard well.

KNOW WHY YOU MOVE

There are many possible reasons to move in a sketch: you need variety and change so it doesn't look dull; one of the characters is excitable, and the actor needs room to convey this; there's a funny part in the middle that could be made funnier if the actors dance. Whatever the reasons to move, there is always one reason that wins the day and one rule that must be obeyed: Every movement needs a motivation. No one should move unless the character has a reason to move. Now, that reason could be that another character is irritating you with his cloying arguments and you must step away from him in order not to slap him. Or it could be that you are thrilled to see the character who just entered stage right. It might even be that you want a better look at another charac-

ter's Bible verse. Whatever the reason, it must be a reason to be a movement and not something else. Having actors move arbitrarily around a stage is confusing and even in a short sketch will make the audience tired. Move with a motive. Only. Ever.

RAISE THE TENSION

If you've ever been in an argument, you know that our proximity to one another shifts with the rise and fall of tension. If you are in a yelling match, you might stay away from one another until you need to close the distance for the sake of being heard yet more loudly, probably at the climax of the argument. If you are seething, you might express your anger by creating more distance between you and your opponent, even turning away. When the argument is resolved, there may be a swift physical approach to one another in a desire to reestablish the relationship. And this doesn't just happen in arguments. An awkward goodbye, an unexpected greeting, a discovery of something new—every story includes tension. If it doesn't, it's not a story.

The actors' objectives will play an important role in blocking. They are motivated, remember, to get something, to get someone to do something or to make someone do something for them. How will they pursue their physical goals on stage? One character might pursue being loved by waiting, seated on a couch, for her friend to sit next to her and talk. Another character might go after her goal by physically confronting another character. Daniel did a play in which he (the bad guy) and another actor (the good gal) moved and countered each other in a subtle cat-and-mouse pursuit: he working to destroy her, she begging for mercy. (I know . . . Nice, huh?) The overall effect was to create a stage picture of the script—the threats and pleas interwoven in both words and physical actions.

If the characters get what they want, you can bring the tension back down, in line with the way the characters relax or rejoice. Sometimes sketches leave us hanging on purpose. If that's the case, we don't want to resolve anything, because that would detract from the sketchwright's vision for the piece. If you need to leave it hanging, consider having characters simply freeze, then dim the lights so they can move offstage.

In any case, you can use distance, speed and position to express and heighten tension. There is no one formula for doing this; try it and see what works. To build, you have to start somewhere far below your highest point of tension and work your way there. One of the best ways to set this up is to first decide how you want to express the tension (that is, close together? loud? turned away?) and at what point in the dialogue it hits its peak. You can block the top first and work backward from there. Of course you'll want to check it by playing it forward too.

STRENGTHS AND WEAKNESSES

Some parts of the stage feel stronger than others. The audience perceives these subtleties without really being aware of them, which means *we have to*. Because we read from left to right, the audience's left (SR, or stage right) tends to feel stronger—more primary—than the audience's right (SL, or stage left). Center stage feels strongest. What is the most important moment in the sketch? It should take place at SR or C, not the extreme USL. If you want to build tension, danger, conflict or trouble, have the actor enter from SL—so that they travel opposite of the way we read. If they enter from SR, you will communicate peace and well-being, since the left-to-right movement seen by the audience will feel natural, as it should be.

How actors stand also creates levels of strength. Someone standing full-front, or turned straight out toward the audience, will generally look strongest. An actor turned a quarter turn away from front (called one-quarter open, left or right) will still be perceived as strong. Profile position is achieved when the actor stands at a ninety-degree angle to the audience. People see the side of their face—a less strong position. The weakest position of all is, surprisingly, not full-back (also called full-closed, with back facing the audience) but three-quarters closed (left or right).

When your actors share the stage, make sure they can all be seen and that the person with the most, or most important, lines is positioned where he or she will be the center of focus. In an uneven conversation where one actor carries the most important lines while the other listens, you want the speaking actor to face mostly downstage and the listening actor to face mostly upstage. If two actors share dialogue equally, they can both cheat out—that is, stand at one-quarter open, faced toward each other. This will give the illusion of them talking face-to-face but allow them to include the audience. If you are using microphones or working in a small space, it's okay, and looks more natural, to have actors face one another more directly.

You'll have to experiment with your space and actors to discover what looks balanced, emphasizes the angles of the sketch, and allows everyone to be heard and seen. Unusually shaped buildings, nontraditional stages and the specifics of each drama can complicate the relative strength and weakness of stage areas.

Finally, you can develop stage pictures for your sketch. For example, when we performed the story of Jairus and the bleeding woman (Mark 5), we set up a stage picture with Jesus at SR and Jairus's daughter, a disciple, and the bleeding woman at DC, staggered slightly diagonally, one in front of the other. Jairus's daughter (the "greatest") sat on a stool in the front, and the bleeding woman (the "least") stood in the back. The disciple, full of angry energy at Jesus' faux pas, moved horizontally between the daughter and the woman during his lines, just enough to keep cutting off the bleeding woman in the back (what the disciples actually did). We arranged it so that just before the woman's lines, the disciple stopped in a position that made her visible and audible to the audience. The stage picture told the story without anyone saying a word.

FROM THE ACTORS' PERSPECTIVE

I like to let actors move around a bit in the first rehearsals. I can cull ideas from what they've done and sometimes, with just a bit of refining, leave the blocking as they did it. In other cases the rehearsal space accentuates a problem—say, actors who are struggling with confidence or who haven't understood what their character wants.

It's crucial to watch for bad habits and unnecessary or unmotivated movement. Moving onstage is something like singing: You have to attack the note, on the note, and stay with the note. Unless you're Aretha Franklin and can slide magically into the pitch, you start on the pitch. There probably are some Aretha-like actors out there who can slide to their marks, but don't count on them showing up on your team. Movement on the stage is very distracting if it's not clear. This is an area you should afford actors no opportunity to shuffle in. If I see someone wandering around the stage—something new actors are prone to do—I know they need help being disciplined about their movements. In fact, giving newer actors something definite to do and somewhere definite to do it can help them develop discipline and a sense of presence on the stage that will pay off for years to come.

Other actors may thrive on the opportunity to explore possible objectives for their characters. Giving people some freedom and then honing in and pulling things together is great if you have enough rehearsal time. If you don't, of course, the inexperienced actors will probably feel relieved at the direction, while their experienced teammates will understand the demands of time and be willing to go with what you present.

DIRECTING TRAFFIC

One more task related to blocking is called "crossing": getting the actors to their positions without collisions and without awkward readjustments. You don't want people diving and darting to avoid one another; this will be—*Whoa, oops! Sorry*—distracting. Once you've established positions for various moments, go back and make sure everyone can get where they're going smoothly.

The direction you give the actor is, "Bob, cross DL (down left, or moving downstage and to your left) above chair (upstage from the chair) to DL (the down stage left area) and speak line A; cross UR (up right) to chair C (center), speak line B, then sit."

This means Bob will walk from his current position (somewhere either center or right, and upstage—because he's crossing down and left) to a new position at downstage left. He'll say his line, then cross up right to center stage. He will speak his second line, then sit in the chair positioned there. Any movement to a new position is a cross—even if no one crosses in front of anyone else. And remember, every cross is motivated—the character needs a reason to move.

If there's even the potential for a problem, it's best to address it early and rearrange. That way the actors will memorize the new movement or position and get on with it. Pay attention to crosses in which two or more players must pass each other; no one should be blocked from sight, tripped up by furniture or walking behind another person who is speaking (this is very distracting). Inexperienced actors will do better if they stand firm while they're speaking.

Always take notes on blocking. People will forget some of it. I ask actors and crew members to take notes on their own scripts. But I always keep a copy of our blocking decisions on mine. (By the way, if you make changes in rehearsal, remember to change them in your script!) If you have a stage manager, he or she will need to keep meticulous notes for you.

The easiest way to keep your notes readable is to draw a straight line from the margin to the exact place the cross or turn is to occur. In the margin write the stage directions: using X for cross, "XDR to C," that is, cross downstage right to center stage. This way you'll know exactly what's supposed to happen and on which line. There are few things more tedious than having to go back and try to reconstruct a decision you made last week in the throes of a glorious, artistic moment that you cannot retrieve now. Keep notes, and keep them updated.

AN EXERCISE IN DIRECTION
Have each actor follow these directions as quickly as possible. Once everyone has gotten the hang of directions, you can create your own workouts and include multiple people crossing multiple directions at the same time. What fun!

Call out these directions for the actor to follow. At "line," he or she may say, "Aha! It's you!" or, "Have you seen my taquito?"
◆ Stand full-front at C.
◆ Cross to DR—line.
◆ Turn three-quarters closed—line.
◆ Cross to C profile.
◆ Cross to UL, turn one-quarter open right—line.
◆ Cross DR, full-front—line.
◆ Cross UL to C full-front.
◆ End.

35 REHEARSING WHEN YOU DON'T REALLY HAVE TIME TO REHEARSE

Daniel Jones

It is advisable to think in terms of two kinds of time: clock-time and energy-time. Energy-time is the more valuable, for the director can get as much from actors in two hours of inspired, excited rehearsal as in six hours of boredom and fatigue.

VIOLA SPOLIN

At a church that I helped plant, we had what you might call a worship-drama team. This was not because we didn't want two separate teams, but because it was a new ministry, resources were limited and the best people to lead the drama were also leading worship. These are problems many of us face in ministry: limited resources, scant time. We found that after pulling together our rented worship space, transporting and setting up equipment, and rehearsing the worship team, we had only fifteen to thirty minutes to prepare the sketch.

Though normally I'd consider this a result of poor planning, because of logistics in our case there just wasn't any more time. And while I wouldn't recommend making minimal preparation a long-term practice, we worked to make the most of limited time, our relationships of trust and our improvisational skills (which grew a lot). In the end we developed tactics that allowed us to handle performing on such a brief rehearsal budget and still thrive. Here's some of what we learned.

SET EXPECTATIONS

If you know ahead of time that you will be limited in your rehearsal time and space, choose scripts that cater to your limitations. If you or someone else is writing specifically for your community, write the parts to your actors' strengths. Write so that scripts can be read or held in hand. Or place the sketch in a setting where scripts can be hidden or incorporated. You can also incorporate offstage voices. (See "Scripts" on page 175 for examples.)

If you are choosing outside material, go for something that's not too ambitious. It may be the perfect companion piece for the talk that day, but if you don't have the time, you don't have the time. Scour through scripts and have some on file that you can use if you're short on time.

As you gather to run through the sketch, be up front and realistic about the time you have and what you need to accomplish during that time. Someone needs to lead, and you are that person. You may be dealing with an anxious, fritzy team. You must lead people out of that wacky (yet understandable) emotional space.

Here's how:

◆ Keep your cool and your focus. What needs to happen in the time you have? Stop and think. If you haven't already done so, gather the actors who'll be part of the sketch. It's best to go with your best under pressure. If James starts to sweat and his voice goes all crackling Peter Brady, it's not gonna help. Choose people who won't freak out!

◆ Talk through (concisely, because, well, ya don't have a lot of time to rehearse) the order of what you will do in the next however many minutes you have. "All right. Let's read through from the top. Then we'll block and read again."

◆ Create expectations about what God can do through your work. It's crucial for people to remember that this isn't about them, that the sketch will be really useful. Even when rehearsal is short, the result can be something beautiful—if you take courage and go for it.

PRAY

Now that you've gathered the team and created beautiful expectations, by all means, pray. Ask God to hold onto you as you rehearse and perform. And then walk in the truth: God will work in and through you. While prayer may seem like a no-brainer, I find that the moment I'm crunched for time and most anxious is when I'm most likely to forget to take a deep breath and ask Jesus for help. Then, halfway into the rehearsal, when things feel like they are falling apart, I catch myself: "Ooohhh, prayer would be good here." So, take that breath early on, before anxiety sets in. Choose to believe God will speak through the sketch. That's what we're hoping for, right?

READ

Have people read through the sketch. Allow them to hear each other and get a sense of the piece. This is probably the most important practical thing you can do. If the actors can understand where the sketch is going, you've already done a good bit of the work. If you possibly can, have the group read it twice. Now that they've heard it once, it will build their confidence to go back and let the lines sink in without any other distractions.

BLOCK

Move your actors into position onstage and begin to block out the scene (for more on blocking, see chapter thirty-four on page 131). Even when you don't have the time to create glorious stage pictures, you can think through a simplified plan that gives the sketch movement but doesn't overwhelm the actors. They've got a lot on their plates, so give them clear, simple movements that get them where they need to go. Less is more, because—in this case—less can be done better.

Use creative blocking: have your actors on benches, couches or stools, or around coffee tables, with minimal rising and crosses. Limit the stage space you are working in to create a smaller, more focused area that doesn't require big, sweeping crosses. Or approach the sketch as a reading and have each actor in a solitary space, perhaps staggered on the stage, speaking directly to the audience.

We used this approach at a conference where we had little time to block and rehearse a sketch on racial and ethnic identity. The lack of movement actually helped the sketch: it put the focus on the words of the text, while our positions onstage created a jagged picture of distance and separation that illuminated the racial tensions of the story. With simple direction we took a rather complex sketch and made it accessible both to the audience and ourselves. The response was huge. God was at work. The audience responded to the honesty of the sketch and the questions it raised about ethnic identity.

TO MEMORIZE OR NOT TO MEMORIZE

It is always difficult for actors to get onstage in front of an audience with scripts in hand. We tend to assume the audience will think we are slackers who just chucked this thing together. Well, the audience is less likely to think this

than you are to fear it. And while it may have been, um, slightly chucked, you still worked hard and the sketch still has something to say. In fact, if the actors don't act weird about having scripts in their hands, the audience will most likely go with them on it. It's always best to memorize the script, but if that is just not an option, here are some ways to deal with this pesky problem.

First, know that it's okay to use a script in some situations. In the instances you need scripts, find ways to make them less obvious. One way is to use tables or desks on which the scripts can be placed mostly out of sight. One time the script called for me to sit at a computer, so I taped it to the monitor, which faced away from the audience. I realize this is starting to sound like the private confessions of a skimping actor, but really, sometimes in the throes of ministry, one thing needs to be sacrificed for another.

Bruce and I did a sketch that was written for us, but we were in different locations and couldn't rehearse until about an hour before we performed. The sketchwright actually wrote it to be performed with scripts in hand, from two ladders. Given our brief rehearsal, it was a better use of our time to focus on saying the lines well than on saying the lines from memory. It was no disgrace to us as actors— Bruce does the whole Gospel of Luke from memory, and I've done plenty of memorizing in my career. But in this instance, the writer and actors aimed to make the sketch work with scripts unabashedly in our hands, for all the world to see.

If your actors are using a script, make sure they handle it well. They should be confident about it. The audience would much rather focus on the sketch than on the scripts the actors are juggling. Instruct the actors not to fidget with it. Work out a way for them to turn pages without rustling. Help them not to stare at it. If the audience hadn't really noticed, they would now. The audience will give its attention to the thing the actors give their attention. Most audiences will be kind to actors when they use a script. If actors don't make it a distraction, it won't be one.

CHARACTERIZATION . . . DO I HAVE TIME FOR THAT?

Do you have time? Well, not so much. Don't worry about your actors finding their character's deepest pains and what happened in their character's childhood to make them who they are today. Let your actors know, "You should work out of who you are. You are interesting; and in any acting, a part of you will come through." Make some quick observations about each character. Is he patient or frantic? Sad or silly? Does she think highly of herself or have poor self-image? How might his voice be pitched: high? low? How quickly or slowly would she speak? walk? These basic questions can be answered fast and will give your actors something work from. Essentially, they need to give the audience a glimpse of this character in relation to the main point of the sketch. Actors need to flesh the characters out the best they can, but not become overwhelmed. In many cases it may be just as effective for them to play themselves. If the script allows for that, then hey, rock on.

REHEARSE IN THE PERFORMANCE SPACE

Try to rehearse in the space you'll perform in. It is always a bit funky to go from the third-grade Sunday school room with flannel-board Nebuchadnezzar cheering you on, to the main sanctuary with real live people. Sometimes it can be hard to schedule time for rehearsal space, but what you are doing for your congregation is as important a piece of communication as anything else. Create in your community the expectation that you will need this rehearsal time every week. Especially under pressure, it is helpful to have a feel for the actual arena you will be performing in. You will get a sense of what it will be like when people are there, how much room you actually have to work in and any other potential snags that might arise.

I was performing at a crowded conference and had limited time to rehearse on the rather large stage. Though I would have loved more time to get a feel for my environment, the half hour I had helped me adjust and prepare to be there with a lot of people. It was still a bit nerve-racking, but I knew how far I could move without falling off the stage, where the stage was uneven and how bright the lights would actually be. It may seem simple, but being surprised by physical elements can throw off a performance.

I heard the story of a performance at the Sydney Opera House that required live chickens onstage. The company never rehearsed with the chickens in the actual space. On opening night the performance was briefly stalled because the chickens wouldn't stay on the stage, flew around the performers and kept plummeting into the orchestra pit! We are not chickens, but the point still stands: rehearsing in your performance space will help you in the end.

DO ANOTHER RUN-THROUGH

Once you've prayed and read and blocked and rehearsed, run through the whole thing again if time allows, so everything stays fresh and you are ready to go.

PRAY AGAIN

Pray again. God knows what's up and will redeem mishaps. Remember, you are choosing to step out in faith. None of us loves to do things, especially art, on the fly, but sometimes it's good for us to go for it without our normal securities. Winging it pushes me to edges that cause me to either trust God to do his thing or crumble in my own fear. I've learned that God always comes through.

BE CONFIDENT

Be confident about what you are doing. Nourish confidence among the actors, so that when they step onstage, they stop fidgeting and avoid staring blankly into space, thinking, "What am I gonna do next?" If they wander out of the sketch, they'll yank the audience out of it with them. Encourage the actors to go with what they've got. It may not be memorized, it might not be Chekhov, but it may be what God has for your community.

ENJOY YOURSELF

Finally, enjoy directing and performing the sketch. That will communicate a lot to the people watching. They'll enjoy you enjoying yourself. They'll be confident that what you are offering is good if you are confident in it. Rehearsing with no time to rehearse often feels to me like what I imagine the feeding of the five thousand felt like to Jesus' disciples. There isn't time, you've been doing a ton of other work, and the last thing you want to do is feed a bunch of people—I mean, *you* haven't even had time to eat! But no, Jesus wants to serve lunch. Or a sketch. Now you have one more thing to do.

The disciples had a hard time with this, but the cool thing is that Jesus was with them—and he is with you. He will stretch what needs to be stretched, and people will eat their lunch. And cooler yet, you will get to serve and bless people along with Jesus.

36 PROPS AND SETS

Susi Jensen

If a character says he's reading Shakespeare, be sure that the book he's holding doesn't say in big bold letters *The Cat in the Hat.*

DAVID GROTE

All stories take place in a certain space and time. A stage is a rectangular space (usually) with width, height and depth. To the audience that sits in darkness, the lit stage takes on the dimension of depth when the space is filled with a few well-chosen sets and props.

In the early stages of creating your dramatic piece, bring a visual artist into discussions of the set design and prop usage. Set designers have an eye for what creates space and mood. Sometimes they can imagine simple solutions to awkward staging problems, especially when you are not performing in a professional theater. Indeed, many of us are doing drama in lecture halls and churches, often sharing the stage with an unsightly volume of worship equipment—space that lacks design.

Recently I wrote and produced a play set in the mansion of a wealthy Asian American woman living in a Bay Area suburb. We performed the play at a conference center. The wall behind the stage was painted with an amateur artist's rendition of a mountain scene, waterfall included. This was not an ideal backdrop for the play, but I was ready to ignore it, because as the director of the play I didn't have the time and energy to give attention to the wall. The most pressing matter for me was to get my actors rehearsal time. However, my wonderful set designers went to work and covered the wall with translucent white paper and used black electrician's tape to create the illusion of Japanese rice paper, shoji screens. They added a table, a vase with orchids, a Chinese warrior statuette, and the set was complete.

As a general rule, the more props, the more tech people you need for your production and the more expenses you incur. For a one-act play with two simple sets, I spent about fifty dollars on props. If you have no money for props in your budget, make sure your writer isn't scripting extravagant sets. And when writing, keep the stage in mind. If you don't, you might write an impossible world for the stage. For example, once I wrote a scene that involved two people walking along a sidewalk, talking. In TV and film, this could work. Onstage my characters were walking around in circles looking ridiculous. This is one of the limitations of the stage: movement from one setting to another in one scene. So, I rewrote the scene with my characters sitting at a café.

FURTHERING THE STORY

When writing a dramatic piece, try not to put props in where they are not absolutely necessary. Use props if they further your story; otherwise, get rid of them. Great drama happens all the time without props. It's amazing how well pantomiming works. You don't need a pot and two cups to put a tea party on stage if your actors go through the motions of a tea party as if they had the pot and two cups. Quality in your writing, directing and acting are the essentials of drama. In general, I try to write stories that could play anywhere. If there are any props,

make it so the actors carry them on and off stage. A chair, a cane, a hat, a bag of microwave popcorn can be enough.

I learned this the hard way. In my first full-length play, I made such extensive use of props that they became cumbersome and took away from the flow of action. Without a real tech crew, some of the scene changes were more than a minute long. As my first large production, I chalk this up to a helpful learning experience. If I were to produce this play again, I would design three set stations on stage, because most of the action took place in one of three places: a restaurant, a van and a pier. With the right lighting effects, the actors could have moved from station to station with hardly any interruption of the action. I would also let the actors pantomime more.

The stage, like any medium, has limitations. Writers and directors learn how to make the limitations an asset. The more plays you read and see, the more you will become acquainted with the medium. If you cannot afford theater tickets, volunteer at a theater for a summer and learn from the professionals, or watch soap operas on television. Low budget television imitates stage action better than film.

GIVING THE ACTORS SOMETHING TO DO

A significant advantage to using props in drama is the potential for the actor to show emotion through the objects. Alison created a series of dramatic vignettes for a conference. One of the pieces that generated the most intense emotion was a scene where a young couple begins to argue over the lack of passion and love in their relationship. Throughout the scene, they fold laundry. In fact, the argument emerges over gender and roles as the male character comments that laundry is a woman's job, while taking out the trash is a man's. You can see the intensity build in the way the actors handle the laundry. Shirts are violently folded and thrown into the laundry basket as the words grow cruel and finally hateful. The scene is poignant because the argument erupts and the relationship breaks up in the midst of a mundane domestic activity. The scene would not have been as powerful without the laundry and the laundry basket.

The laundry is an excellent example of prop usage because it serves all three purposes for props outlined above and is easily carried on and off stage by the actors. The prop sets the scene, gives rise to the tension in the story and provides the actors another means through which to communicate their emotion. When in doubt, hold up your props to these criteria. A prop should meet two of the three. If it doesn't, try going without or imagine some better options.

37 EVALUATING PERFORMANCES

Alison Siewert

God gave us two ears and one mouth so we can listen twice as much as we talk.

YIDDISH PROVERB

If you're a director, your team will likely check in with you to see how you think they did. They might come ask. They might hang out, hoping you'll mention it. But directly or indirectly, they need to hear from you. They'll also talk with each other. And their friends in the fellowship will have lots to say. My rule is that our team will not critique performances until at least twenty-four hours after they're over. People come offstage having just bared their souls to a crowd. They're raw. It is not the most constructive, rational time to process the details of improvement.

PRAISE FIRST

So initially, I offer praise. Even if it went badly, I can at least tell people they put in a good effort or that one line really worked or that it was a good first sketch. I don't lie to the team. I want them to develop appropriate self-assessment and a willingness to critique their own work. But critique needs context. I don't sling every possible problem at the group, because when people have been slung at they usually want to shower off instead of talk.

Praise first. Think of everything you can call good: effort, lines, how the costume worked, that Bob remembered not to pick his nose. Spend ample time filling people in on all the stuff they did right. What's right is more powerful reinforcement than what's wrong. We are more strongly motivated to do more of what we do well than we are motivated to do less of what we did wrong. I found this out when I switched voice teachers.

I started with a technician who constantly

told me how not to let my tongue rise, how not to place the vowel there, how not to lose breath support. I struggled to sing while *not* doing all the things I was not supposed to do. Later I worked with a slightly crazy guy who would jump to his feet and yell (loudly—he was an opera singer), "Yes! That's it! Do that again! Again!" At first I was so startled at someone jumping around while I sang, I wasn't sure what to do. But soon enough his excitement took over my attention and I improved very quickly. I was thinking all the time about doing the right thing—except that I wasn't really thinking about it. I was just "doing more of that!" and my teacher was jumping around, so I knew "that" was good. Once I quit worrying about what not to do, I stopped doing it. Magic. Performance makes people self-conscious. If you can draw your artists' attention away from themselves and into the process of doing it more and better, they will improve quickly and confidently. The wrong things will go away because they're not reinforced.

CORRECTION

What about the stuff that really shouldn't be praised? Of course there are some things that we don't want repeated—ever!

I start with myself. Part of every evaluation examines my directing. Did I help the actors adequately? Did I appropriate rehearsal time well? Was I clear about where we were going? Did we negotiate that scene until everyone understood their roles? Did I forget anything? Did the important things show up as important? How was the pace?

I take a careful look and get some input from others—though not just any others. I invite specific people, both inside and outside the drama circle, to give me feedback. Often they will notice things I didn't, both good and bad. I might think something was completely distracting but find out that no one else even noticed it. Because the intensity of the process can skew our perceptions, it's important to hear from other people.

I also evaluate the script, the appropriateness of the sketch for the context and the technical support. I assess whether the script held up: Was it self-explanatory? Did people follow the humor? Did it move through the story quickly but thoroughly? If there was anything lacking, I make note. If I chose (or wrote) a script that was too hard for the team, that didn't work in general or that didn't work in the context, I want to choose or write better next time.

Sometimes I watch a videotape of a performance. But in most cases I don't encourage actors to watch videotape of themselves, because I find it inculcates self-consciousness. Unless you have sophisticated videography available, the videotape of a sketch, usually shot from a balcony with a single camera, reduces the overall effect of the art quite radically. No one looks that good. I find it more helpful to watch the tapes myself and then give feedback to performers about what I observe.

Soon after the performance, usually at our next team meeting, we engage in evaluative conversation. We review what went well, including comments we've heard from others. We critique with a present-to-future focus. In other words, we are not going to go on about how bad something was, how embarrassing and how we should never have done it that way. Rather, we critique in terms of "next time." "Next time we need to work harder on blocking." Or, "Next time, you must memorize your lines more solidly." "Next time remember your cue." These critiques lead to immediate correction: there is something constructive the team members can *do*.

It's important to keep track of patterns. If an actor slurs her speech for the third week in a row or someone drops lines in four out of six sketches or the microphones have been late more than twice, that's a pattern. Dealing with habitual or ongoing issues is different from correcting one-time gaffes. You might find that a performer is struggling with fear or approaches his job slothfully or that a technician doesn't really know what she's doing. These require more corrective conversation and more pastoral or training involvement than a single mistake.

Sin is part of our life together, and sometimes it shows up in the artistic process. Perhaps an impatient word, an angry look or an inappropriate joke has been lobbed from one team member to another. If this is the case, the team needs to talk about it. Sometimes confession, repentance and forgiveness need to happen in the meeting. Sometimes they need to be offered privately. With sin, we really must dwell on how bad something was—and that means dealing with it before we move on. Never sweep sin under the stage. Once we've dealt, we move forward with Jesus' help to restore and serve each other.

Finally, we evaluate the use of the sketch in the service. The drama team talks first and forwards its thoughts to the planning team. Did the tone and timbre of the sketch work? Did it fit in its time slot? Did the speaker and other leaders connect with the sketch without trying to explain it?

The evaluative process helps us develop. It points out areas in which we feel defensive and self-conscious; it shows where we have trouble receiving praise; it can also hurt. The director can help the team hold successes and failures in balance. Keep things in proportion. It's pretty rare that any artistic endeavor is entirely bad or entirely good. There's always room to improve.

Your example affects your team's reception of critique and praise. You model growth by embracing criticism—"Wow! That's a great point. Let's think more about how we might do that better." And you model humility and hope by receiving praise. "Yes, I think we've done a good job building that area. God is working with us."

BIBLE STUDIES FOR DRAMA TEAMS

STUDY 1
GOD GETS STARTED
GENESIS 1:1—2:3

Alison Siewert and Daniel Jones

PURPOSE: This study will help us see how God sets the stage for artistic and dramatic expression.

One of the scariest things about being an artist is that you have to actually start the art. To go from blank to concept to image to the fullness of expression is daunting. Imagine God's canvas: endless nothingness. That is how God starts his project. Even with nothingness as a starting point, God is able to create something really good. It is good because it expresses who God is, and because it expresses it not just to emptiness but to creatures made to be like God himself. God makes the whole creation and puts people at its zenith. Then he gives it away! God gives away his art.

In the midst of pressure not only to get to rehearsals and meetings but also to find time to actually be creative, it helps to stop and look at God as a creator. To pause and consider God's courage, his thoughtfulness, his intelligence, his ability to make beauty that defines beauty—this is a discipline that will serve us as we engage in the artistic process together.

INTRODUCTORY QUESTIONS
◆ What part of the creative process do you enjoy most?
◆ What part of the process scares you?

BACKGROUND
The Hebrews lived among many other tribes, all of which had their own creation stories, often detailing convoluted squads of deities running the universe through greed, force and selfishness. Many created entities were thought to have been made through conflict—for example, one god cutting another in half to form the skywaters and the groundwaters. The stars were thought to be communication from the gods about human fate—which was inescapable—and humans were regarded as less than real, only phantoms. People were created to serve the gods "that they might be at ease."

Genesis is the statement by God's people, in the midst of those cultures, of the meaning of human existence, the order of the universe and the character of God. We are going to look at the first of the two creation accounts in Genesis, the more structured and formal of the two. It was part of an oral tradition before it was written down.

FOR STUDY
◆ Have one person read Genesis 1:1—2:3 out loud. Pause, and have another person read it again. What words, phrases or images jump out at you?
◆ Consider what it might have been like for the Hebrews to hear this story in the context of their life among the nations. What might have been notable or outstanding?
◆ How is this account put together? (How does it move along?)
◆ What do you appreciate about God in this text?
◆ Verse 27 says that God made humans in his image. From the text so far, what do you think that means?
◆ What does this passage tell you about God as Creator? Artist?

FOR LIFE

◆ If you were going to stage this story theatrically, how would you do it? Assuming no limits on budget, time or talent, brainstorm how this would go.

◆ This account was written during a time when Israel lived among many other stories. What models does it suggest to us for sharing our story in the midst of our culture's many stories?

◆ We mentioned that God takes courage to create—he is not stopped by the barrenness or darkness as he begins. What do you need courage to do as a creator? Ask God for this courage.

STUDY 2
YOUR NAME IN LIGHTS
GENESIS 11:1-9

Daniel Jones and Alison Siewert

PURPOSE: This study will help us think about the temptation to provide for ourselves rather than letting God provide for us.

The first time I (Daniel) studied the account of the Tower of Babel with a group of artists, my heart pounded and I clenched with conviction. I have been a tower builder: methodically considering how I can make a name for myself and reach the heavens—not through or with God, but by my ability and desire to be known. Something in me wants to be defined not by my dependence on God (as his creature) but by my independent ability to make my life. I yearn for external things (looks, talent, achievement, money) to build me up when I know—in my head—that I need God to build me, not from external stuff but from the inside out.

Coming out of the study, I thought, *How often do actors and others use the art they love to build themselves up, get the pat on the back, and become well-known and wealthy?* Pretty often. In our culture, name recognition and exposure are big. Even in Christian contexts, where I and others can claim, "I'm doing it for the Lord and he just keeps opening those doors," I have to wonder, *Is that really true? Am I really in it for God—or am I attracted to making a name for myself?*

INTRODUCTORY QUESTIONS

◆ When you look at famous people, especially dramatic artists, what is most appealing about their fame?

◆ Have you ever been drawn to being famous? Or have you ever been famous? What do/did you hope for? How did it turn out?

BACKGROUND

The Tower of Babel story shows up after Genesis has laid out the "table of nations" (chapter 10), the list of seventy nations on the earth after the flood. Everyone could communicate because there was only one language, and people were all clumped together in one general area, what is now the southern Tigris/Euphrates plain. They decided to make a tower, probably a *ziggurat*—a four-sided staircase with a room at the top (bed and food included) where the gods could stop by for a rest. *Ziggurats* were filled with rubble; it was all about the stairs.

The towers were built using burned bricks and tar (for mortar) and were neither solid nor long lasting.

FOR STUDY

Have three people read the story aloud: one as the narrator, one as the Babylonians and one as God. Have fun telling the story. (If you're having snacks while you do this, feel free to employ cheese puffs or something as a building material and try it out . . .)

◆ What do you imagine it was like for everyone to have "one language and few words"? (What might the dynamics of that society have been?)

◆ Why do the Babylonians want to build, and what are they trying to avoid?

◆ How does God respond? (Is he actually scared, or does that inference seem rhetorical?)

◆ What's the effect of God's response?

◆ Contrast how the tower builders were defined at the beginning of the story with how they are defined now.

FOR LIFE

◆ The Babylonians' tower—what they create (their art)—represents their spiritual reality. What does your creation look like? In other words, how would you like for people to see and define you? Create a collage or picture to illustrate your tower when you're making a name for yourself. Next to that one, make another "tower" out of God's names for you.

◆ Why does God divide people from one another? What is the effect of our separation from one another—and how does God use that for our good?

◆ How can you get down off the tower-building project? Where will you go from here? Pray together.

◆ Find someone who has struggled with letting go of making his or her own name, in whom you can see God has worked to make *his* name. Talk with this individual about this passage and about how you might resist tower building and instead choose the humility of creaturehood.

STUDY 3

I WANT WHAT THEY GOT
PSALM 73

Daniel Jones

PURPOSE: In this study we'll consider some of the temptations to compare and covet that can beleaguer us as performers.

Even though we can shrug off Hollywood as bogus, in the backs of our minds we know that our drama gets compared to the standards set by movies and TV. Actually, we don't even need Hollywood to make us feel bad; most of us compare ourselves to each other, to the other (better) actor, to other churches—we can always find some comparative standard.

We can become acutely aware of others' abundance and our own lack when we see well-produced theater and wonder what it would be like to have all that space, time, money, attention and education, plus all those amazing pros who know what they're doing . . . And here we are, rehearsing in the third-grade Sunday school room. Or perhaps we see people around us who fit the good images of our culture—thin, fit, beautiful, young and so on—and wallow in our shortcomings.

It's a simple thing to covet what we perceive others have; it's a more difficult discipline to trust that what God is giving us is exactly what we need.

INTRODUCTORY QUESTIONS

◆ What is one thing you truly love about yourself?
◆ By what standard do you evaluate yourself? It could be another person, a different life path or even your picture of yourself as you "should be."

BACKGROUND

Psalm 73 is addressed to the people of God assembled in worship. Asaph, the founder of one of the main musicians' guilds among the Levites, is the presenter.

FOR STUDY

◆ Listen to the psalm, then go back and study quietly for a few minutes. From the text, what can we understand about the community's situation? (What surrounds them? What might they be experiencing?)

◆ Review the list of characteristics of the wicked. What can you identify in our own culture?
◆ Which indignity or struggle seems the worst to you?
◆ Describe the wrestling process of the psalmist: How does he go back and forth and finally let God win?
◆ When God does win, what does that look like?
◆ How does it change things for the psalmist?

FOR LIFE

◆ How have you "come close to stumbling" as you've envied the arrogant and seen the prosperity of the wicked?
◆ What is the psalmist's remedy for envy?
◆ How does the psalmist call us to continually combat the temptation to covet and compare?
◆ How have you seen God bring true abundance to your life? your art? your team? And how could you work together as a team to focus on God's gifts to you? Think of some specific disciplines you could do together.
◆ Create a psalm of your own about the ways God is at work in your life; share them at the end of your study or the next time you meet.

STUDY 4
DR. JESUS
LUKE 5:29-32

Alison Siewert

PURPOSE: In this study we'll seek to identify how God works through our weaknesses to bless others and heal us.

Healing is all over the Gospels: lepers, blind guys, bent-over women, the lame, the deaf and the bleeding all find their way to Jesus. The Gospel writers certainly had something in mind when they included those stories in theirs. They had seen lots of people healed by Jesus—they experienced him as the

Great Physician. How does Jesus the doctor show up in our lives?

One challenge for drama teams is that we are often portraying broken, hurting people, but many of us have been taught to keep our game faces on, to look for the good in every situation and to keep our struggles to ourselves. Admitting our weakness, frailty and pain is part of letting Jesus in and allowing him to shape our innermost being. It's also part of becoming effective actors and communicators, because it is our own brokenness that informs our ability to portray true characters.

INTRODUCTORY QUESTIONS

◆ What is the sickest you've ever been, and how did your doctor treat you?

◆ What do you like least about going to the doctor?

◆ When has someone else's difficult experience, illness or struggle informed or encouraged you?

BACKGROUND

At the outset of Luke 5:29-32, Jesus has just called Levi to follow him, and Levi turns around and throws a huge party for Jesus at his house. As a tax collector, Levi had betrayed his own people by extracting Jewish money for the occupying Roman government. Tax collectors had to collect their own salaries: In effect, they provided for themselves by adding extra amounts to the legal taxes. Many tax collectors became very wealthy, essentially by stealing from fellow citizens.

Jesus is, then, at a party at Levi's with Levi's friends—mostly other tax collectors and their crowd—a patently unpopular, irreligious crew. The Pharisees are zealous and legalistic; they wanted to see Israel return to God by keeping the law. To them, Jesus' presence at a dinner of tax collectors is scandalous, distasteful and leaves him discredited. But Jesus apparently carries enough weight to make them attempt to engage him in dialogue over the in-

cident, rather than ignoring him altogether.

FOR STUDY

◆ Read the story out loud. Then take turns relating it in your own words from the perspective of various people in the room: Jesus, the Pharisees, Levi and the other guests at dinner. What stands out? Surprises you? Delights you?

◆ This conversation takes place in front of a crowd, and it's likely politically charged. What questions beneath the questions do you hear?

◆ Who is well and who is sick?

◆ What response is Jesus hoping for?

◆ What response does Jesus get? (Keep reading to discover this.)

◆ If you were in the room, how do you think you would have responded?

◆ What are the implications of Jesus' being a doctor?

◆ What are the implications of being a patient?

FOR LIFE

◆ No one likes to be sick. Some of us avoid even admitting when we're sick. Why?

◆ It's great to get diagnosed, but being diagnosed means becoming aware of our weaknesses. How might your awareness of weakness help you as an artist?

◆ How can you work with your weaknesses to connect with characters you're playing? What challenges might you encounter as you try to do that?

◆ One thing teams can do for each other is pray. Not just quick, chirpy prayers but deep, healing prayers. Spend some time sharing with one another about your brokenness and weaknesses, one at a time. Then lay hands on each person who has shared (a sign of God's blessing) and pray for healing. Appeal to Jesus the Great Physician. (You might need to do this in smaller groups or over several weeks. And if you run into something too overwhelming for your team, confidentially, and with the person's permission, seek a pastor or counselor for help.)

◆ Once you've done some sharing and praying together, talk about how you can help each other to be vulnerable, to allow the broken places to show as you portray broken people onstage.

STUDY 5

MAKING GOD'S NAME KNOWN
ACTS 17:16-34

Alison Siewert

PURPOSE: In this study we'll explore how we communicate the gospel in terms our culture can understand and pursue.

Paul visited Athens after a close call in Thessalonica and then Berea. Some believers brought Paul to Athens, where he waited for Silas and Timothy to join him. While he was there he took note of the city's idols and also its sincere yearning for a God they did not know. This passage has been studied a great deal as a model for contextualizing the gospel—making the message connect with people in ways they understand.

Making the gospel connect with people in ways they understand is what we're trying to do with drama. One of our main goals is to refresh things people have heard a million times and to introduce things they've never heard—all in a way they can comprehend and even enjoy.

INTRODUCTORY QUESTIONS

◆ How did you first hear the gospel? Did it make sense? Why or why not?
◆ What's the best way you've ever heard the gospel preached? The worst?

BACKGROUND

Athens was a major crossroads and center of culture, and, as the text says, was full of idols. Paul usually went to the synagogue first wherever he was, to bring the gospel to the Jews before going to the Gentiles. Epicureans were committed to hedonism and were famous for their feasts, at which people ate until they threw up, then came back for more. To them God was irrelevant. Stoics were nearly the opposite, holding altruism and self-sacrifice as their standards; they believed the universe dissolved back into God but had no active faith.

The Areopagus was a council, the center for debate and discussion—an intellectual gathering place. Paul was invited to talk there about his "new teachings" about "strange deities." Look carefully at the way Paul explains the faith in their terms.

FOR STUDY

◆ Break the passage up and read it aloud. You can take parts if you like. As you listen, what themes seem to wind through the whole story?
◆ How does Paul regard the city? And how do

the people of the city regard him? (Note: "Idle babbler" means, literally, "seed picker," or perhaps "birdbrain.")

◆ How does Paul connect with the crowd at the Areopagus?

◆ How does he connect the Athenians' story with the gospel story?

◆ How does art figure in?

◆ If you were going to create a sketch for Athens, what elements would you include?

FOR LIFE

◆ If you were walking through your town or campus, what artistic expressions or symbols could you identify that express people's longing for, but lack of knowledge of, God?

◆ How could you incorporate one or more of those expressions or symbols into a sketch? Consider writing something.

◆ If you were trying to lay out the gospel in a culturally contextualized way, something akin to Paul's preaching here, how would you do it? (What media would you use? What would be the important characteristics of the work?)

◆ How does this passage encourage you to continue building artistic communication in your community?

THE SPIRITUAL LIFE OF DRAMA TEAMS

PERFORMERS AS DISCIPLES AND DISCIPLES AS PERFORMERS

Daniel Jones

"Nobody else," Anthony went on, "sees you as you are. Nobody else will give you such a difficult and unpleasant time as I do. You'll never be comfortable, but you may be glorious. You'd better think over it."

ANTHONY TO DAMARIS IN "THE PLACE OF THE LION"
CHARLES WILLIAMS

I became interested in acting at about the same time I started going to church. I was baptized and smacked the new label "Christian" on myself. It was an exciting time and a confusing time. One world held riding buses into New York, pounding the pavement, going on auditions, getting a gig here and there and trying to feel out the art of becoming an actor. The other world held youth group meetings, choir robes, weekend retreats and Wednesday night dinners. Neither world made sense to the other. I found myself asking the question, *How can I be in both?*

It felt like some freak split-screen world, like in the movie *Sliding Doors*—this is what your life would look like if *this* happened, and this is what your life would look like if *that* happened. I knew I really liked art and acting, but when I looked around church, I didn't see anything deeply artistic. Sure, there were Easter cantatas and musicals, but nothing theatrical that satisfied me fully. At the same time, I wasn't fitting into the acting world because of the whole Jesus thing. I wondered if God even thought it was okay to for me to act.

I didn't know how to be a disciple of Jesus and a performer; I didn't know how to be a performer and a disciple of Jesus. I felt duplicitous. And not good. I came to the conclusion that I probably had to choose one or the other. I chose for a time to live in the land of duplicity and continue performing, calling myself a believer. But I was never fully given over to being a disciple.

I think that is where many of us begin. We have the clear call to follow God. Is there anything better than that, really? But then we have this artsy, performer side that doesn't have much room to stretch in the Christian community. And if we venture out, we face the struggle of knowing how to be disciples while being performers.

FOLLOW ME

In the beginning of the Gospel of Mark, Jesus says to a group of fishermen, "Follow me, and I will make you fish for people" (Mark 1:17). Immediately, the dudes drop their nets and leave everything behind to follow Jesus. At that very moment, Simon and Andrew, and then later James and John, become disciples of God. When we choose to follow Jesus, we choose to become disciples. It's a good deal: we get to see miracles, healings, other folks being changed by God. And we get in on the hard stuff, the costly things that come with following God. The things we see and hear prompt our growth if we continue to trust Jesus. As long as we follow him, we are his disciples.

The call is always to be disciples. We only change that when we refuse to be discipled. Jesus says, "Come. Follow me." And we're all, "Okay Jesus, I'm gonna drop my nets, except for that performer, actor, artist thing . . . yeah, I need that." The Savior of the world calls out to us; and although we may respond immediately, we continue to hang onto other things we want. How crazy is that?! I am truly convinced that in order to be a performer and a disciple as a whole person, you have to hold the performer thing pretty lightly and, if pushing and shoving gets started, be willing to let go of it altogether.

We must be willing to let go because some of what has been raised up in us as performers is unhealthy. Many of us worked at performing long before we gave ourselves to following Jesus. We have to restructure to become disciples. Our performance training sets up expectations that don't necessarily match Jesus' plans for our good. When I think about art from a Jesus angle, for example, it seems important to consider whether we could make art differently, with new meaning and purpose. Could our art look different from the way Hollywood or Broadway produces art? There's nothing in my artistic training that would help me think that way. But Jesus does.

I've seen some performers become unrealistic about who and what God wants us to become. They equate worldly success with blessing from God. We know the way to be successful has nothing to do with "success," but it's so hard to remember that. I see people who have wanted Jesus but have never given themselves over to him. Unless we release our art into his hands, no success will be whole. And we may miss God's blessing, his unique call on our lives.

MAKING A DECISION

I remember the moment: I was deciding whether to go to graduate school or to do ministry in which I had the opportunity to be both performer and disciple. Had I gone to grad school, I would have been part of a prestigious conservatory program. I would have had top-quality training for three years straight and little time for anything else—not really even a church community (maybe Sunday morning—but is that really enough?).

The other option was doing ministry—building a new community, and learning to disciple, lead bible studies, communicate the gospel, receive healing and have accountability. And part of my job would be developing art and theater and performing in multiple contexts. It seems like a no-brainer now. But at the time, it was a mighty struggle to decide.

I remember sitting in the car in front of my church with my pastor. We talked about my struggle to decide what I wanted to do. All the pieces were out on the table (or dashboard), and I was resisting a decision. I wanted Jesus, but, dang, I wanted the art thing as well. It made me so mad. She read this Scripture to me: "God has a future with hope for you" (Jeremiah 29:11). And the more truth I heard, the angrier I became. I rolled my eyes. I squirmed in my seat, opened the door, shut the door, opened the door again, shifted and tried not to really listen. The pastor wasn't telling me what to do. But I knew what God was saying. The competing voice in my head asked, *What will I lose out on if I don't continue training as an actor?* and *What will my life look like if I don't go about it in the expected way?*

My pastor asked, "How do you want your life to be useful?" In that moment, clarity smacked me. That was the question. I wanted to be useful both as an actor and as a disciple, but I wasn't willing to let go of the art thing as I knew it and according to my plan. It was mine and I was entitled to it. I wasn't taking into account that it was something God had given me in the first place, that he knew me and knew that part of me . . . and that he might even want to bless me through drama. I thought that perhaps God had different ways for me to do acting. I didn't really trust that if I took the risk to let go of it, God would honor that decision and redeem what I had let go of. I questioned whether God could really bless me and make me a blessing.

CAN I REALLY BE BOTH?

We can see ourselves as one or the other: actor or follower, artist or disciple. I thought I had to set up strict boundaries (sometimes we *do*) to separate my performer world from my Christian world. We wouldn't want the two intermingling! They're like Uncle Jarvis on your Dad's side and Aunt Bernice on your Mom's—the relatives you work hard to keep from sitting at the same table at the wedding reception. It would work better, in an attempt to help them get along, to acknowledge that we can't control them. I thought I could control each of my realms separately, but I couldn't. And looking back, I'm glad I couldn't.

We need space to be disciples, to trust God with our futures, knowing he is faithful. We can let go of anything in our lives for the sake of the gospel and know Jesus will give us what's better. Without Jesus as Lord—fully in charge—we remain in pieces and unable to integrate our realms. God wants blessing for us, but if we choose to operate in fear and distrust, we cut ourselves off from what God may have for us as performers.

What I've found is that, as Scripture and countless stories of faith lay out for us, when we surrender the parts of our lives we cling to the most, God redeems us and allows us to do and see and be part of extraordinary things. When we really become disciples, when we stick close to Jesus, we get to see the most and be in on the most. Being performers is part of our story, which becomes part of God's story. It's good to hope that God does something with the performer in you. And it is good to become a whole person with all of you integrated as a follower of God. You can be both performer and disciple.

A GLIMPSE OF HOPE

A little over a year ago, we were performing a play on Mark's Gospel at a conference. Natalie, a student who was in a study I led on the first half of the Gospel of Mark (yes, it was a packed week) came to see the performance. What she had been discovering in the Scripture met the story she saw unfold on the stage. She saw Jesus in a completely new way. That night she went out by the lake, sat on a rock for a long time and prayed. As she listened to God, she realized that she had been around Jesus but had never made an adult decision to follow him. She then took the risk to follow Jesus.

That story overwhelms me for so many reasons. For starters, it's been wonderful to watch Natalie grow as a follower of Jesus and leader of others. But it is also a sign to me of God's faithfulness. That week I was doing the two things that I took a risk to do instead of full-time performing: teaching the Bible and acting in a play. In that week, God wove my life together. I taught the Scripture and I did a theater performance. God spoke to Natalie and she became a follower of God. And he spoke to me, still more deeply, about how I am becoming a follower too.

WORKING WITH THE THEATER COMMUNITY

WORKING WITH THE THEATER COMMUNITY

Nina Thiel

Be absurdly generous.

PETER BARKWORTH

What a great party! Four hours of pure relaxation, conversation, tables spread with food, coolers stocked with drinks, kids splashing in the Jacuzzi and adults unwinding. After this spring's dance company concert, it was our pleasure to invite the entire cast and crew over for barbeque. My husband, Larry, was happy to grill a ton of chicken, our kids were happy to play with the kids of the other dancers, and I was happy to care for my friends in my home, to pray that they would connect their good memories of time spent with us (a Christian family) to Jesus. It was a blast. You would have loved it.

I have never really connected in Christian theater circles, so all of my experiences in theater and dance are in the secular realm. The theater community in your city or on campus is a great place for professional development and an incredible place to bring Jesus' presence as you get to know and love the people there. My initial launch into performing my quite evangelistic show on campuses across the country came from my work and alliances in the "secular" theater community. And because I have returned to theater and dance after an absence (and years of wonderful ministry and spiritual growth as a campus minister), I re-approach the theater community with a new vision and sense of purpose. I feel like I'm learning new things

every day. What follows are some things that I have come to know. I hope you will find some insights for your particular situation, whether you're new to theater or thinking about it with new eyes.

A SERVANT'S HEART

Whoever wants to become great among you must be your servant, and whoever wants to be first must be your slave— just as the Son of Man did not come to be served, but to serve, and to give his life as a ransom for many. (Matthew 20:26-28 NIV)

My first experience back in the theater community was to stage manage a New Dance Company concert four years ago. Because there weren't many of us backstage, I did more than just put on the headset and let the booth know when the dancers were in place (and get them in place!), and call lights and music. I mopped the dance floor before every performance. I set props. I handed dancers props during pieces. I helped with quick costume changes. I changed lighting gels (the colored plastic sheets that go over the lights) between dances. I once even put my finger in a stagehand's face during a dress rehearsal and said, "Never do that again." My mission was simple: to do my job well, to serve the dancers so they didn't have to worry about a thing and could simply dance.

Serving others is something we work at in the Christian community. We value the opportunity to be like Jesus. We believe him when he says that serving is the way to true greatness. And I have been amazed at the impact our serving—even just doing things that come naturally to us—has on my dance and theater friends. The night I had a bunch of dance friends over for dinner when a former teacher was in town for a visit, they went on and on about how wonderful my husband was to help prepare dinner and to do all the dishes while we sat and talked. And there was the morning I offered myself to the director of *The Sound of Music* at the local community theater (our son was in the production) and became her new best friend as I crafted hair pieces for the children for the wedding scene, dusted furniture on the set and mopped the rehearsal hall floor. Any production, from your child's dance re-

WAYS TO SERVE
THE THEATER COMMUNITY
Nina Thiel

- *Bring food to people, even just a well-timed soft drink or sandwich. No one ever has time to eat during productions.*
- *Have people over for meals.*
- *Volunteer your home for cast parties.*
- *Sew costumes.*
- *Sew buttons, snaps, hooks and elastic on costumes.*
- *Be someone's dresser (help people change costumes).*
- *Help prepare mailings (stuffing envelopes, putting on stamps).*
- *Make copies.*
- *Usher at performances.*
- *Help with set construction.*
- *Bake for the snack bar.*
- *Staff the snack bar.*
- *Help lay the dance floor (for dance performances).*
- *Organize costumes.*
- *Help with strike (after the last show, the cast and volunteers take apart sets and put away lights, etc.).*
- *Manage the house (the audience and their portion of the theater).*
- *Be the stage manager.*

cital to your roommate's spring musical, provides incredible opportunities to serve and, with these opportunities, a sure way to get to know people, learn from them and love them. Volunteers are almost always needed and embraced. See the sidebar for a list of things I've found myself doing in the last four years. I'll bet you can see yourself doing many of them!

SHARING THE GOSPEL AND OUR LIVES

> We loved you so much that we were delighted to share with you not only the gospel of God but our lives as well, because you had become so dear to us. (1 Thessalonians 2:8 NIV)

As I write, I am in rehearsal for our community theater's production of the musical *Footloose*. I have a great part—the one I wanted! I've also just finished my second full year with a new job description that allows me to intentionally pursue performing, not only my one-woman show but also local theater and dance. When I'm not with my family, most of my time is spent in some sort of theatrical pursuit. Just the other night I was talking with my husband about how good this is—because I really love what I'm doing and I really love the people I get to spend time with—but how strange it feels to be immersed in this sort of community.

I have jumped all the way in so I can learn all I need to and have an impact—but sometimes I wonder if I'll drown. I wonder if this is how Jesus felt when he became one of us and immersed himself in humanity. Well, he certainly is my model here. I don't know how to just stand at the edge and hope to accomplish anything! Here's my top three list of how to share your life and the gospel in the theater community:

Go to performances. If you have theater friends in your life, you will show them your love and support by seeing everything they're in. I know who has planned and showed up at *my* performances (and my kids' performances)

and who hasn't. It means the world to me when people come and see; it saddens me when they don't. So I, likewise, try to be in the audience for my friends. Here's what my spring was like:

◆ April 4th: Seeing Gary in *The Miser* at Stockton Civic Theatre.
◆ April 12th: Seeing Michael in *Cat on a Hot Tin Roof* with the American Blues Theatre Company.
◆ April 19th: Seeing our daughter Catherine in *The King and I* at St. Mary's High School.
◆ April 20th: Seeing Justin in *Twelfth Night* at University of the Pacific.
◆ May 9th: Seeing our son John in his elementary school play.
◆ May 12th: Seeing Erin, Beau, Sara and Chloe in *Fiddler on the Roof* at Delta Community College.

And when you go to your friends' performances, realize that theater has quite a culture of gift-giving: notes, cards and flowers are all kept, displayed and treasured by your performing friends.

Take classes. This is where you'll meet the people—your teachers—who can really help you grow as a performer and where you'll get to know fellow travelers in your artistic journey. I was lured back into performing with my dance company because I decided to take a couple of dance classes at the studio where they rehearsed. My class with Bruce launched me into performing Scripture drama, but my acting teacher from college helped me form the vision for my one-woman show *Always the Women*. And my friend from those college acting classes, then the producing director at the local civic theatre, shepherded ATW right onto the stage. Further training from another acting teacher in town developed me and the piece, propelled me into a ministry of traveling to perform it and led me into some great friendships with theater folks in the region. Teachers are honored to be asked to help— like if your team has a sketch you're having trouble with, or if you'd all like to take a class or get coaching together. A whole campus drama team could take "Acting I" on campus. A church team could take a class at a local theater. The financial cost is nothing compared to the quality training, relationships and opportunities that emerge from those alliances.

Be in shows. The best way to really get to know and love people is by actually being in shows with them—either onstage or backstage (see section on serving). All the rehearsals, all the blood, sweat and tears, and all the working together and celebrating together can't be reproduced. You have to be there. I have had the most wonderful conversations about Jesus and other deep issues (rearing children, working hard in marriage, transitioning in jobs) in between rehearsals. And always, always be on the alert for chances to do things together outside of rehearsals and performances. Going out with everyone after a dance company concert this spring yielded fruitful conversations and deeper connections. I am really looking forward to all that being in a play this summer will bring for me and for the kingdom as I bring Jesus' presence into the theater and into my relationships there every night.

SETTING YOUR CORE

> I appeal to you therefore, brothers and sisters, by the mercies of God, to present your bodies as a living sacrifice, holy and acceptable to God, which is your spiritual worship. Do not be conformed to this world, but be transformed by the renewing of your minds, so that you may discern what is the will of God—what is good and acceptable and perfect. (Romans 12:1-2)

My kids' ballet teacher also teaches mat classes based on the methods of Joseph Pilates.

I love these classes, so I go whenever I can, and I am more aligned and strong than I've ever been! The first thing Elaine says as we start new exercises is, "Set your core" (belly scooped, ribs closed, pelvic floor muscles tight, head aligned, pelvis not tucked nor back arched). Once our "core" is set, we can do anything she asks us to do, because we use the proper muscles and we won't hurt ourselves.

Last fall a ministry colleague gave a wonderful talk on caring for our souls. As I listened to him and reflected on my life lived out in the theater community these days, I heard Jesus saying to me, "Set your core." I need not fear that drowning feeling if I am closely connected to Jesus, if my rhythms of attention to my soul (time alone with God, time in worship with others, time growing in Christian community) are not only in place, but are truly sustaining me.

With my core set, I recognize my tendency to gossip with everyone else backstage, and I can repent. With my core set, I notice opportunities to enter conversations with spiritual encouragement and offers to pray. When my core is set, people seek me out for listening and praying. When my core is set, I discover and embrace those opportunities to serve much more quickly and with a better attitude. When my core is set, I do a much better job of fielding the inevitable sexual innuendo and even temptation that seems to hang in the air backstage. When I take the time to discern "what is good and acceptable and perfect," I live a fully integrated life wherever I am—in church on Sunday or in the theater on Saturday night—serving others and sharing my life with them. I want this to be my hallmark—for my own growth and influence, for the sake of the kingdom, and for the community, the theater community, to which God has called me.

WORKING WITH DRAMA TEAMS

PART 1
FOR PASTORS AND LEADERS

Alison Siewert

Would to God that I could persuade the rich and mighty that they would permit the whole Bible to be painted on houses, on the inside and outside, so that all can see it.

MARTIN LUTHER

Sometimes people want drama to happen but don't know how to supply resources or advocate for the people doing it. Listen to one person's story:

> I wrote and directed several theater pieces for a national church event. Two of the actors were delayed by a late plane and arrived parched and hungry. I went to the event's command center where there was food left on the lunch table, explained the need and asked if the actors could make themselves sandwiches. The manager said, "No. That's just for our setup team." When I asked if we could at least procure a couple of bottles of water, his answer was, "No. That case has to last our team for the whole conference." Hospitality had to be found a long walk away at the coin-op soda machine.
>
> And over the course of the week, there was more difficulty. The drama team was housed far from each other and far from the meeting site. There was never time to go back to our rooms, even for a quick nap. The small rehearsal space we used before the event was needed for other meetings—and without notice we found our scripts, props and other belongings stacked outside. There was literally nowhere to rehearse, nowhere even to gather for prayer. We had to circle up in public. Someone suggested we could rehearse in the hallway behind the stage. It turned out to be the garbage area for food services. We tried, but it was so dark and smelly, it proved useless. In the end, amazingly enough, the drama went beautifully, and people felt it was a resounding success. There were some really powerful moments. Yet afterward, we received fewer than five pieces of direct feedback, though they were all positive, from the church leaders and event organizers.

Drama is a new phenomenon in many Christian contexts. It's not something we've embraced, or even allowed, for very long in recent history. In every situation we can probably assume people want to be helpful and encouraging but in many instances don't know how. I'll outline some of the things that church leaders, staff workers, pastors, speakers and others can do to work well with a drama team and to help drama ministry grow strong.

HOW ART AND ARTISTS FUNCTION

Art does its best work when it is allowed to flourish, and when artists are allowed to flourish, in a community of trust. When artists are given space and told, "We believe you can help us by telling this story," they can evoke both life as we know it and life as it shall be in the kingdom's fullness. The invitation creates an opportunity for artists to engage.

Drama evokes what's unexplainable. Theater artists help us discover what's beyond our perception. Artists can get out on an intuitive edge, looking ahead to things which we find hard to describe but which we know are true and real. But this doesn't happen without nurture: artists must be raised up, discipled, trained. This is crucial because theater leads people, especially when it takes place in the context of gatherings and worship. In order to serve well, artists need to understand and be helped into the holiness and responsibility of their role.

ENCOURAGING ARTISTS AS LEADERS

Figuring out how to shape, encourage, challenge and bless artists is a challenge for leaders who work with them. Our investment in artists as followers of Jesus is the single most important way we build art and open space for artists. There are regular life issues with which artists, like anyone else, need help. Developing disciplines of prayer, Scripture study and character is key. Artists need some input about leadership too. They need help answering questions like, *As a performer, how do I think about being "up front"? What can I do to receive both criticism and praise without having either one topple my heart? Can I find courage to perform from a vulnerable place?* Drama team members need to work through many of the same questions as more typical

up-front leaders in a fellowship. But sometimes we don't consider this because they are not doing traditional leadership such as preaching. If you want to develop a good drama ministry—or any other arts ministry—disciple artists.

DISCIPLING ARTISTS

Art is not just about self-expression. In fact, one of our primary calls as artists is not to focus always on ourselves. However, performers in particular are actually taught to focus on themselves, to draw attention to themselves. They have been rewarded for this. They are good at it. They are often attractive, interesting people—it makes sense for others to direct attention their way. When you add to that the way our culture treats well-known actors and the way it exalts self-expression, you can see how quickly and easily performers can develop prima-actor complexes.

Drama teams need help developing the daily, human, outwardly focused sides of ministry: basic servanthood, communal experiences of hearing God in Scripture, love for the lost, intercessory prayer. It's good for performers to commit to regular, unglamorous service. Some of our team members did laundry for others in their dorms, tutored kids in urban after-school programs, made food for new students during finals weeks. Basic, hands-on work is good for the souls of those who deal most of the time in the abstraction of ideas. One team did several ministry projects together in order to learn ministry, experiencing great community and connection as a bonus. Pastors and other church leaders can model, and support drama teams in developing, this type of communal spirit.

Dramatists need help knowing and trusting that God really loves them. Many performers struggle with poor self-image—that is, with the notion that they should, by their own effort, power and talent, be able to do everything set before them, and do it right. Many artists wrestle with a perfectionism that tells them they'll never be adequate. These wrestling matches nearly always leave them less certain of their call, gifts and passion. Of course, we say, "You don't have to pull it together by yourself." But artists will still feel an obligation to make beautiful, useful art. You can help them come to know God's love and the freedom of the gospel on a deeper level. Most of us will soak encouragement right up because we don't often get it. (Of course, that was before we knew you, but knowing you're reading this book gives us hope!) And the good news is that regardless of our artistic performance, the God who thought of us and art and life considers us worth his life. Feel free to remind us.

Artists also need challenge. Think of it this way: leaders can support people, holding them up from behind. They also challenge people, urging them to greater things from the front. If the levels of support and challenge work on more or less equivalent terms, people are faced with new and sometimes difficult things to work through but also find the strength to face them. Challenge without support can leave people defeated; support without challenge creates stagnation. Artists need reassurance and encouragement; they also need to be urged on to more. People grow when others press on them. "Iron sharpens iron, so one person sharpens another" (Proverbs 27:17 RSV). Do not, for fear of hurting feelings, avoid telling dramatists the truth. They need to hear it. Remember when you were in junior high and your friend told you about the orange thing hanging off the end of your nose—after the dance was over? It's never happy to hear the truth way after the fact. Tell people what they need to know right away and while they have power to make adjustments.

TALKING TO GOD AND EACH OTHER

Drama teams need people to pray for them, to bring them before God. Consider developing a prayer team to work either just with the drama folks or perhaps with all your artists or worship leaders. A wise mentor once told me, "Get prayer before *and after* public ministry." Praying before seems obvious, and many of us have always done this. But afterward? Ah, she was right! It is often after performances that we feel most uncertain. Having exposed our deep inner selves to a roomful of people, performers (as well as preachers and worship leaders) often come away feeling raw, tired and shaky. It's tempting to regret every second that didn't go as planned, to second-guess every move we made or to gloat in our apparent success. But it's unfruitful and only leads to a kind of spinning self-defeat and poor self-image or inappropriate self-adulation. It is wise, indeed, to find some people who will agree to meet with the team before and immediately after a performance. Prayer can be brief, but you will see the effect of getting folks to God. Team members may also find deeper issues coming up as they work. Acting, particularly, taps into some vulnerable places in our hearts. Be on the lookout for people who need pastoral attention, prayer and encouragement.

Performers need feedback. That might sound completely obvious, but you'd be surprised how infrequently we hear much in response to our work. A church that wanted one of my sketches contacted me. I asked clearly, in writing, that they let me know how it went—that's how I learn to write better! I never heard another word. Even when I sent a second note asking about it, I got no response. Sometimes pastors and speakers are so focused on teaching, preaching and administration that they lose sight of art, even if they're enthusiastic about it. When drama is a newer component of ministry, people tend not to know how to evaluate it or what to say. Audiences sometimes love what they just saw but feel awkward letting an actor know they appreciated the performance. Fellowships need help learning how to speak encouragement, reflection and correction back to artists. Teach folks how to do this, and while they're learning, you can help your team by giving your feedback.

OFFERING SPACE
AND SUPPORT

For their temple project, Ezra and Israel received a decree from King Cyrus:

> Whatever is needed—young bulls, rams, male lambs for burnt offerings to the God of heaven, and wheat, salt, wine and oil, as requested by the priests in Jerusalem—must be given them daily without fail, so that they may offer sacrifices pleasing to the God of heaven. (Ezra 6:9-10)

Think of yourself personally or communally as King Cyrus.

Drama teams need several kinds of space in which to do their work. Physical space for rehearsals is an absolute necessity. The best situation is a room that can be set up for rehearsal and left undisturbed from week to week. Of course, this is not always possible. But if a team can use the same space for all its rehearsals, this is most efficient. Moving equipment from room to room, marking off a floor plan and reorienting everyone takes a bite out of already tight time. It's also important for rehearsal rooms to be closed to public wandering and visitor viewing. Teams need to be able to work where they feel safe trying things without pressure to perform. Finally, a rehearsal room must be relatively comfortable: adequately heated and cooled and well lit.

Your drama folks will also need access to the main staging area. If that's in a church, they'll need to get into the chancel. If it's a community room, they'll need to get inside ahead of time—perhaps even ahead of your regular setup. Sometimes drama teams, musical worship teams and speakers need to be in the same space around the same time—particularly right before the event. Work out a schedule and make sure people can set up their stage area, props, and whatever else is needed, in time to prevent last-minute panicking. If another group precedes yours in a public space, be sure you know what their

contract says about their departure time and ask them to stick to it. Your teams don't need the extra stress of negotiating with other groups and advocating for their own preparation time. This may sound like an unlikely collision—but it's happened to us more times than we can count. Whether it is you or another fellowship representative who negotiates such things, allocating space and time for preparation will be a tremendous service.

THINKING TOGETHER

A great deal of the team's experience in your fellowship will depend on how and how well you work together to integrate what they are doing with the overall program. One church I know gathered all its program staff—music director, drama director, pastors, children's directors and chief sexton—and worked through the entire schedule of presentation programs a quarter ahead (e.g., they brainstormed about September, October and November at their meeting in May). They brainstormed ideas for talks, art, special media and music for half a day. During the second half of the day, they secured the details for the immediate quarter (e.g., they worked out details for June, July and August at the May meeting). Set yourselves up to create a team atmosphere in which artists can receive meaningful input from, and give meaningful input to, the whole of the process. This will produce a much better end product and a much happier working relationship.

When a group of friends and I planted a church, we were most of the team. We talked constantly about possibilities in a sort of ongoing brainstorm. We also met formally with preachers to discuss worship plans, not quarterly but rather a couple of weeks ahead. As in our case, a smaller team can work more quickly and flexibly than a large one. Our situation dictated compact scheduling. Though in most cases having more planning time will help, you can improve your life together even with short meetings close to events, if that's what you have available.

The key is to talk things through, understand each other's hopes and expectations, and know together what you believe God is saying to you as leaders and ultimately to your congregation. Artists do much better when they can share their work with the confidence that it will be a meaningful part of what's going on and not simply an afterthought.

When a dramatic piece will be part of a worship service or other event, the planners must work to ensure the sketch will not be cut. Think of this as programmatic space we offer to the drama team. There is nothing so demoralizing as having worked hard to prepare a piece and being told at the last minute, "We'll have to do it next week." (Note: It's an equally bad experience for worship leaders to be told to cut songs. They have worked as hard as anyone else, including speakers, to prepare and, except in highly unusual circumstances, should be honored by having their offerings included as planned.)

Leaders and planners must also work hard to communicate to the team what the talk and/or other presentations are focused on, so that what the team does enhances the overall communication. To do a sketch followed by a speaker who makes no use of the sketch leaves the audience puzzled and the drama team wondering if it has wasted its time. The preacher doesn't have to mention the sketch—under no circumstances should he attempt to explain it—but a dominant image or a quote from one of the characters might be woven into a talk, or the mood or theme might be developed. Art not only enriches communication; it shapes it. There are lots of "sermon-booster skits" out there, but that's not primarily what we're talking about here. Even if a preacher has a definite angle and approach to a passage, artists may be able through their process to elucidate it—that is, if they have access to the conversation and space to suggest.

PROVIDING FUNDING

Finally, artists need space in your fellowship's budget. A drama team should have some rehearsal boxes, music stands, stools and lights. These basics will make it possible to rehearse. But you should also consider making money available for

◆ purchase of scripts

◆ purchase of educational books and subscriptions

◆ trips to see professionally produced plays

◆ trips to visit other churches and ministries

◆ professional training, including voice lessons, acting and directing classes

◆ purchase of props and costumes

◆ purchase of lighting and sound equipment

◆ pay or honorarium for someone who is leading a very active drama team (In other words, consider making it a job for someone.)

Understanding what artists do and how they do it will help you work well with them. If you know how their process works, you'll be able to make important connections at key moments along the way. The right words well placed can make a ministry soar; the wrong words or no words at all keep the jets grounded. Spend time with the team. Get to know individuals. Watch them work. Find ways to express affirmation, encouragement and challenge. And watch as things really take off.

PART 2
WHAT ISN'T DRAMA?

A conversation with Jason Gaboury, Bruce Kuhn, Daniel Jones, Lisa Harper, Scott Brill, Nina Thiel, Alison Siewert and Susi Jensen

Jason: What isn't drama? Propaganda. Attempts to emotionally manipulate an audience. Lectures.

Bruce: So much of the "Christian drama" I have seen is dull: propaganda in story form. The story is only the message bearer.

Daniel: Drama is not art when it belittles reality and ties things up in neat little packages. It shouldn't preach or attempt to manipulate.

Jason: Yes. Drama shouldn't try to preach a sermon. One of the things that drama does well is bring up the complexity of life . . . so it shouldn't be used to try to over-simplify situations.

Lisa: When a drama is preachy, it weighs the action of the play down and prevents the most beautiful moments from surfacing. I saw a Christian production once that was hard to watch. In theater we get to know and care for the character through what she does to get over her obstacles to get what she wants. *This* character preached at and tried to convert his non-Christian friend through the whole play. He flawlessly endured persecution, then judged others who weren't as strong as he. So, what did we learn about the character? He's preachy, self-righteous and comes off pretty arrogant . . . he wasn't likeable.

Daniel: I watched a sketch at a conference about dealing with conflict. Aside from the fact that it was waaay cheezy, it also tried to be a sermon. We got to watch the man hide something from his friends, then have it exposed, then have a fight about it, then have everyone say, "That's okay, we still love you" in the end. It was sort of like, "The Five Steps to Conflict Resolution" in skit form. And, of course, nobody is going to walk out of that room and have conflict the way the sketch presented it.

Scott: Drama fails when it becomes a "tool"—when there's nothing of the artists' or audience's soul involved.

Nina: Yes, drama wants to say something— but it's the saying it that matters, not the focus on a specific outcome in the audience (e.g., everyone signing up).

Scott: I hate drama that I think is trying to influence me toward some preplanned action: "Watch this dialogue. Now invite Jesus into your heart." As though I can't be trusted enough to be truly emotionally engaged by what I see and therefore need a sort of prepackaged set of emotional responses.

Nina: That seems more mercenary and manipulative to me than I believe drama is or should be.

Alison: It uses the audience.

Jason: To leave the audience out of the relationship so that an actor can vent a lot of emotion may feel good for the actor, but it's abusing drama.

Daniel: It is one thing for the author of a play or sketch to demonstrate what he or she would do, but if the sketch preaches, then the audience isn't left with anything to discuss. When the audience is shown how to respond, they are cut off from taking ownership. We need to let the drama seep in and swirl around them, and then they can respond.

Nina: There are commercials I would consider drama—"This is your brain on drugs . . . and this is your family, relationships . . ."—but most are just commercials designed to get us to buy stuff, even the Kodak commercials. What's the difference? The first is sort of a performance art picture of how things really are. The second are moments choreographed to get a specific audience response rather than to tell a true story. I still cry during Kodak commercials, but I know I'm being manipulated. The fact that we joke about it (Kodak moment, anyone?) means we know exactly what the writers were after.

Scott: If the writers were trying to get something from us, then it's bad drama. Bad drama denies the mystery of God and our souls; good drama invites us into that mystery.

Susi: Drama isn't spectacle. Public gags, extravagant art and special effects on stage do not constitute drama. Story is essential to drama. Drama isn't private. Drama takes private thoughts and feelings and puts them on the public stage. Drama is a form of proclamation.

Alison: Sometimes it seems like drama isn't always bad but, rather, badly used. And sometimes both. It's critical that we know what we are hoping the drama will do in the context. Is it telling a story, straight up? Is it pointing at something prophetically? Is it making Scripture accessible? That affects what and how we write.

Nina: There are also just plain badly written sketches and shows—superficial, going for the easy connection or communicating what could easily be said in a sentence: "Jesus died for my sins," or, "Life is meaningless." These are deep concepts but often communicated quite superficially in our churches and even onstage. Most people aren't gripped or provoked by that sort of drama.

Bruce: Are you sketching out a quick cartoon for a family joke? Then much is forgiven and more is not needed. Are you trying to get a stranger's heart with an art form? Don't embarrass yourself with quick and shoddy work, and don't be gulled by the compliments of friends.

Jason: Exactly. Often, well-meaning Christians ill conceive drama. They desire to illustrate biblical truth and use a combination of different theatrical techniques (most often a combination of allegory and melodrama) to try to illustrate a point or emotionally stir an audience. As an audience member, I am left guessing, *Am I watching an allegory (a very complicated thing to do well theatrically) or a melodrama? Is this behavior symbolic? Is it supposed to be real? Who are these characters? Why are they wearing signs? Is this hokey? Am I supposed to laugh? Cry?*

Alison: I've heard plenty of talky stuff, where the sketch is supposed to explain the entirety of the gospel or missions or a person's life. But life is just not like that. None of us talks our way through—we *do*. We act. Bad drama is often bad because it says too much.

Susi: Although the words *are* important. I enjoy going to the Museum of Modern Art and looking at static art pieces, but if I go to see a drama, I expect words. That doesn't mean it must be lots of words. It does mean that the drama onstage hangs together by a story.

Lisa: If I'm writing a play, it's not meant to be read. It's meant to be seen and experienced.

Alison: So our hope for drama is to have it taken in through the experience rather than just the hearing. But both what we see and what we hear is crucial. That has application for every aspect of communicating the gospel to postmoderns, doesn't it?

Susi: Actually, the traditional Mass comes close to postmodern hearts, with the experience of taking the Eucharist as the climax of the worship service. I believe drama also can be this climax. Good drama can take the sermon to a higher plane. This is not to say that the sermon isn't important. It is to say that the Word becoming flesh before the eyes of the audience will have more impact than three points of application.

Alison: So the key is *experiencing* the hearing rather than simply hearing *from* the drama. Words are important—but it's much more than words. Words have a job to do.

Lisa: The minute characters launch into long speeches explaining the past and how they got to this current place, they stop the action of the play. Action moves drama. Exposition stops it. When I say "action," I don't mean action as we see it in action movies. I mean what the characters do to get what they want. So, you only want to include necessary exposition. Sketches that try to preach say too much and miss the movement of the story.

Jason: Once I saw a play that was "semi-autobiographical" put together for an outreach. In this particular case, the woman who wrote the play was also starring in it as the main character. Two-thirds of the way into the play the woman was crying and screaming and ranting about how bad her life was. At the point that the woman was the most emotionally intense, much of the audience left. Or sat awkwardly waiting for this part to be done. Why? Because she was abusing drama. The drama seemed to serve her need to vent a lot of emotion, but it didn't invite the audience into discovering some truth.

Daniel: It's kind of like Jesus telling parables. Jesus doesn't just lay it out there for all the world to see. He keeps things hidden so that they can be found. So that people take ownership by seeking and finding. That is the response we should be hoping for.

Alison: It's not dramatic to spill all the info right from the start. People stay in their seats because they expect something still to come. Yakking everything from the stage from the beginning leaves the audience no reason to keep listening. And it overexplains realities that can't be explained—and, in fact, are misrepresented by explanation.

Daniel: You often have a character in the play that functions as the mouthpiece for the playwright. But that only works when it is not forced on the audience. It's usually pretty clear, in most good drama, where the author stands, but then the author trusts his or her audience to come to some of their own conclusions.

Alison: Perhaps our problem is that it's hard to let go and allow people to draw their own conclusions. Maybe in the church we've exerted ourselves toward controlling things—so we can have orthodoxy with the outcome we want and the gospel preached just so. I mean, not that we'd want it preached sloppily—but maybe we've thought God to be less able than he is to ensure the right outcome of communication. I mean, people's hearts are God's, not ours, to shape. Our job is to tell the truth the best we can.

Scott: I've seen a good bit of drama that I think would be better classified as propaganda shows—sort of a Christianized version of why we are all happy on the collective farm. It strikes me as a somewhat ironic attempt at maintaining some of those controls.

Jason: Seeing bad Christian drama and hearing suspicion of non-Christian theater from other believers caused some serious problems for me. I felt like in order to do good art, I needed to be outside the church, but in order to be connected at church, I needed to stay away from the theater. The false dichotomy between good theater and the church caused me to resent both communities and feel out of sorts. When drama is abused or ill-conceived, I get frustrated and angry. Others I know have become suspicious of using drama in church.

Daniel: Yes. And when bad art gets produced, it strengthens people's assumptions that all art done by Christians will be bad. I've experienced the difficulty of walking into a performance and having it assumed that it is going to be bad because I am Christian and what I am performing has the label of Christian theater slapped on it. Christians have the best story to tell, but we haven't yet learned how to tell it well.

RESOURCES FOR DRAMA TEAMS

RESOURCES FOR DRAMA TEAMS

SCRIPTS AND SITES

1. Write your own.
2. Read this book.
3. Find *Drama Team Sketchbook*, a companion to this volume.
4. Curt Cloninger, a veteran—and very good—solo performer, has two books of scripts for worship available on his website: <www.curtcloninger.com>.
5. *Image Journal* publishes scripts and interviews with writers, actors and other artists. You can visit their site at <www.imagejournal.org>.
6. There is a massive number of websites, including <www.willowcreek.org>, <www.mustardworks.org>, <www.ridinglights.org> and <www.cita.org> (Christians in Theater Arts), offering training, journals, scripts and other materials for free and for purchase. But remember, it's a wildly mixed bag o'quality out there, so for scripts, consider number 1 above.

A FEW GOOD BOOKS

Some are Christian, some are academic; we've found them all useful.

On Directing

Ball, William. *A Sense of Direction.* New York: Drama Publishers, 1984.

Bogart, Anne. *A Director Prepares.* New York: Routledge, 2001.

Dean, Alexander, and Lawrence Carra. *Fundamentals of Play Directing.* 5th edition. Orlando: Holt, Rinehart & Winston, 1989.

On Acting

Bruder, Melissa, et al. *A Practical Handbook for the Actor.* New York: Vintage, 1986.

Hagen, Uta, with Haskel Frankel. *Respect for Acting.* New York: Macmillan, 1973.

Morton, Craig, and Ken Hawkley. *Word of Mouth.* Scottsdale, Penn.: Herald, 2000. Includes readers' theater scripts.

On Writing

Buechner, Frederick. *Telling the Truth: The Gospel as Tragedy, Comedy, and Fairy Tale.* New York: Harper & Row, 1977.

McKee, Robert. *Story, Substance, Structure, Style, and the Principles of Screenwriting.* New York: Regan Books, 1997.

On Putting Things Together

Dyrness, William A. *Visual Faith: Art, Theology, and Worship in Dialogue.* Grand Rapids: Baker Academic, 2001.

Siewert, Alison, et al. *Worship Team Handbook.* Downers Grove, Ill.: InterVarsity Press, 1998. Includes scripts.

SCRIPTS FOR DRAMA TEAMS

WORD

Alison Siewert

I wrote this sketch for an event that focused on Scripture study. As I worked on it, it occurred to me that the Hebrews talked directly about God's Word all the time and delighted in it. But I couldn't think of many contemporary ways we deal directly with delight in the Word. So . . . the language in this sketch is meant to be enjoyable, to go quickly and lightly.

CAST OF CHARACTERS

Player 1, Player 2

Two actors speak—each one treats his or her lines as a contiguous thought, a stand-alone unit; but the two voices are timed so as to allow for space and overlap, so that both may be heard in interplay, as one elucidates the other. Toward the end (the last 14 lines) the two players take on clear rhythm. Keep the pace up and have fun.

PLAYER 1	PLAYER 2
Word	
	What word?
The word	
	Word what—
Say "word"	
	[smarmy accent] The Holy Bible
Let's talk	
	God talked
Write it down	
	People wrote
Every word	
	What they got

Heard a word

        Lots of words

How many

        They described

In there?

        What they got

When things happened

        God talked

Stuff happened

        God acted

Heard a word

        Like a story

Saw a word

        (as movie title) *The Epic Adventure of God and People*

It was real, though

        God's thing

It went down

        People saw

Some days I wonder

        People listened

What's in that book?

        I wonder

In that book—

What was it like to hear God talk?

Yeah, what's in there?

How did they know it was him?

I dunno

I guess they knew . . .

Stuff really happened

People wrote

God laughing

Not knowing, of course

God shouting

That their words

And whispering

Words became huge

Whisper and shout and in the middle

Words turned into—

God said stuff

—Life

Life happened

God talked

Stuff happened

So now I wanna know

Just imagine

What's in that book?

What's in that book

> *[evangelist accent]* In the Bible

A lot of words

> *[smarmy accent]* In the Scripture

How many?

> I wanna know

I dunno

> Tell me everything

A very large number

> Can someone please explain this to me?

Loads o'words, stuff God did

> I wanna know

You gotta know

> What it was

What people hear

> What it's like

What God said

> What's in there

What you hear

> 'Cause the Word

It talks

> When God picks up a voice

He talks

                        Right here

Here—well, there

                        In the middle of people

There in their language

                        Like a local

God picked up on the dialect

                        He says stuff

And told them a little about himself

                        Says a lot of stuff

So they could

                        Very funny, sometimes

Get an idea about God

                        Like once he talked through an ass

Get a picture of God

                        And one time he explained stuff from a little shrub

Get an idea about God

                        And then, this once, God showed a guy his behind only

Get an idea about God

                        And that deal, where he did little wheelies in the air

What an idea about God

                        God talks a lot

God's idea about God

                        In that book, God says stuff

For one, he said, they could

        That's one thing, when you listen

Get to know him

        Listen up if you want to

Find out what's up

        Listen up if you want

It's the Word

        Take it in

Like a local

        Soak it up

'Cause God picks up a voice

        Pay attention

Wraps words in voice

        Cause it's everything

Has a beautiful voice

        All your ears ever hoped for

Sometimes he sings it

        Your ears get full

In our dialect

        (together with Player 1) And the rhythm kicks in

(together with Player 2) . . . rhythm kicks in

        [next twelve lines in rhythm] God tells

[in rhythm] Like a local

What he's like

Listen up

What word

It's the Scripture

That word

It's the Bible

In there

God talks

That book

Listen up

What's up?

Take it in

God's up

Think it over

God's voice

God talked

Voice box

God talks

Voice book

In our voice

In a guy

Like a local

God picked up sound

In our dialect

> We can hear him

(slower) Can you feel God's voice?

> > *(slower)* And it's in that book

The end.

SKETCHIMONY

Micah Trippe and Chris Hull

Here's a prime example of using a sketch to make an announcement. It stays light but also communicates a lot of information in a short time because the lines get traded quickly. A 'Mark Study' is an intensive inductive Bible study of Mark's Gospel. Use this as a model for writing your own announcements.

CAST OF CHARACTERS

Micah, Chris

CHRIS: Hi, I'm Chris.

MICAH: And I'm Micah.

CHRIS: And together we are

MICAH & CHRIS *[together]*: Two white junior men.

CHRIS: Two years ago we embarked

MICAH: On what some might call

CHRIS: The never-ending story

MICAH: Others have called it

CHRIS: Mark Study

MICAH: Why, Chris, whatever is that?

CHRIS: Why, it's the story of a man who changed the world. A story full of

MICAH: Violence

CHRIS: Madness

MICAH: Racism

CHRIS: Passion

MICAH: Suffering

CHRIS: Elation

MICAH: Fear

CHRIS: Intrigue

MICAH: Danger

CHRIS: Betrayal

MICAH: Murder

CHRIS: Hope

MICAH: Rescue

CHRIS: Restoration

MICAH: Joy

CHRIS: Tears

MICAH: Despair

CHRIS: Conviction

MICAH: Healing

CHRIS: Miracles

MICAH: Risk

CHRIS: Curiosity

MICAH: Power

CHRIS: Hypocrisy

MICAH: Evil

CHRIS: Death

MICAH: Resurrection

CHRIS: Wow, Micah; that sounds better than *The Godfather*.

MICAH: Yeah, it's better than *Gladiator*.

CHRIS: Yeah . . . it's better than the World Series.

MICAH: It's better than the Super Bowl.

CHRIS: It's better than the Oscars.

MICAH: It's better than an A on a midterm.

CHRIS: It's better than writing a paper.

MICAH: It's better than a road trip.

CHRIS: It's better than a weekend at home.

MICAH: Man, I'm going. You going?

CHRIS: Yeah, I'm going.

MICAH: All right.

CHRIS: Well, Micah, we should really go.

MICAH: Later, Chris.

THE DREAM

Lisa Harper

This sketch was written for a gathering of African American college students. The text could be adapted to a different ethnic culture and situation.

CAST OF CHARACTERS

Jerry, Tina

Lines are interwoven, sometimes spoken spontaneously, as each character shares. They only turn toward each other as noted. And yes, the actor playing Tina really did shave her head.

JERRY	TINA
I saw this movie, man.	I saw this movie with my boyfriend.
Tina really wanted me to see it. Yeah, yeah, yeah. I know. Don't ever let your girl drag you to—	
	Real Women Have Curves He fell asleep.
I fell asleep.	
	I couldn't believe that girl. I mean she was . . .
So, I see this fat girl walkin' down the street in the first scene, and I'm thinkin', "She ain't curvy. She fat! Give me J. Lo!"	
	But she was confident. She didn't take no crap from no one! I wish I could be like that! *[TINA looks at JERRY.]*
See J. Lo. She got that voice and that attitude and that . . . that body—*that's a real woman*—Blam!	
	He doesn't think I notice when I see him lookin' at other girls. We'll be walkin' down the street, I'll be talkin' to him about . . . whatever, and his head is turnin' like it's a radar.

I can't help it. I mean curves get me . . .

[Her head turns like a radar.] Oo oo oo . . . oo oo oo.

J. Lo gets me. See I like it when my girl Tina dresses in those tight dresses and her booty be all like . . . *Bling!* You get me?

He's a mystery to me. You know, I mean we can have the deepest conversations — I mean about our dreams and the world and politics — and he looks me in the eyes when we talk. And there's this connection, you know? And I know I want to be with him, nobody else but him . . . and then he goes oo oo oo walkin' down the street. I don't get it.

You get me?

So I started studying the girls who catch his attention . . . and I started dressin' like them in the tight dresses! I had to buy a dress two sizes too big and have my mom take in the top to get my butt into one of those deals! And I got a weave . . . I mean ain't no straight hair coming out of this head! But you know the only thing is I've been permin' my hair for so long I don't even know what it's really like. . . . And I'm afraid to find out.

Long hair . . .

Skin like honey . . .

And I got some of that Porcelana fade cream stuff too . . . I mean . . . if you can't beat 'em, join 'em . . . but I couldn't do it, girl. I opened the jar and stuck my fingers in, and it hit me . . . I'm about to burn my skin. I'm about to burn off my blackness.

My mom gets on me some time about the pictures I have hangin' in my dorm room. I mean I tell 'er it ain't no thang. Ever guy in the place has the same honeys hangin' on their playpen walls. *[JERRY indicates where his "honeys" hang on the imaginary wall — surrounding him.]* I mean we got Georgette and Charlize and Tamika. Gotta give 'em some love, ya know?! Hey!

I was about to burn my soul . . .

But you know I was talking with Tina a couple of nights ago. We were talkin' about how wacked out the world is that justice doesn't mean anything anymore . . .

And then she's forming the word "justice" when in my mind it was like the Tina I knew just burned away and in my mind's eye. Tina was like one of the honeys on my wall.

That was it.

That was it.

I saw it like a flash, you know? I'm turnin' into the one person in this world I don't want nothin' to do with — my father! He's a playa, you know? Goes from one woman to the next . . . never there for us. *[deliberately]* I don't want to be like him. *[pause]* It's just all this pressure, you know? I mean, in music videos and magazines all I see is guys lookin' at women like they're nothin' but accessories. I mean here comes *[NAME A CURRENT MALE RAP STAR]* rollin' up. He slides outta his ride and here come his two honeys. One on each arm . . . And now I'm lookin' at Tina like she's . . . nothin' but an accessory. I mean either I see Tina as just a body, or I see her as a body . . . with a soul. And if I see her with a soul . . .

I was about to burn my soul . . .

Then I have to look at mine . . .

And it's no good.
It scared me

It's no good.

I don't want this anymore!

I mean what am I really lookin' for? Do I really want an accessory? No . . . I want Tina . . . I want a wife . . . I want to be a father . . . I want to raise a family . . . I want God. . . . And I want to be a man of God.

I'm tired of jumping through hoops to be loved. I'm tired of paying $200 for hair that ain't even mine. I want to stand up like the girl in *Real Women Have Curves* and yell at the world, "This is me! Take it or leave it! I don't care!" I want Jerry, but not at the expense of myself!

But I never felt so far from God. It's like I know what I want and I see all the lies, but I'm stuck.

I had a dream last night. I dreamt that all the women on TV looked like me. And they all had skin like mine . . . and noses like mine . . . And I couldn't believe it. *Friends* was black! *ER* was about a black hospital! *The Practice* was about a black law firm! And the world was black like me! And black was beautiful!

And my shape was beautiful!

And my hair was beautiful! . . . My hair like wool . . . like Jesus' own hair . . . was beautiful.

But my heart is saying, "God, help."

And he does . . .

Then I woke up. And I looked in the mirror and I saw my weave.

He says [*JERRY sings the chorus of "I Am the Lord, Your Healer"*]

And I got my scissors.

Ahhhh . . .

And I cut it all off. All of it!
[*TINA takes off her hat and throws it to the ground.*]
The weave and the perm.

I feel clean.

[*TINA doesn't see JERRY at first, but then realizes he is looking at her. TINA turns to face him.*]

[*JERRY turns and sees TINA. He realizes how much he loves her.*]

[*honestly, gently*] I love you.

[*Lights fades to black.*]

MARY
A MONOLOGUE ON LUKE 1:26-56

Alison Siewert

CAST OF CHARACTERS

Mary

MARY, a very young woman, sits, pregnant and showing, to talk with an unseen hearer.

MARY [*as though talking to a supportive counselor*]: It's . . . it's been really hard around home. I mean, my parents are great and everything but this . . . they're having a hard time. I mean, they don't believe me. They think I must have gotten drunk or whatever and like blew it with some guy. But I didn't. It wasn't like that. I was walking back from my cousin's house . . . and this, [*pausing, uncomfortable, trying to find a word*] this, this wind—I mean, I guess it was like a wind. I don't know what to call it. This wind hit me right here [*touching her right cheek*]. It was warm, and . . . and I just kind of . . . I knew. I knew it was something. And it blew around me—the wind—and then I just felt like I was supposed to kneel down, like it was God. And it was . . . [*pausing, then quietly continuing*] God.

He asked me, he asked me if I would do it, if I would carry the baby, if I could carry the baby to term and not get scared and back out and . . . [*pause*]

[*taking a deep breath*] So I said, "Yes . . . okay. I will."

That was the beginning of . . . things being hard. I felt kind of sick, but I couldn't tell anyone, so I had to, you know . . . I mean, I had to pretend everything was normal. And my fiancé, Joey, he was really nice because he thought I had like, mono or something, I was so tired. But then . . . [*pause*] . . . then I started, you know, showing, looking like I was gaining weight, and then all of a sudden it's huge, my middle is huge. And everyone's talking. And Joey—everyone thinks he's such a nice guy, and his dad's a pastor, so they believed him when he said, "Hey, it wasn't me." But they didn't believe what I said . . . "Who'd she—?" "Whose baby?" "Why did she go an' blow such a nice engagement? Think of how her parents must feel." "That Joey's such a sweet boy and she's just a tramp."

A couple of nights ago—maybe it was last night, I can't remember—Joey came over while I was in class and talked to my mom and dad . . . Then when I got home, they all told me to sit down and they told me the wedding was off. My mom made this big show of taking the dress—the wedding dress she made me, and putting it away in a bag. My dad said how they were so disappointed in me, and how they hoped I'd figure out a way to make something better of myself, and how sad it was for me to lose such a nice man like Joey.

And then Joey left, without even talking to me . . . *[pause]* He just walked away, down the street, and didn't say anything. Not even goodbye.

So . . . now it's just me and . . . the baby.

I'm moving out this weekend—I think to my aunt Liz's, a couple of towns over, where people don't know me.

[pause]

[touching her cheek] That wind—did you feel that, just now? *[looking above the crowd]*

Music begins quietly. MARY stands and dances a little, turning . . . then stops, looks out, reflecting. As song continues, she sits, backlit in shadows.

Lights fade to black.

SHALOM LIKE JAZZ
A MONOLOGUE

Jess Delegencia

Biblical peace, what we call shalom, is like jazz
Complex, multi-layered, hard to pin down
A beautiful dissonance, perfect imperfections
That bring about the wholeness
The wonderful totality
That is shalom, or jazz

Shalom is wholeness
Of a collective that goes beyond just two parts
It's encountered, affirmed, experienced
Between every player and every group
Like the perfect groove of everyone's improvisation

Shalom is revelation
When the totality of existence is whole
Like rhythm without melody
And melody without rhythm
Like jazz without the blues

Shalom is not the opposite of war
Though war is the monster that attacks shalom
Jazz is not the opposite of classical music
Though classical music is the prison of a jazz musician

Shalom is health
Order amidst disorder
Now winning the past
Like a Negro spiritual
In the midst of slavery

Shalom is the future
Hope of things meant to be
Like the highest hallelujah of a gospel choir
It takes you there
Shalom is real peace
An experience of heaven
The best jazz Miles ever heard

HEBREWS 11
PRETTY MUCH THE WHOLE THING

For Five Readers
Arranged by Alison Siewert

Here's an example of straight-out Scripture as script. This is a collage-style piece that's easier than a full-on collage: a good starting point with enough challenge to get a team moving, but not an overwhelming task.

CAST OF CHARACTERS

Reader 1, Reader 2, Reader 3, Reader 4, Reader 5

This may be read from one location or with readers scattered around the congregation. It must be read as a story and with life in it, or it will be deadly boring.

READER 1:   Now faith is the assurance of things hoped for, the conviction of things not seen.

READER 2:   By faith people in the past gained God's approval.

READER 3:   By faith we understand that the worlds were prepared by the Word of God, so that what is seen was made out of nothing, by God's Word alone.

READER 4:   By faith Abel offered to God a better sacrifice than Cain, and God testified that Abel was righteous. Through faith, though he is dead, Abel still speaks.

READER 5:   By faith Enoch was taken up so that he did not see death; for God confirmed before he was taken up that he was pleasing to God.

READER 2:   And without faith it is impossible to please God, for the one who comes to God must believe that God is and that he is a rewarder of those who seek him.

READER 3:   By faith Noah, being warned by God about things not yet seen, prepared an ark for the salvation of his household, and became an heir of the righteousness that comes from faith.

READER 4:   By faith Abraham, when he was called, obeyed by going out to a place he was to receive for an inheritance; and he went out, not knowing where he was going. By faith he lived as a foreigner in the land of promise, living in tents with Isaac and Jacob; for he was looking for the city that has foundations, whose architect and builder is God.

READER 5:   By faith even Sarah received the ability to conceive a child, even as an old woman, because she had considered the God who had promised her to be faithful.

READER 4:   So from a man so old he was practically dead, and his equally ancient wife, were born as many descendants as the stars of heaven and the grains of sand at the shore.

READER 1:   All these people died in faith, without receiving the promises, but seeing and welcoming them from a distance, and openly admitting that they were strangers and exiles here on earth.

READER 3:   People who believe and talk about these sorts of promises make it clear they are seeking a country of their own. If they had been hoping for their home country, they could have turned around and gone back . . .

READER 1:   But they desired a better country, that is a heavenly one. So God is not ashamed to be called their God—

READER 3:   —he has prepared a city for them.

READER 4:   By faith Abraham, when he was tested, offered up Isaac. He considered that God is able to raise people even from death—and he received him back as a foreshadow.

READER 5:   By faith Isaac blessed Jacob and Esau about the things to come.

READER 3:   By faith Joseph foretold the exodus of Israel out of Egypt.

READER 4:   By faith Moses' parents hid him; and by faith, Moses, when he was grown up, refused to be called the son of the Pharaoh's daughter, choosing rather to endure ill treatment with the people of God than to enjoy the passing pleasures of sin; considering the reproach of the Messiah greater riches than the treasures of Egypt; for he was looking to the reward.

READER 5:   By faith the walls of Jericho fell down after they had been encircled for seven days.

READER 3:   By faith Rahab the harlot didn't perish along with those who were disobedient, after she had welcomed the spies in peace.

READER 2:   And what more shall we say? For time will fail us if we tell of Gideon, Barak, . . .

READER 3:   Samson, Jephthah . . .

READER 1:   . . . of David and Samuel . . .

READER 3:   . . . and the prophets, who by faith conquered kingdoms, performed acts of righteousness . . .

READER 2:   . . . obtained promises, and shut the mouths of lions . . .

READER 1:   . . . quenched the power of fire, escaped the edge of the sword . . .

READER 3:   . . . From weakness they were made strong, and became mighty in war, and put foreign armies to flight.

READER 5:   Women received back their dead by resurrection, and others were tortured, and others experienced mocking and scourging, yes, also chains and imprisonment.

READER 3:   They were stoned, they were sawn in two, they were tempted, they were put to death with the sword . . .

READER 2:   . . . they went about in sheepskins, they were destitute, afflicted, badly treated—people of whom the world was not worthy—wandering in deserts and caves and mountains.

READER 4:   And all these, having gained approval through their faith, did not receive what was promised during their earthly lifetimes, because God had provided something better for us, so that apart from us they should not yet be made perfect.

[READERS 2, 3, 4, & 5 speak in simultaneous layers with READER 1 here.]

READER 1   *[slowly]:* Therefore, since we have so great a cloud of witnesses surrounding us, let us also lay aside every sin which so easily entangles us, and let us run with endurance the race that is set before us, fixing our eyes on Jesus: the author and perfecter of our faith, who for the joy set before him, endured the cross, despising the shame, and has sat down at the right hand of the throne of God.

READER 2:   Cloud, cloud, great cloud . . .

    READER 3: We have a cloud of witnesses . . .

        READER 4: Abel, Enoch, Abel, Enoch . . .

            READER 5:   Noah made an ark for salvation.

READER 2:   Abraham, Sarah, descendants as the stars of heaven in number, innumerable as the sand by the seas.

    READER 3: A cloud of witnesses, great cloud, a cloud of witnesses . . .

        READER 4: Isaac and Jacob and Joseph and Moses . . .

            READER 5: Rahab trusted God.

READER 2:   We have a great cloud of witnesses surrounding us.

    READER 3: Gideon, Barak, Samson, Jephthath, David, Samuel . . .

        READER 4: The women, the martyrs, the women, the martyrs . . .

            READER 5: In prisons and goatskins, in caves and holes, in deserts and graves.

READER 2: We have so great a cloud of witnesses surrounding us.

    READER 3: We have a cloud surrounding us, witnesses.

        READER 4: Jesus, author and perfecter of our faith.

            READER 5: Surrounding us, a cloud.

READER 1: We have so great a cloud of witnesses surrounding us . . .

READER 2: Surround.

    READER 3: Witnesses surrounding.

        READER 4: Surround.

            READER 5: *[sotto voce]* Surround.

BIRTHDAY BREATH

Jenny Vaughn Hall

Here's a slice-of-life piece. You might use this for a retreat about relationships, grace or being real with one another.

CAST OF CHARACTERS

TANI, a young woman; STEVE, her boyfriend

[TANI walks into the room, lights the candles and straightens everything out.]

TANI: OK, come in.

[STEVE opens the door and comes in].

STEVE: Oh, wow. Oh Tani, this is great.

TANI: I know it's my birthday and you're technically supposed to do stuff for me, but I just thought we could end our night like this. *[hesitant]* I—Do you want to dance?

STEVE: Sure.

TANI: I burned a couple of songs onto a CD. *[Music begins. They slowly start to dance. She looks at him as she speaks.]* I wanted to do something kind of romantic. I've always loved this song. Have you ever heard it? *[He shakes his head]* No? Really? It's totally a classic. *[She begins to sing part of the song "The Way You Look Tonight."]* There is nothing for me but to love you. *[Their faces are close; she is looking right into his eyes. STEVE is trying hard not to look uncomfortable.]* Are you OK?

STEVE: Yeah, yeah, this is great, I mean—

TANI: Are you sure?

STEVE: Well, I don't know. Can we take a little time-out on the dancing?

TANI: OK.

[They sit.]

STEVE: I'm just not that great a dancer and—

TANI: Steve, I don't care. I just thought we'd have fun.

STEVE: Right, right, I know. It's really sweet of you, the candles, the wine, I just—

TANI: Just what?

STEVE: The thing is Tani, I have this . . . you know what, never mind, it's stupid.

TANI: No, go ahead.

STEVE: Well, when I was a kid my mom would always wake me up in the morning for school.

TANI: *[confused]* OK.

STEVE: She would wake me up before she brushed her teeth, and she had this awful . . . really bad morning breath. *[remembering]* Ohwww. It was painful.

TANI: So, what exactly does that have to do with us?

STEVE: Well, while we were dancing and you were singing, and we were just really close up and . . .

TANI: Are you saying I have bad breath?

STEVE: Well, yeah. I mean, I'm sorry. I wish it didn't bother me, but it was just . . . kinda . . . stale.

TANI: I don't know what to say. Ummm . . . sorry, I brushed my teeth. I didn't think it was that bad.

STEVE: Yeah, Tani, it's just me. I have a sensitive nose . . . it's me. OK, I know I gotta get over it. *[pause]* It's stupid, I'm being a jerk. I know I gotta get over it. Forget it, let's keep dancing; let's keep dancing.

[He stands up and offers his hand to her. She is hurt, but she takes his hand and they start dancing again. As she is talking, he still can't handle the breath. He goes over her shoulder to take a breath and holds it while he faces her. He tries to be subtle but it's loud.]

TANI: *[doesn't notice yet; she awkwardly tries to make conversation]* The House of Blues was really cool. Had you ever been there before?

[STEVE is holding his breath and gives a muffled "Yeah."]

TANI: Oh you have? You know who would really love it?

[STEVE gives another muffled "No." TANI notices.]

TANI: What . . . what are you doing?

STEVE: Nothing, nothing. *[He tries to hold her close. She breaks away.]*

TANI: Oh! What are you doing? Steve, you are seriously messed up. I can't believe you. It's my birthday. My birthday. Thanks. Happy 25th Tani, your breath smells like—

STEVE: —I know, I know . . . I was hoping you wouldn't notice.

TANI: Wouldn't notice that my boyfriend sounds like Darth Vader?

STEVE: I'm sorry, I am. I just have this breath thing. Don't take it personally.

TANI: How could I not take it personally?

STEVE: But Tani, you've just gotta know that I really am into you. I am. I mean, I think you're great; you look great, beautiful. It's just kind of a turnoff to have you singing and breathing and—

TANI: Oh, I'm sorry for breathing. I'll really try to work on that.

STEVE: That's not what I meant.

TANI: I think we should just call it a night.

STEVE: But I didn't give you your present yet.

TANI: Why don't you just throw it to me so you don't catch my halitosis?

STEVE: *[chuckles despite himself]* Tani, don't say that. I'm sorry. I feel like a complete jerk.

TANI: Good. You are being a jerk.

STEVE: I'm sorry. I am. I wish I wouldn't have said anything.

TANI: Yeah, well, I wish I wouldn't have done anything.

STEVE: What do you mean?

TANI: I mean I wish I wouldn't have done any of this. The candles, the stupid music, the singing. *[long sigh]* I've wanted to do something like this for so long. I've never had a boyfriend before.

STEVE: I know, I know. And then I have to go and talk about your—

TANI: Please don't. Don't say that again. *[pause]* I just feel like I'm putting myself out there, y'know? It's like I'm daring to be romantic, and for a few minutes I was thinking that maybe I could be really beautiful to someone.

STEVE: Tani, you are beautiful. I love that you wanted to be romantic with me. I'm just . . . I'm not used to you being so . . . human.

TANI: Oh, stop it. I can only handle so much charm in one night.

STEVE: No, I don't mean it the way it sounds. I'm used to being with girls who look and act all perfect . . . not that you aren't . . . or . . . but . . . what I am trying to say is that . . . you're really . . . real. You're real and I love that . . . I really love that. I'm just not used to it. And I want to keep trying to get to know the you that is real, even if it means occasional bad breath.

TANI: Really?

STEVE: Yeah, really. So as my first step—*[getting really close in her face]* Go ahead, breathe.

TANI: *[turning her head away]* No, no, no, you don't have to do that . . . I believe you!!

STEVE: Come on, breathe.

TANI: No Steve, no, I don't want to, please.

STEVE: Come on, please.

TANI: *[covering her mouth slightly, she asks hesitantly]* Are you sure?

STEVE: Positive, come on.

TANI: OK. *[She sings "The Way You Look Tonight" again]* . . . and your cheek so soft there is nothing for me but to love you, just the way you look tonight.

[While she sings, STEVE is taking deep breaths. All of his lines overlap with the song. The song should end after he says his last line.]

STEVE: *[deep inhalation and exhalation]* I'm breathing deeply. *[deep breath again]* And it's not perfect but I'm still liking you. *[slight pause]* I still like you.

[They laugh, and keep dancing.]

Lights fade to black.

ZACCHAEUS WAS A WEE LITTLE MAN
THEME AND VARIATIONS INTRODUCING LUKE 19

Alison Siewert

This is a collage. Change cultural references (Dave Matthews Band, Moravian Love Feasts, Bethlehem Parking Authority) to fit your context.

CAST OF CHARACTERS

ADAM (could also be EVE if that works better for your team) and ELO (short for Elohim)—friends and running partners

ZOE—girl on the phone

FRAN and STAN—coworkers and Dave Matthews Band fans

Each conversation is played independently and in its own stage area, but runs together as though it were one larger conversation. Use very small adjustments in lighting to indicate focus; do not bring lights fully up and down.

ADAM: Shoot! Here he comes. *[to himself]* Hide, Adam, hide! D'oh!

ELO: Yo! Adam! Where are you? Adam! Hey—don't you wanna go for a run, dude? Come on!

ADAM: *[to himself]* Geez. OK. Here goes. *[to ELO]* Over *[resigned pause]* here.

ELO: What? Where?!

ADAM: Here. Right here.

[They freeze. Lights up on STAN.]

STAN: D'you hear Dave Matthews is coming to town today?

FRAN: Uh-huh.

STAN: They blocked off Main all the way up to Union. Dave Matthews. Can you believe it?

FRAN: What? Here? Why? Oh—wait, I know—*[sarcastically]* He collects Moravian Love Feast memorabilia, right? I'm so sure, Dave Matthews coming to Bethlehem. Nice try, joker man.

STAN: Doubt me if you must, but just wait . . .

[They freeze. Lights up on ELO.]

ELO: Where exactly is "right here"? You got any map coordinates on you? And why are you hiding in the first place? What's wrong with you?

ADAM: Uh . . . umm . . .

[They freeze. Lights up on ZOE.]

ZOE :   *[on the phone]* Yeah, I would love to go to your brother's party, but all those people hate me. *[pause]* No, not that—Remember that letter to the editor I wrote a couple of weeks ago? Yeah, the one they printed? Yeah. The one I wrote that they printed. About how we just need to love and respect the Bethlehem Parking Authority more and more?

[Freeze. Lights up on ELO.]

ELO: "Ummm" what? *[startled, almost running into ADAM]* Oh! Aack! Here you are. Anyway, what's "ummm"?

ADAM: Well, I, uh . . . I was hiding.

ELO: You were hiding.

ADAM: Yep, that's it. *[as though all done explaining]* I was hiding.

ELO: No—wait a minute. You're not getting off that easy, dude.

[They freeze. Lights up on STAN.]

STAN: Look down there—See that mob? *[visionary]* He's somewhere in there, I'm tellin' ya.

FRAN :   *[without looking up]* Uh-huh.

STAN: Oh, come on. You could use a brisk walk to wake you up! Let's go check it out.

FRAN: If I come with you, will you stop hassling me?

[They freeze. Lights up on ZOE.]

ZOE: Look, I just can't show up there. I'd be humiliated. It's bad enough I see people just around—at the gym and stuff. But at least there, I can pretend to be all focused and sweaty and into Tae-Bo-ing or something. *[pause]* No, not actually tying bows. It's a kickboxing—never mind. Anyway, it'd be embarrassing and uncomfortable. Sorry, I'm not going.

[*She freezes. Lights up on ELO.*]

ELO: What's really up? I thought we were friends.

ADAM: OK. I screwed up.

ELO: And?

ADAM: Real bad. That's why—well, I was afraid you'd see me.

ELO: Well, I'm pretty much looking right at you.

ADAM: I know, believe me. I was afraid you'd see me, and then—

ELO: And then—?

[*They freeze. Lights up on FRAN.*]

FRAN: [*stunned, breathless*] Omigosh. I can't believe we just had coffee and donuts with Dave Matthews. Can you even believe it? I can't believe it!

STAN: [*self-satisfied*] Life is good indeed.

FRAN: Life? Life will never be the same! [*huge, completely cut loose*] I-HAVE-PASSED-SWEET'N-LOW-PACKETS-TO-DAVE-MATTHEWS!! I!—AM!—CHANGED!!

STAN: [*kicked-back*] What a great guy, inviting us out for coffee. I was a little surprised about the seven donuts, though.

FRAN: Seven donuts?

STAN: Dude, he ate seven donuts.

FRAN: Have you ever seen him play? [*demonstrating*] All that wiggling? He uses up seven donuts in one song.

STAN: I guess. Dude, that was so great. Coffee. Dave. Us.

[*They freeze. Lights up on ADAM.*]

ADAM: I guess I don't really have a "then—" I didn't really know what would happen next.

[*They freeze. Lights up on ZOE.*]

ZOE: Neither do I. Look, how about this. We'll do something after the party. I'll lay low at home and then I'll come by a little later—say, 10:30? *[pause]* I know the party'll be half over. That's the point. I can park at the corner and sneak around the back. Just look for me—Then we can take off and go see a movie or something. *[pause]* What? Wait, did you say Dave Matthews? Like, the band? Here? Totally! I'm there. [pause] OK. See you around 10:30. Don't forget to look for me!

[She freezes. Lights fade.]

THIS IS MY JESUS
A ROUND

Jason Gaboury

This is performed as separate conversations but contiguous lines, in these pairs:

A and B

C and D

F and G

H and I

E, on its own, mid-audience

Actors stand so they are interacting without being in one another's space. The illusion is of separate spaces at the same time.

A   My Jesus . . . if you don't know my Jesus, I feel bad for you.

B   Listen to her talk. It's like she got Jesus in her book bag. *[mocking]* "Look everybody, here's Jesus."

C   Smelly feet, I don't know what this has to do with smelly feet.

F   Man, this whole thing stinks: Don't you know that more people have been killing each other over Jesus than any other figure in history?

G   Exactly.

F   This whole religious thing, Jesus and all the rest. In the end it is just a matter of people with power trying to push their agenda on everybody else.

G   No freedom.

F   No doubt.

D   No, it's a poem I read in a book called *Jesus with Dirty Feet*.

H   The thing that I like about Jesus is the fact that he was a freedom fighter.

I   What are you talking about?

H   Man . . . like, he was an oppressed minority . . . fighting in the struggle for justice. That's
        why they killed him.

I   Who?

H   The power players . . . big government . . . the police state of the day . . . they were scared.

C   What's that on your arm?

D   This?

C   Uh-huh.

D   It's my WWJD bracelet. What would Jesus do . . .

C   You are into this Jesus thing, aren't you?

A   But you gotta know Jesus . . . personally . . . down in your heart.

B   How you gonna know Jesus in your heart—she don't even have a Bible.

A   It's a personal relationship.

B   I got relationships with people.

G   When I was younger, my mom made me go to church. I couldn't deal . . . people were
        so hypocritical.

F   True.

G   So I thought Jesus was like this cosmic Mr. Rogers . . . you go to this "land o' make-
        believe" every week and think of stuff you're sorry for . . . then he says "You're special,"
        and then you get back to real life.

F   That's it.

G   One day I thought, *This is really stupid.* So I may be less religious now. But at least I'm
        more honest.

I   I thought Jesus was into . . . peace and love.

H   No, man. Think about it. The man was executed as a political prisoner . . . he pissed the
        wrong people off, and bam!

I   I never thought about it like that.

*[As soon as one round is completed, all groups begin talking at once, continuing their conversations, but with some ad lib
and louder, more intense—until E stands up from the audience, walks to center of room and opens to read Luke 4:16-19.]*

E   And he came to Nazareth, where he had been brought up; and as was his custom, he en-
        tered the synagogue on the Sabbath and stood up to read. And the book of the prophet
        Isaiah was handed to him. And he opened the book and found the place where it was writ-
        ten, "The Spirit of the Lord is upon me because he has anointed me to preach the gospel
        to the poor. He has sent me to proclaim release to the captives and recovery of sight to
        the blind, to set free those who are downtrodden, to proclaim the favorable year of the
        Lord."

TRUTH OR DARE
A SKETCH INTRODUCING CONFESSION

Alison Siewert

Here's a group of young adults "confessing" their worst stuff to each other but not really dealing with it. This sketch was designed to open conversation about confession

CAST OF CHARACTERS

Margo, Emily, Andy, Shane, Will, Jason

Six friends sit in a circle, eating, drinking and playing "Truth or Dare," throwing a die to decide each person's turn. Players should voice appropriate oohs, ahs, etc.

EMILY: So . . . then I just went and put the dead trout in his closet . . . and I guess he didn't notice it.

ANDY: Oh, that's so gross!

SHANE: Wait—How long didn't he notice it?

EMILY: Well . . . kind of a while.

SHANE: *[leading]* Uh-huh.

[Everyone stares at EMILY, who capitulates.]

EMILY: *[gives in, takes a deep breath]* Um . . . three weeks.

ANDY: He didn't notice for THREE WEEKS?!

MARGO: Eew. That is ultimate gross.

WILL: Talk about skanky. Dude! Three weeks of dead fish in his closet and he didn't notice! Argh!

SHANE: Skank-o-rama. I didn't think you had it in you, Emily!

EMILY: OK, OK. Who's next? *[throwing die]* Number . . . four. Andy! Truth or dare, love?

ANDY: Um . . . Truth.

EMILY: Tell us . . .

WILL: Get 'im, Emily!

EMILY: Worst thing you ever did. That you never told anyone about.

ANDY: You mean absolute worst? Wow. Lemme think . . .

WILL: There are so many to choose from!

ANDY: Oh, I know. There's this one time I was playing with my slingshot—like a kid's one—
             I was sitting on the balcony. And I was just, you know, firing around for fun. And then
             I saw the neighbor's cat walking around, and I sort of, ya know, aimed around it. But
             I figured, *I'll never hit it; it's small and it moves fast.* But then—

WILL: I can't believe this—

ANDY: I couldn't really see through the trees, but like eight or ten seconds later the cat . . .
             it just sort of fell over dead. I mean, it was like completely still. Not breathing. The
             next day my mom told me the Millers' cat had just suddenly up and died. She said
             they thought it must have had a heart attack or something and—gonzo.

MARGO: Whoa. That's serious, Andy. And you never told them?

ANDY: Would you tell them?

EMILY: That's so . . . cruel. *[starting to get kind of upset]* I can't believe you!

WILL :   *[intervening to keep it light]* Ohhhkaaay. Who's next?

ANDY: I dunno. But we can find out—*[throwing die]*—Two! It's Shane's turn! Truth or dare,
             dude.

SHANE: All right. Truth.

ANDY: Oooh. I already have so much information to exploit. Let's see. Tell us . . . the weird-
             est girl you ever liked. Like, had a crush on.

MARGO: Oh, now is that really fair?

ANDY: It's Truth or Dare—C'mon!

SHANE: The weirdest girl . . . OK. I guess it was Portia Romalitis.

WILL: Portia? Gnarl! Are you serious?

SHANE: Hey. She was nice, she was kinda cute . . .

ANDY: She used to pick her nose all the way through third period.

WILL: Daily. All the way through geometry. And her hair, it was like dyed—

MARGO: It was dyed orange.

EMILY: Ooh, and that black lipstick she used to wear.

SHANE: Hey. We were freshman soul mates. What can I say? OK—Whose turn? *[throwing die]* Margo! You're on, babe! Truth or dare?

MARGO: With you guys?—I would never take the dare. Truth.

WILL: Truth it is. First place you ever made out, and with who.

MARGO: That's easy. In the social studies section of the library, with Pete Barnes.

EMILY: Really?

MARGO: What?

EMILY: Pete Barnes? Pete—Barnes?

MARGO: Yeah. What's the problem with Pete Barnes?

EMILY: Nothing. Never mind. It's just that I . . .

MARGO: You've always had a secret crush on Pete Barnes?

EMILY: Oh, yeah, right. No. That's not it. Never mind. Let's move on. Who's next?

MARGO: *[to EMILY]* I wanna hear more about that later, Em. OK . . . *[throwing die]* Ladies and gentlemen, it's a three. Will, you're on.

WILL: Truth.

MARGO: Truth . . . OK. Let's see. Mr. Will, tell us the worst thing about you.

WILL: *[thinks for a moment, takes a deep breath]* Well . . . to be honest—

ANDY: He's tellin' the truth, folks.

WILL: To be honest, I guess the worst thing about me is, I don't really care about other people very much. I mean, I kind of tend to kind of hurt the people I'm closest to. Like,

I'm insecure, and I use other people to feel better about myself. *[He pauses to look for reactions.]*

[All four friends are silent and uncomfortable; they wait for WILL to continue.]

WILL: Um . . . like, to be more specific, um . . . I kind of tend to judge people around me, like, I'll think, *Oh, I'm so much smarter than them.* Or maybe, *Geez, I'm glad I'm better looking than* [interrupting his own gaffe] *Sha—him.* Or, *Glad I'm going out with her and not her.* You know, I'm judgmental and harsh toward my friends. Kind of a lot. I mean, not openly, just in my mind and behind their backs.

MARGO: Ohhhhkaaay.

EMILY: Omigosh. I can't believe you're admitting that.

WILL: I know. I'm such a scum.

MARGO: *[kind of tranced-out, in shock]* Yeah, OK.

[They sit in completely uncomfortable, long silence.]

WILL: OK. So—Who's next?

EMILY: *[in shock, but attempting to move on]* I think Jason's the only one who hasn't gone.

ANDY: So . . . Jason, truth—or dare?

JASON: Oh, believe me—dare! So definitely, dare.

[EMILY hands off the die as friends make eye contact with all but WILL—they are still shocked. Lights dim. Players exit.]

SHHH!
FOR PSALM 46

Alison Siewert

Sometimes we use sketches that deal only indirectly with the idea of the Scripture or a topic to be explored. Here's one that gets us thinking about being still.

CAST OF CHARACTERS
Andi, Carter

ANDI and CARTER, a married couple, meet for lunch. ANDI sits down to study; CARTER comes up with a drink, approaching for something more social.

CARTER: Hey, hon . . . mind if I sit with you?

ANDI: Yeah, but— *[cut off]*

CARTER: *[cutting her off, enthusiastic]* Ya know, it's so much more fun now that my office moved—I like being able to see you at lunch.

ANDI: Well . . . I'd love to hang out and talk, but I've really gotta work. Is that okay?

CARTER: Sure. I'll just people-watch or something and sit here quietly.

ANDI: Cool.

CARTER: Ooh! Look at that guy! See him?

ANDI: *[looking up]* Which guy?

CARTER: The one with the orange hair but it's balding and combed waaaay over and— *[cut off]*

ANDI: *[cutting him off]* Yeah, yeah. I see him.

[She returns to her work, and there is a pause.]

CARTER: So . . . what do you wanna do this weekend?

ANDI: Oh, I dunno. If I get this report finished, we can go dancing. I've been wanting to go.

CARTER: Yeah . . . *[distracted]* Oh! I can't believe that!

ANDI: What?

CARTER: That guy in the Porsche almost just slammed right into that woman in the Jetta! It was like *this* close!

ANDI: Great.

CARTER: No, it wasn't really great. I mean, if it had been any closer . . .

ANDI: *[not really paying attention]* Mm-hmm.

CARTER: Wow! Now, she is really . . . *[lustily admiring]*

[ANDI glares silently.]

CARTER: *[rescuing it]* . . . she is really eating a bagel. *[sheepishly]* Sorry.

ANDI: Carter?

CARTER: Yeah?

ANDI: I gotta finish this.

CARTER: Yeah, yeah. You should finish that. Then we can go dancing. Like you were saying.

ANDI: Right.

CARTER: *[pauses for a long time, trying really hard to be quiet]* Whadoyou think about that Middle East peace thing?

ANDI: Carter?

CARTER: Yeah.

ANDI: The report. I'm working on the report.

CARTER: Sorry. It's just so hard to sit here and not talk to you.

ANDI: Apparently.

CARTER: *[after managing another long, disciplined pause]* Where do you wanna go for dinner?

ANDI: Carter!

CARTER: Yes! I will be quiet!

ANDI: Thank you!

CARTER: *[a shorter, more antsy pause]*

ANDI: *[Looks up, nods.]*

CARTER: Your hair looks gr—*[cut off]*

ANDI: Shhh! *[cutting him off]*

CARTER: Right! *[pause]* How many more pages do y—*[cut off]*

ANDI: Shh! *[cutting him off]*

CARTER: Yes! Quiet. *[pausing, looking at the computer]* Is that new software yo—*[cut off]*

ANDI: Carter! Shh! Report due! Must finish! You—shh! *[cutting him off]*

CARTER: Okay! It's just that it's—*[cut off]*

ANDI: *[cutting him off]* It's time for me to do my work! Now shh!

CARTER: *[putting a hand over his mouth—a disciplined pause]* Andi? . . .

ANDI: *[angry]* What?!

CARTER: I was just gonna tell you—

ANDI: Shh!

CARTER: I'm going back to my office.

ANDI: Shh!

CARTER: Bye.

ANDI: Shh!

[CARTER leaves quietly. ANDI finishes her report and closes her laptop with a flourish, looks around for CARTER.]

ANDI: Carter? *[looking]* Carter?! Where'd you go? Oh! *[frustrated, calling him on her cell phone as she exits]* Carter? Hi, it's me. Where'd you go? I just wanted to make dancing plans. I'm done. Oh—sorry to interrupt your processing time. Okay . . . I'll call you back later. Bye.

[She exits.]

The end.

LOVE AMERICAN STYLE
A SKETCH FROM *RACETHNICITYOU*

Jenny Vaughn Hall and Phyllis Wong

CAST OF CHARACTERS

Christine, John

CHRISTINE and JOHN, a romantic couple, are at her house—for him, the first time.

CHRISTINE: *[in Chinese]* OK, Mom, we're coming. Just a minute.

JOHN: What did you just tell your Mom?

CHRISTINE: I told her we're just going to be making out in here a little before dinner.

JOHN: What? Your parents are gonna kill me!

CHRISTINE: I'm just kidding; I told her that we'll be coming to dinner in a minute.

JOHN: Christine, I'm freaked out enough already about the forgetting the whole shoe thing. That's really not gonna help. I'm really sorry I forgot.

CHRISTINE: No, it's okay, but didn't you see me take off my shoes when we came in?

JOHN: Yeah, but I just thought you were getting comfortable. And I remembered at the last minute that I have a hole in my sock. Do you think they're offended?

CHRISTINE: No, I think it's all right. Don't worry—they're gonna love you.
[She gives him a kiss on the cheek and rests her head on his shoulder.]
But just in case, maybe you should take them off now.

JOHN: But what about the hole?

CHRISTINE: What hole?

JOHN: The hole in my sock?

CHRISTINE: I guess you could take your socks off too then.

[JOHN starts taking his socks off.]

JOHN: I thought you said that your family is not very traditionally Chinese.

CHRISTINE: Well, I didn't think we were until you came home with me today.

JOHN: *[kind of laughing]* Yeah, well, it's weird. I mean all this stuff in your house. Taking my shoes off. Even how it smells. Your house even smells kind of funny.

CHRISTINE: *[laughing]* What?

JOHN: Yeah, it smells like sushi or something.

CHRISTINE: Stupid! That's Japanese. I'm Chinese, you freak. And you're being rude. You know you are talking about MY house. I do live here.

JOHN: I know, but it's all so weird, you know? I mean, you have to admit that this is strange, right?

CHRISTINE: *[getting a little more serious]* Well, not really, no. What do you mean?

JOHN: I mean, I don't mean strange in a bad way. I mean strange in a good way. I mean different. Yeah, different, that's what I mean.

CHRISTINE: *[kind of goes with him]* Different. Right. Right. *[hesitant pause]* Well, it's okay, right?

JOHN: Of course it's okay. Of course! I mean, I still love you.

CHRISTINE: *[overlapping, confused]* Well . . . yeah!

JOHN: *[realizing he's digging himself into a hole]* I mean, it doesn't change anything about how I feel about you. I still love you.

CHRISTINE: Yeah. I wasn't questioning that, John.

JOHN: I know, I know. This place is just new and I just need to get used to it, you know? It's just weird.

CHRISTINE: *[getting angry]* It's not weird!! Stop calling it weird! When you call this place weird, you're calling me weird!

JOHN: But Christine, you're different. You're . . . I know you. I know you.

CHRISTINE: *[pauses]* You know me? Well, I take my shoes off when I come into the house, John . . . *[begins to rant and get upset]* And I speak Cantonese and watch Chinese soap operas with my Mom. I love roast duck over rice, with Chinese broccoli and oyster sauce. And I celebrate the mid-autumn festival and Chinese New Year, and I was born in the year of the Tiger. And . . . and that's important to me. These things are important to me, John.

JOHN: I like rice.

CHRISTINE: *[laughing, upset]* Oh my gosh, John. You've really outdone yourself this time.

JOHN: What?

CHRISTINE: Did you hear anything I said?

JOHN: Yeah, you like eating tiger and you were born in the year of the duck.

CHRISTINE: John! That's not funny!

JOHN: I'm not trying to be funny. Did I get something wrong?

CHRISTINE: Yes! It's wrong. It's all wrong. All of it.

JOHN: But I love you.

CHRISTINE: Love me? You can't even see who I am. How can you? *[responding to her mother, in Chinese]* There in a minute, Mom! *[to JOHN]* We better get in there for dinner.

JOHN: Can we talk . . . later?

CHRISTINE: *[exiting]* Let's eat. C'mon.

[They exit.]

The end.

THE BRANCH

Susi Jensen

This was written as an illustration for a talk on repentance. The idea that the character Cliff would rather cling to his branch than be pulled from the side of the mountain compares to the absurdity of our lives when we cling to the petty comforts that, if taken in perspective, give very little security but can be difficult to give up.

CAST OF CHARACTERS

Jane, Cliff

PROPS

JANE: Hiking gear, binoculars, bird book
CLIFF: Hiking gear, bush, plastic bottle, hat, book

The director will need to develop something convincing to portray one character hanging on a sheer side of a mountain and another character speaking to him from above . . . within reaching distance. Names and genders may be changed at the director's discretion.

The scene: CLIFF hangs on the edge of a mountain. He holds a small shrub with one hand and with the other drinks from a plastic water bottle. JANE, wearing her hiking garb and carrying binoculars and bird book, is bird watching as she enters. She is gazing up into the sky and around, enjoying the scenery. She sees a bird and quickly gets her bird book out to see what species it is. All of a sudden she looks down and notices that the path she was walking on has come near a drop-off. She stops abruptly.

JANE: Whoa!

[Jane peeks over a ledge where CLIFF is hanging. At first she doesn't see him.]

JANE: That's quite a cliff.

CLIFF: It's true in more ways than one.

[JANE looks around to try and figure out where the voice is coming from.]

CLIFF: I'm down here.

[JANE looks down and slaps her hand over her mouth, aghast.]

JANE: Oh my gosh! Are you okay?

CLIFF: Sure. I'm fine. The name's Cliff. I'd shake your hand, but . . .

[JANE hurriedly sets her binoculars and book down. She squats and peers over ledge.]

JANE: What happened?

CLIFF: I was walking up there one moment, and then in the blink of an eye I was here. Lucky son-of-a-gun, too. I managed to grab this here branch and find a couple of footholds.

JANE: Well, let's get you up. I'm pretty sure I can reach one of your hands. Oh . . . by the way, my name's Jane.

[JANE lies on her belly and reaches down with her hand. Her hand comes within reach of CLIFF's.]

JANE: Can you grab ahold?

[CLIFF ignores her hand.]

CLIFF: Say . . . You have any sunscreen?

JANE: What?

CLIFF: Sunscreen. Do you have any?

JANE: Ah . . . no. I left mine in the car. I put it on before my walk, you know . . .

CLIFF: Darn! It gets mighty hot here around 2:00.

[JANE pauses as she takes in this comment.]

JANE: I'm not sure I know what you mean.

CLIFF: *[impatiently]* The sun shines against this side of the mountain in the afternoons. I get baked pretty much every day. It's the only complaint I have about this situation I've been in.

JANE: Oh. I get it. You're some kind of protester? You're living on this ledge to save an endangered . . .

CLIFF: No. That's what everyone thinks. I'm just here because I slipped, okay?

[JANE sits up and scratches her head.]

JANE: Okay. You mean you want to spend time on this ledge . . .

CLIFF: I don't necessarily want to, but I have to.

JANE: Did you notice that I put my arm over the edge here and that I could reach you? I mean, if you stretched your arm . . . you could grab my hand and I could pull you up.

CLIFF: How do I know that?

JANE: It's obvious, isn't it? What about a helicopter?

CLIFF: Oh, they've tried . . . FOUR TIMES! Each time, same thing. They come down on the ladder, asking me to let go of my branch. And I say . . . "NO." I mean, they could drop me . . . and . . . and . . . they've come on foot too . . . just like you, reaching over, asking me to let go. But I can't let go. You're asking the impossible of me.

[JANE slaps her forehead with her hand and groans.]

JANE: How long have you been here . . . Cliff?

CLIFF: Three months.

JANE: How do you . . . ?

CLIFF: My friends bring me food and water, books . . . everything I need, really. I'm grateful to them . . . grateful to be alive. I could have died that day.

JANE: *[under her breath]* I know . . . Not a bad alternative . . .

CLIFF: What? I can't hear what you're saying.

JANE: Oh, nothing.

[JANE gets down on her belly to talk again. She reaches her arm down.]

JANE: Look here, Cliff. I believe I can lift you up onto the path. You see my arm. You know you can reach it. Why don't you grab it and let me help you.

CLIFF: Look, ahh . . .

JANE: Jane.

CLIFF: Look, Jane. I know you mean well. But I'm just not up to it. This shrub has held me for three months. To be honest, I'm kind of attached to it.

JANE: *[under her breath]* You're right about that.

CLIFF: What?

JANE: Look, Cliff. You must see how absurd this is. You're going to hang onto this branch . . . and stay here indefinitely . . .

CLIFF: Yes.

[JANE stands up and paces impatiently.]

JANE: What about when the storms come? What about winter? Have you thought that far ahead?

CLIFF: No, I haven't. A wise man once said, "Take one day at a time . . ."

JANE: Well, a wise woman is telling you today, "Get your butt off the mountainside, you idiot!"

CLIFF: You see. Why should I trust you? You're not such a nice person! You'd probably drop me!

[JANE moans as she rolls her eyes. She stands with her hands on her hips. Finally, she picks up her binoculars and bird book.]

JANE: I guess you'll just have to keep holding onto that branch. I can't force you to let me help you.

CLIFF: Won't you stay and talk for a while longer?

JANE: No. I really have to be going. [beat] Goodbye, Cliff.

CLIFF: Goodbye. Come again . . . Visit any time.

[JANE walks off, shaking her head.]

[CLIFF picks up his book and reads.]

The end.

LIFEDESIGN
A CONVERSATION BETWEEN MOSES AND MIRIAM

Alison Siewert

CAST OF CHARACTERS

Moses and Miriam

Players mostly talk past each other.

MOSES: My older sister grabbed me one day and she said, she said, "Come here. I need to talk to you."

MIRIAM: Moses, we have to talk.

MOSES: She said, "Moses, you are not them. You are us."

MIRIAM: You're one of us. You are not from them.

MOSES: I . . . am . . . not them?

MIRIAM: You're us. You're one of us.

MOSES: You are not them.

MIRIAM: You are one of us. Look! See the design of your skin, your hair—

MOSES: What? . . . I didn't know what to think, to say. I'm not Egyptian. I'm not—

MIRIAM: You are not them.

MOSES: She told me, I . . . was saved. My mother—

MIRIAM: They were throwing all the baby boys into the water, into the Nile.

MOSES: They were drowning baby boys.

MIRIAM: You would have been one of them.

MOSES: They threw all the Hebrew boys into the river and drowned them.

MIRIAM: Thousands of babies dead and floating and . . . drowned by Pharaoh.

MOSES: Egypt—my family—killed . . . my people—

MIRIAM: You are not them.

MOSES: Our mother saw and she knew . . .

MIRIAM: Our mother knew you were different.

MOSES: I was different, saved—I was not dead.

MIRIAM: And she could have been punished, but she hid you.

MOSES: It was a huge risk for three months, a secret.

MIRIAM: Do you know how hard it is to keep secret a screaming baby?

MOSES: But she did it.

MIRIAM: And then you grew, you got too big to keep hidden—so she sailed you in the river.

MOSES: Then she sailed me down the Nile.

MIRIAM: She designed a little basket boat—

MOSES: A basket?

MIRIAM: —and sailed you in it.

MOSES: Floated me.

MIRIAM: I followed her down to the river, and watched.

MOSES: She hid me, in my sailing basket. And she watched.

MIRIAM: I watched our mother feed you one last time.

MOSES: She kissed me in secret, goodbye, shalom.

MIRIAM: She filled you up and kissed you: shalom, goodbye.

MOSES: And she watched.

MIRIAM: She stood there for a long time, watching and praying. I stayed and watched.

MOSES: And watched.

MIRIAM: You cried, and they heard you . . . your other mother.

MOSES: My other mother heard me, the Egyptian princess and her friends.

MIRIAM: They had come to the river to bathe.

MOSES: She was with her friends, coming to the river, and they heard me . . .

MIRIAM: You were loud—like someone stepped on a cat.

MOSES: They couldn't mistake a baby's cry.

MIRIAM: They looked and found you, sailed there into the reeds.

MOSES: And when they looked, they found me in my basket.

MIRIAM: Right in the reeds, like you had sailed your little boat into harbor.

MOSES: There I was.

MIRIAM: A basket full of screeching boy.

MOSES: They picked me up.

MIRIAM: They took you out and held you.

MOSES: I guess they liked me.

MIRIAM: You were so beautiful, they had to like you.

MOSES: She—my other mother—she wanted me.

MIRIAM: She had to love you.

MOSES: She adopted me.

MIRIAM: The Egyptian—Pharaoh's daughter—adopted you.

MOSES: She parented me.

MIRIAM: But someone else had to feed you.

MOSES: My birth mother watched.

MIRIAM: I watched when she picked you up, and then I said,

MOSES: My sister made her way over and said,

MIRIAM: I said, "Would you like me to find someone who can feed him for you?"

MOSES: Would you like me to find a Hebrew to nurse him?

MIRIAM: I know someone . . .

MOSES: My sister knew my birthmother would . . .

MIRIAM: So I called our mother and she became your—

MOSES: My mother would feed me.

MIRIAM: She became your mother again.

MOSES: My Egyptian mother dressed me and played with me.

MIRIAM: She got to feed you all day.

MOSES: But my Hebrew mother fed me.

MIRIAM: Then you got too big to feed.

MOSES: I grew up.

MIRIAM: You were taught and trained.

MOSES: They gave me every good thing.

MIRIAM: But you are not them.

MOSES: I am not just them. I came to them from a basket.

MIRIAM: You are not them.

MOSES: I came from somewhere else, from someone else.

MIRIAM: You did not come from Egyptians.

MOSES: But I came to Egyptians.

MIRIAM: You were not meant to be Egyptian.

MOSES: I was meant to grow up in Egypt.

MIRIAM: Your life is designed by Yahweh.

MOSES: Yahweh designed that I should be raised Egyptian.

MIRIAM: Your life is designed by Yahweh.

MOSES: Yahweh designed that I should go with his people.

MIRIAM: You will lead the people of God.

MOSES: Switch sides.

MIRIAM: Take the side of God's people.

MOSES: They gave me good things; they gave me my life . . .

MIRIAM: Yahweh designed it.

MOSES: Pull apart the kingdom that saved me.

MIRIAM: Pull together God's people.

MOSES: Yahweh designed me for his people.

MIRIAM: Yahweh built your life for his people—

MOSES: I will lead the people of Israel.

MIRIAM: To take them from Egypt to new land.

MOSES: The people of God are slaves.

MIRIAM: We don't really know who we are.

MOSES: Egypt is built on slavery.

MIRIAM: We are oppressed.

MOSES: I saw an Egyptian beating a man into the ground.

MIRIAM: We are beaten.

MOSES: I hated him . . . I hated the Egyptian. I hated Egypt.

MIRIAM: It has been so long . . .

MOSES: Israel has been oppressed here for so long.

MIRIAM: We don't know what it means to belong to God anymore.

MOSES: Their oppression seems normal.

MIRIAM: The Egyptians don't know Yahweh.

MOSES: Our economy is built on it.

MIRIAM: What does it mean that we belong to Yahweh?

MOSES: We force them to build our kingdom.

MIRIAM: Our lives are labor for a kingdom that doesn't know God . . .

MOSES: The people of God are disposable here.

MIRIAM: And our babies are dumped into the Nile and drowned . . .

MOSES: The Egyptian beat up a slave.

MIRIAM: Grabbed from their mothers.

MOSES: So I killed him.

MIRIAM: They are carried away by men we don't know—

MOSES: I didn't even know his name.

MIRIAM: We don't know them and we don't know why.

MOSES: Some overseer, a low-level manager. I didn't know him.

MIRIAM: They come and take the boys.

MOSES: I saw him, and then I grabbed him by the throat.

MIRIAM: They come and take them away.

MOSES: And threw him on the ground.

MIRIAM: And throw them in the river.

MOSES: And beat him.

MIRIAM: They throw them in the river.

MOSES: And beat him.

MIRIAM: You can hear them for a moment.

MOSES: And beat him.

MIRIAM: They cry as they're thrown.

MOSES: Until there was blood on my hands.

MIRIAM: And then you hear the thudding splash.

MOSES: And then . . .

MIRIAM: And then . . .

MOSES: Then he wasn't resisting anymore.

MIRIAM: Then it's very quiet.

MOSES: He was . . .

MIRIAM: Because . . .

MOSES: He was dead.

MIRIAM: They're dead.

[Pause]

MIRIAM: You arc not them.

MOSES: I knew that. I have heard that in my head for so long. I am not them. I am . . .

MIRIAM: You are—

MOSES: An Egyptian dressed me and played with me.

MIRIAM: Your Hebrew mother fed you.

MOSES: An Israelite fed me.

MIRIAM: Your Egyptian mother raised you.

MOSES: I came from somewhere else, from someone else.

MIRIAM: You did not come from Egyptians.

MOSES: But I came to Egyptians.

MIRIAM: You were not meant to be Egyptian.

MOSES: I was meant to belong beyond Egypt.

MIRIAM: Your life is designed by Yahweh.

MOSES: I was meant to belong to Yahweh.

MIRIAM: Your life is designed by Yahweh.

MOSES: Yahweh designed my life.

ABOUT THE WRITERS

SCOTT BRILL is Associate Regional Director with InterVarsity in New England. After a promising start in Darien High School's "Theater 308" company, his artistic interests kind of died out in engineering school. His passion for writing drama and dialogue reemerged as he tried to engage college students about life and God in a variety of campus settings. His most well-received works at the moment are nightly readings for his three daughters, with whom he has the reputation of producing passable character renditions of Gandalf, Gollum and others. He currently lives in Worcester, Massachusetts, with his family. Find him at Scott_Brill@ivstaff.org.

JESS DELEGENCIA got talked into an audition, got the lead and kept acting. He has been team leader for InterVarsity at UC Berkeley and has acted with the Filipino American theater company there. A native of Quezon City, Philippines, he has explored the relationship of cultures and theater and currently enjoys working with hip-hop forms in theatrical settings. Jess performed Scripture drama at Urbana 2000 and continues to develop this art—but his secret dream is to be a lounge singer . . . or at least to eat some good *lumpia* and adobo now and then. Jess lives in Oakland, California. You can contact him at jess_delegencia@ivstaff.org.

JASON GABOURY does student ministry at Hunter College in New York City. He graduated from Springfield College and studied acting and directing at The American Musical and Dramatic Academy of New York City and the LOST Theatre in London, England. Jason is slightly embarrassed to have been in the show "The Magic School Bus—Live." He's

also acted and directed in more serious and educational/historical theater and is part of the Urbana 03 Theater Team. Jason's big passion (beyond Jesus and the deep life) is café con leche (don't get him started). He lives in New York City with his wife, Sophia, also a campus minister. He's at jdgaboury@aol.com.

JENNY VAUGHN HALL grew up in San Diego, California, taking dancing lessons and attending performing arts schools through high school. She took her show on the road to UCLA as a theater major where she appeared in plays, including *The Wedding Band* directed by Debbie Allen. Jenny likes musical theater and has done *42nd Street*, *A Chorus Line*, *Into the Woods* and, as she says, "a lot of *Nutcrackers*." She works with InterVarsity at the University of Southern California, studies at Fuller Seminary and directs and performs *RacEthnicitYou*. Jenny once worked as Fred Flintstone (in costume—whew!) and enjoys outdoor adventures with her husband, Scott. She is known—despite all that ballet training—as a bit of a klutz. Reach her at javavaughn @yahoo.com.

LISA HARPER went to Rutgers University to become an actor and ended up writing plays after an argument with a friend provoked her to find a way to get Christians to pay attention to homeless people. She found her way to the University of Southern California playwriting program, and her thesis play, *An' Push da Wind Down*, was mounted at the Kennedy Center after it won a national collegiate competition. Lisa works as director of reconciliation ministries with InterVarsity in Los Angeles and specifically with First Nations and black students. She writes, acts and directs in

RacEthnicitYou as well as other works and enjoys helping people develop their artistic and inherited cultural gifts. Her e-mail address is LisaSHarper@alumni.usc.edu.

SUSI JENSEN earned her degree in creative writing from Stanford University and has worked in the San Francisco Bay area with InterVarsity as campus staff and volunteer intercessor. Currently a coach and writer for several drama teams, she has written both sketches and full-length works and is working on a children's novel. Susi balances disciplined, faithful writing with raising the two children she shares with her husband, Jason. Contact Susi at SusiJensen@aol.com

DANIEL JONES is a campus staff worker and theater specialist with InterVarsity and is a member of the Urbana 03 Theater Team. He is an actor with credits in stage, film, print and television. He is a cofounder of ransomTHEdonKey, a theater group that performs *markproject* and *beginning,* as well as other stuff for college campuses and churches. He studied acting at the American Conservatory Theater in San Francisco. With a group of friends, Daniel planted and led worship for a church for people who aren't from church. Once a ranking gymnast, he can no longer touch his toes, but he *can* still do a handstand. He enjoys wearing orange shoes. If he can get the tux on right, Daniel will be married to Jamie by the time this book is published. You can contact Daniel at danielcjonze@aol.com

BRUCE KUHN was on Broadway in *Les Misérables* and performed in the resident company of Actor's Theatre of Louisville. He now tours his one-person performances to universities, churches and conferences across North America and Europe. The repertoire includes *The Gospel of Luke* (in KJV), *The Acts of the Apostles, Tales of Tolstoy, Paul and the Philippians* and *The Cotton Patch Gospel.* The conservatory graduate was on staff with Inter-

Varsity as an evangelism specialist. Bruce has taught storytelling at Regent College, Oxford University and for the International Fellowship of Evangelical Students (IFES) in seven countries. He and his wife, Hetty, a landscape painter, have two children. You can contact Bruce at <www.brucekuhn.com>.

ALISON SIEWERT started out in this whole theater thing as a preschool tap dancer. Trained as a musician, the Occidental College graduate cowrote and edited *Worship Team Handbook* (IVP) after leading worship at Urbana 93 and 96. She directs the Urbana 03 Theater Team and is the cofounder of ransomTHEdonKey, a theater group that performs *markproject* (on Mark's Gospel) and *beginning* (on Genesis 1—3), as well as shorter works, at campuses, churches and events around North America. After working in lots of different churches, often directing music and art, Alison and some friends planted an arts-integrated church for people who don't do church. She lives with her husband, Dan, and two sons. You can reach her at AVSiewert@mac.com, and at <www.ransomthedonkey.com>.

NINA THIEL lives in Stockton, California, and performs at colleges and churches around the United States. Her show *Always the Women* explores Jesus' encounters with women in the Gospels. Nina's training in acting and dance undergird her roles in local theater and dance productions. She is a member of InterVarsity staff and cowrote *The Small Group Leaders' Handbook: The Next Generation* (IVP). Nina and her husband, Larry, have a daughter and two sons. Wearing her red plain slippers to rehearsals, she repeats her motto: "Why put on shoes when you're just going to have to change them when you get there?" Nina can be found hanging out at her site: <www.ninathiel.com>.

MICAH TRIPPE sometimes walks backwards just for fun. A film studies graduate of Occidental College in Los Angeles, the Atlanta native works at a film production company in Hollywood and is writing a screenplay. He can be reached at mrtrippe@yahoo.com.

PHYLLIS WONG grew up in Toronto, Canada, where she learned not only English but also Cantonese and French. She graduated from UCLA where she studied literature and began to act and write theater. Phyllis has worked with college students as an InterVarsity volunteer and is preparing for film school. She is a fan of broccoli, and her e-mail address is Phyllis1Wong@aol.com.

NOTES

Chapter 2: Waking Up
[1]Stanley Hauerwas and William H. Willimon, *Resident Aliens* (Nashville: Abingdon, 1989), p. 128.
[2]Anna Deveare Smith, *Talk to Me* (New York: Random House, 2000), p. 9.
[3]Murray Watts, *Christianity and the Theatre* (Edinburgh: Handsel, 1986), p. 31.
[4]Hauerwas and Willimon, *Resident Aliens*, p. 149.
[5]Watts, *Christianity and the Theatre*, p. 31.
[6]For a helpful review of theater's history, see Anne Bogart, "Memory," in *A Director Prepares* (New York: Routledge, 2001), pp. 21-41.
[7]Bogart, *A Director Prepares*, p. 31.

Chapter 3: Drama and Worship
[1]William A. Dyrness, *Visual Faith: Art, Theology, and Worship in Dialogue* (Grand Rapids, Mich.: Baker, 2001), p. 21.

Chapter 7: Drama and Evangelism
[1]C. S. Lewis, "The Weight of Glory," in *The Weight of Glory and Other Essays* (New York: Collier, 1980), p. 4.
[2]William A. Dyrness, *Visual Faith: Art, Theology, and Worship in Dialogue* (Grand Rapids, Mich.: Baker, 2001), p. 20.

Chapter 8: Drama Across Cultures
[1]Anna Deveare Smith, *Talk to Me* (New York: Random House, 2000), p. 12.
[2]Anne Bogart, *A Director Prepares*, (New York: Routledge, 2001), p. 32.
[3]Frances Rings, choreographer's notes in *Walkabout* (Pymble, Australia: Playbill/Showbill, 2002). See <www.bangarra.com.au>.
[4]Ibid.
[5]August Wilson, quoted in George Plimpton, *Playwrights at Work* (New York: Modern Library, 2000), p. 353.

Chapter 9: Building a Performance Team from the Ground Up
[1]Anna Deveare Smith, *Talk to Me* (New York: Random House, 2000), p. 9.

Chapter 11: Sketching Life
[1]Phyllis Trible, *God & the Rhetoric of Sexuality* (Philadelphia: Fortress, 1978), p. 16.

Chapter 13: Telling the Whole Story
[1]Robert McKee, *Story: Substance, Structure, Style, and the Principles of Screenwriting* (New York: Regan Books, 1997).
[2]*Silverado*, dir. Lawrence Kasdan (Columbia, 1985).
[3]*Superman*, dir. Richard Donner (Warner Brothers, 1978).
[4]*Star Wars*, dir. George Lucas (Twentieth Century Fox, 1977).
[5]*The Empire Strikes Back*, dir. Irvin Kershner (Twentieth Century Fox, 1980).
[6]*The Return of the Jedi*, dir. Richard Marquand (Twentieth Century Fox, 1983).

Chapter 14: Context Isn't Everything, but It Sure Is a Lot
[1]David Mamet, *True and False: Heresy and Common Sense for the Actor* (New York: Vintage, 1999), p. 19.

[2]Dorothy L. Sayers, "He That Should Come," in *Two Plays About God and Man* (Noroton, Conn.: Vineyard, 1977), p. 124.
[3]Carey Cecil, *Mara* (unpublished). Used by permission.

Chapter 16: Writing Funny
[1]Alison Siewert, *Ed and Laura's Seriously Scary Conversation* (2000).
[2]Alison Siewert, *Wish I Had a Shirt Like That* (2000).
[3]David Bayles and Ted Orland, *Art and Fear* (Santa Cruz, Calif.: Image Continuum, 1993), p. 80.
[4]Alison Siewert, *Chopsticks*, in *Drama Team Sketchbook* (Downers Grove, Ill.: InterVarsity Press, forthcoming).

Chapter 17: Writing Monologues
[1]Arthur Miller, in *The Paris Review Playwrights At Work*, ed. George Plimpton (New York: Modern Library, 2000), p. 163.

Chapter 18: Creating Collages
[1]This sketch can be found in *Worship Team Handbook* (Downers Grove, Ill.: InterVarsity Press, 1999).
[2]Context note: Moravian Love Feasts are a historical remnant of the Moravian Christian community's mission to America in the 1740s. They were dinner and worship events for the believers. The old Moravian settlements, like the one where this sketch took place, attract tourists and history buffs.

Chapter 19: Bringing the Word to Life
[1]Uta Hagen with Haskel Frankel, *Respect for Acting* (New York: Macmillan, 1973), pp. 82-85.
[2]Gerard Kelly, *Retrofuture* (Downers Grove, Ill.: InterVarsity Press, 1999), p. 95.

Chapter 20: Scripting Scripture
[1]Alison Siewert, "Simon's wife," in *Markproject* (2001).

Chapter 21: About Acting
[1]Rob Lowe played this role on the drama series *The West Wing*.
[2]David Mamet discusses this in his book *True and False* (New York: Random House, 1997).
[3]Frederick Buechner, *Telling the Truth: The Gospel as Tragedy, Comedy, and Fairy Tale* (San Francisco: Harper & Row, 1977), p. 21.
[4]William Ball, *A Sense of Direction* (New York: Drama Publishers, 1984), p. 86.
[5]*Chopsticks* is available in Alison Siewert, *Drama Team Sketchbook* (Downers Grove, Ill.: InterVarsity Press, forthcoming).

Chapter 22: Is It Okay for Christians to Act?
[1]Anna Deveare Smith, *Talk to Me* (New York: Random House, 2000), p. 147.
[2]Dorothy L. Sayers, *The Man Born to Be King* (London: Victor Gollancz, 1943), p. 23.

Chapter 24: Using Your Voice
[1]Michael McCallion, *The Voice Book* (New York: Routledge, 1998), p. 3.

Chapter 25: The Unself-Conscious Artist
[1]John Gielgud, quoted in Anne Bogart, *A Director Prepares* (New York: Routledge, 2001), p. 115.

Chapter 28: Remaining Calm
[1]*Star Wars*, dir. George Lucas (Twentieth Century Fox, 1977).

Chapter 29: The Servant Director
[1]Robert Greenleaf, *Servant Leadership: A Journey into the Nature of Legitimate Power and Greatness* (Mahwah, N.J.: Paulist, 1977), p. 16.
[2]Ibid., pp. 15-16.
[3]William Ball, *A Sense of Direction* (New York: Drama Publishers, 1984), p. 44.

Chapter 30: The Director Prepares

[1]Anne Bogart, *A Director Prepares* (London: Routledge, 2001), p. 117.

Chapter 31: The Audience

[1]Viola Spolin, *Improvisation for the Theater* (Evanston, Ill.: Northwestern University Press, 1999), p. 13.
[2]Anne Bogart, *A Director Prepares* (London: Routledge, 2001), p. 120.

Chapter 32: Directing Rehearsals

[1]Michael Bloom, *Thinking like a Director* (New York: Farrar, Straus & Giroux, 2001), p. 17.
[2]Note: Sometimes writers use the term *beat* to mean a pause shorter than a pause—closer to the way we mean it in music, as a small division of time. Check your script, and if this is the case, clarify with your actors. It need not be a problem, as long as everyone knows there are two meanings possible.

Chapter 33: Working with Actors

[1]Dorothy Sayers, *The Mind of the Maker* (San Francisco: Harper & Row, 1941), p. 65.